Fair winds and safe
Land falls. From "Campion"
to "Tarka".
Xmas 95

Sailing Out of Silence

Sailing Out of Silence

30,000 Miles in a Small Boat

by

Peter Hancock

Drawings by David Wright

Published by Waterline Books
an imprint of Airlife Publishing Ltd
101 Longden Rd, Shrewsbury, England

ISBN 1 85310 529 5

A Sheerstrake production.

A CIP catalogue record of this book
is available from the British Library

Printed and bound in Great Britain by
Butler & Tanner Ltd, Frome and London

Preface

The first person to blame for what lies between these covers is Paul Gelder, Features Editor of *Yachting Monthly*. In the course of yet another of my monologues about some islands I had sailed to, he upbraided me — rather tetchily if my memory serves — for going on at a length to fill a fair-sized book. In a fit of pique, I straight away put *Kylie* ashore and set about cobbling together enough verbal jetsam to be passed off as one. Some of the more rebellious interludes which subsequently escaped from my word-processor were recaptured from outer space by the labours of Joss Wright and David G. Smith. That the compilation has an ending at all is the fault of Lynda Childress, Managing Editor of *Cruising World*, who let me filch a couple of thousand words I had already sold her. My thanks to them all.

David Wright, my friend since school-days, has ensured by his drawings that I shall never be out of his debt. Not for the first time, David has put aside his own work to respond to my needs, re-creating moments in my wanderings with such arresting clarity that, however dulled my own recollections may become, his perceptions will always glint with truth.

*

Although here and there I have drawn heavily from three of my articles which appeared in the international yachting press, by far the larger part of the narrative derives from unpublished — even, unpublishable — material: the creased and salt-stained pages of *Kylie*'s logbook, supplemented only by memory.

Should they read what follows, some folk who know themselves to be the rightful owners of flawless complexions will certainly wish to murder me, on the grounds that I have depicted them with a wart or two. And, while others may be hurt because I have not mentioned their presence at all, I guess that several more will breathe a sigh of relief because my kindlier recollections have edited-out their follies or my charity has cloaked them with names that they never in this world possessed. Torn between the contradictory desires to be both honest and humane, sometimes I may have unwittingly been neither. And it is for that fault, above all, I crave pardon.

Peter Hancock
Southwold
1995

In memory of Pip,

who inspired the voyages

but did not live to make them.

Contents

1

Show-down in Port Louis

My life as an impostor terminated in the middle of the Indian Ocean at twenty-three minutes past four by the wheelhouse clock, a timepiece which may still be measuring other frauds on other oceans, for in those days sea-going clocks, like the ships which carried them, were built to outlast their keepers.

The vessel was berthing at Port Louis, the harbour of Mauritius, and I was at my duty station at the engine-room telegraph, with my eyes focussed on the pilot's lips, all ready to decode his next order, when they were distracted by the antics of the Mauritian mountains, which must be the most comical in the world. The funniest act in their repertoire is the one performed by Pieter Both, an eminence with a mind of its own. Having studied an early-learning leaflet and built itself an ordinary sort of summit, Pieter Both had then cocked a snook at geological tradition by tossing a hefty boulder in the air and balancing it on its peak. From where I was standing, the mountain looked very like a seal with a beach ball on its nose. Although this cool volcanic prank had probably been going on for a few million years, it was new to me, and the sight of it plucked my attention from the pilot's face just when the troopship's stern was about to side-swipe the quay. What would happen to the beach ball, I wondered, if someone threw a herring to the seal?

'Gargle red port,' the pilot murmured into his hat.

'Pardon, sir?' I said.

'Grecian urn, larded,' he went on, still with his mouth out of sight.

I gripped the telegraph and dithered. Scenting a crisis, Captain Trump stroked his jowls and regarded me with rising hope. At last, his eyes seemed to be saying, we're going to get some excitement. I lowered my own eyes, mentally spun a coin and thrust both handles of the telegraph to 'Slow Ahead'.

We did not ram the quay, but we came so very close to disaster that an unsupervised platoon of the Mauritius Pioneer Corps mustered itself at lifeboat stations and tried to abandon ship. When order had been restored and the puzzled troops had been herded below decks, the captain remembered his high office and strove to convey the gravity of my sin. However, it is not very easy to play the part of God if you are only five feet six inches tall and lack a beard. To add to the difficulty of his role-play, the captain's usual face inspired as much awe as that of an irritated Pekingese which had been denied its walkies and, as far as his character was concerned, although he was a fine seaman and a gentleman, he was also a bit of a devil. He had started to lark about even before we had reached Gibraltar, haring ten miles from our charted course just to flush a horde of gannets from their rocks. And before the navigator had recovered, on the pretext of semaphoring investment tips to a tax-exiled brother, he had steered so close to Cape St Vincent that the vessel had lurched ten degrees from the vertical because a couple of hundred Coldstream Guardsmen whom we were supposed to deliver to Mombasa fighting fit had flung themselves at the landward rails to get a better view. Nobody saw any sign of the brother, but everybody was able to ogle the pretty girls waving from the cliffs; everybody, that is, except for three guardsmen who had been knocked over in the crush.

The point I am making is that until I manufactured the crisis in Port Louis, the only other times Captain Trump's eyes had displayed a scintilla of pleasure were during his weekly birthday parties, to which he invited all the female nurses. Those whose careers survived the voyage more or less intact calculated that he attained his 49th year of life three times between Liverpool and Port Said. Despite such prodigality, none of the nurses had shown any desire to offer him anything more than a damp handshake. The further east we steamed the emptier became his eyes and the more desperate became the devil within. Yet another birthday party was arranged for somewhere east of Suez, by which time his attention had fixed on a cold but comely Jewish nurse, unconvincingly named

Maureen. We were advised that our attendance at the party was obligatory and that the festivity would peak with the captain doing a new trick devised expressly for Maureen's entertainment. According to information leaked by his steward, this trick had the attraction of both novelty and danger. Moreover, winked the steward, it had sexual overtones too.

Primed with gin and rumour, we crowded into the wardroom. On the stroke of six bells our captain began to heave himself up a three-inch-diameter pipe which ran from the deck to the deckhead, where hung a large revolving fan. Feigning indifference to this display of strength and courage, Maureen clicked her tongue and began to circulate a plate of salmon sandwiches. To gasps of hired adulation from his officers, the captain hauled himself upwards hand-over-hand, quite without the aid of feet or legs until, at a signal from the purser, the steward darted forward and rammed an uncut banana between the captain's open jaws so that, in a fertility rite that he hoped would melt even Maureen's cold Jewish heart, he could offer up the stem for circumcision.

It was far too symbolic for a practically-minded nurse like Maureen to put up with. Her heart did not melt, it exploded. At the moment when the whirling blades seemed about to scalp her grunting suitor, she hurled the sandwiches into the fan and threw herself shrieking to the deck to cushion his fall.

Since that party Maureen had rarely hobbled from her cabin, and until I generated the excitement at Port Louis, the captain's eyes had mirrored nothing but desolation. Indeed, suggested the steward as he stirred my cocoa one night off Madagascar, our demigod's decline might well be terminal.

However, although my activity with the telegraph had rescued him from death by boredom, Captain Trump seemed slow to express his gratitude. From all other angles people were sending out body signals that suggested I was standing some leagues short of sainthood. The pilot's cheeks were a toxic shade of purple, the quartermaster's jaw hung open and the steward had dropped a coffee cup. But none of their opinions mattered much. I could endure the ire of mortals provided I got an okay from the Almighty. Even if I had come close to wrecking his ship, I had at least enlivened his day. Wasn't I going to get just the smallest glint of approval from the devil within?

Apparently I was not. The captain drifted out of the wheelhouse to gaze wistfully at Maureen, leaving me to the mercy of the pilot. When his cheeks had cooled and the stern-lines were snug on the bitts, the pilot removed his hat, wiped his brow and dictated my obituary.

'Write in your logbook the following words,' said he: '16.23 hours:

13

Pilot ordered 'Full Ahead port, Half Astern starboard'. Fourth Mate rang 'Slow Ahead' on both engines.' After checking that I had written down his exact words, before turning away he said in kindlier tones: 'Don't you think, young man, that you ought to see a doctor?'

The shame didn't scupper me all at once, but on that day in 1951 my seafaring career sprang the leak that eventually sank it. I kept my head above water until we had steamed back to Liverpool, but in the paid-off silence of my cabin I thought quite a lot about what the pilot had made me write. The implication was plain: something was altogether missing from what lay between my ears. I was either deaf or daft, or both.

The knowledge was too heavy a cargo to carry. Although there was no written evidence to say so, I knew I was a failure. My seaman's discharge-book was a catalogue of lies. Like all the other skippers who had signed it, Captain Trump had been too easy on me by far. Both before and after the show-down at Port Louis I had been paid off with a double 'VG'. According to what they had written, I was Very Good as regards both Conduct and Ability. But those gradings did not impress me. 'VG's were a debased currency, as common as glass alleys in Birmingham gutters. You had to get the First Mate's wife in the family way, as Brighty did between Balik Papan and Sydney, or attack the Second Mate with an axe, like Ordinary Seaman O'Flaherty did in Willemstad, or almost stuff the Third Engineer into the furnace of his Babcock boiler in the way that George Washington Jones did twice over between Birkenhead and Port Sudan before you missed out on a 'VG' for conduct. And as for ability: even Chief Engineer McDougal, who maimed every engine he put a spanner to, had been awarded a 'VG' for ability. There was no middle ground. Unlike what was written in my school record book, 'Fair' was an inadmissible category of endeavour in the all-or-nothing steamship of life; you came out of the Marine Superintendent's office labelled either 'VG' or 'DR', which last meant 'Decline to Report', 'Dead Rotten' or 'Don't Re-employ'. And if you missed your ship, either by design — like Courteney did in Singapore to live with his Eurasian girlfriend — or quite unintentionally, like those who had been left behind dead drunk on the floors of dockside bars throughout the world, you were sent home to Britain in disgrace as a 'DBS', a Distressed British Seaman. Officially, then, said my VGs, I had never let down my side; but I knew otherwise: whichever way I looked at it, Port Louis had been a disaster. I crawled ashore, and for thirty years kept my feet on dry land and tried to bury my guilt.

For as long as I could remember I had fooled people into believing that

I could hear what they said. At school I always sat near the front, kept my eyes on the teacher's lips and deduced the gist from the visual clues. If I got things wrong, which wasn't often, I pulled a ready-made joke from a sackful of diversionary tricks. Repeated success not only saved the moments but also oiled the wheels of my self-esteem, so that by the age of ten I was convinced that the dreadnought of my seafaring ambitions was unsinkable even by St Christopher, a pop-eyed old spoil-sport into whose collection box I dropped pennies every Sunday but from whose open-toed sandals I never heard a squeak.

On school-days I drew maps of the world and filled the oceans with oddly-assorted fleets. The Indian Ocean was occupied by a flotilla of dhows being chased by an irate whale of such huge dimensions that its flukes had cleaved Australia and converted Alice Springs into a major port. The Pacific was agog with junks and galleons, and the West Indies were in imminent danger of being run down by the liner *Queen Mary*. On summer holidays I was taken to visit my Liverpudlian uncles and aunts, where I divided my time between inspecting the earlier *Ark Royal* rising behind the cranes of Cammell Laird's shipbuilding yard, supervising the Cunarders weighing anchor, and rattling from Dingle to Gladstone on the overhead railway to check on the lading rate of the Mersey Docks and Harbour Board. Even during Christmas holidays spent at home in Birmingham, I managed to see a few ships. Driven a hundred miles inland by gales, every winter some quite famous ones holed up in the Stratford-upon-Avon Memorial Theatre, where I landed on Treasure Island, fought alongside Jim Hawkins against Long John Silver's rascally shipmates and was often mortally injured. By the following Christmas the injuries always managed to heal themselves so that I could fly unassisted to the Never Land, climb up the anchor cable of the *Jolly Roger* and swarm the rigging of the *Hispaniola* to escape impalement on Captain Hook's hook. Fantasy flavoured reality like sugar flavours tea; I drank it by the gallon, licked my lips and prospered. All through my secondary school I was always among the top five in the examination results, and even in the more practical environment of an oars-and-oakum Nautical College I won the Elder Dempster Prize. When the time came for me to leave college and enter what my father called the Real World, native guile and years of practice won me through.

The Merchant Navy medical examination was a walk-over. I skimmed through the form when the doctor's back was turned and saw that 'Hearing' came straight after 'Vision'. When we had flipped through a few pages of red and green dots and he'd vouched for the keenness of my eyes, I could easily guess what would come next.

He stood back from the desk, raised one hand in front of his mouth and turned his face towards a portrait of a buxom-looking Britannia.

'Whore leering formal, thighs up arse?' he suggested.

It was as near to my prediction as made no matter; the tonal gradient at the end signalled that it was a question, and the first part of his mumble was a passable attempt at saying 'Your hearing's normal?'

'Yes, doctor,' I said firmly.

He placed a large tick alongside 'Hearing' and I had passed the medical. My duplicity had succeeded; I could follow a professional career at sea. From that moment until the day I crawled ashore in self-imposed disgrace six years later, quite literally I was in deep water up to my ears.

But after the Port Louis pilot had blown my cover, by the age of twenty-two I had done myself out of a job. When I had washed the salt from my hair and looked around, there did not seem to be a lot of alternative careers open to handicapped ex-seamen who had left school at fifteen. The possibilities narrowed themselves down to two: Politics or Teaching. To the hard-of-hearing, the attraction of the former is that you don't need to listen to what your opponent says. Indeed, deafness — whether feigned or not — is the hallmark of the successful politician. Politics merely requires you to mouth self-justifying answers to self-formulated questions; accurate responses to other people's utterances are not only irrelevant to your function but are damaging to your political health. Likewise, teaching does not imply listening. As in the radio panel-game, when you are a teacher you talk without hesitation or digression till the buzzer goes, and then you bustle out to find a cup of tea.

Unable to choose between the two professions, I went for both, encouraged by the discovery that neither career required any training whatsoever. What was even more musical to my defective ears was that neither of these great circuses seemed to have any medical hoops through which one had to jump before being allowed to perform. If they had, the hoops were never set up for me; I just talked my way into the ring and did my act.

For most of the time the act went well. It wasn't exactly serious clowning, but nor was it a matter of putting my head into the lion's mouth; it was more like a knockabout entertainment, combining the high-wire thrills of popular psychology with swoops on a low-level verbal trapeze that only just missed the spit-and-sawdust. With appropriate variations of swing and pitch, after a few years' practice I could guarantee to bowl 'em over whether my audiences were slouching in schoolrooms, muttering in mansions or frying chips in maisonettes. Both the politics

'......by the age of twenty-two I had done myself out of a job.'
(Oil on canvas by David Wright)

and the teaching had their rewards and their disappointments: I made a living, swallowed failure, drank applause and forgot a few dreams.

But not all of them. Even though I had turned my back on it, I could never live far from the sea. I did not often hear the waves but they were always booming in my brain. I took my family on a holiday to a Scottish sea-loch, shopped for groceries by dinghy and showed them how to sail. Soon, day-sailing was not enough and so we looked beyond the bays. When the kids leave home, dreamed my wife Pip and I, let's sell up and sail away.

Well, the children did leave home, but before we could sail away Pip had fallen ill and died. Other calamities followed her last cortège, stalking me like hit-men through the drizzle: I crashed cars, botched timetables, forgot appointments and became drugged with Valium. Both in the classroom and in the council chamber, my act lost most of its lustre. After the death of my wife I wasn't keen to bowl them over any more. And between my ears, where the dreams had been, the cotton wool seemed to get denser.

In my forties, when the wool was becoming so dense that I couldn't hear one word in ten of what people were saying if they had their backs towards me, I went through another battery of tests, tried out useless hearing-aids and read ancient magazines outside consultants' doors. They looked at the audiograms and told me that things had not changed very much: as they'd said before, I'd got bilateral nerve deafness. The left ear was much worse than the right, but even the right ear wasn't good enough to navigate me through thickets of conversation without tripping over consonants and falling on my face. As far as they could see, 'pat' and 'bad' and 'dab', and 'tot' and 'cot' and 'pot' would always sound the same to me till the day I died.

'But can't you do anything about silencing Semprini?' I asked them.

'Ah,' they said. 'That's what's known as tinnitus.'

'He's at it all the time,' I said: 'playing waily solos on his violin. I wouldn't mind so much, but he does it in my better ear, just behind the cotton wool.'

'M'm...' they said. They tried very hard to think what might be done, and I'm sure that if I live into the 21st century they will be able to stitch a fully-functioning pair of second-hand ears on to my head, but in the mid-1970s, when we first discussed my problems at length, I began to think that if I hadn't got the equipment to match the lifestyle, I would have to change the lifestyle to suit the equipment. If I couldn't hear what people were saying, then why not live either where people never spoke or, alternatively, where there were just no people? It was only a thought among thousands, but it rooted.

Since Christ and I were scarcely on speaking terms, I did not feel I could presume on mere acquaintanceship and become a Trappist monk. Nor did I toy for long with another idea of withdrawing altogether from the sweet stink of society; the solitary contemplation of both my navel and Nirvana had so far revealed nothing more substantial than fluff. And when I looked for unsocial jobs at the lower level of the Real World I was unable to wax warmly about a third career as, say, a night-watchman at Madame Tussaud's. As I dropped my monthly clutter of emptied Valium bottles into the dustbin, I decided that for me the most congenial environment would probably be outdoors and would demand some physical exertion. Most of all, though, it would have to be an environment where I could be away from people for much of the time, but one which did not shut me off from human contact altogether.

By the Nineteen-eighties the doctors were frowning at my intake of sleep-aids and suggested I make a decision about my job. It just wasn't fair to the students to go on masquerading as a teacher when my lessons were little better than one-way lectures. Education, my dear chap, was supposed to be about drawing out their talents; all I was doing was filling them in. I listened to the wave-sounds between my ears and wondered whether I might go to sea again. But this time, I thought, instead of putting other people's lives at risk by being a defective link in the chain of command, as far as possible I would go to sea on my own: crewless, perhaps, but not entirely clueless.

After all, I reasoned, other people had done it, so why shouldn't I? Since Alfred Johnson made the first single-handed crossing of an ocean in 1876, more than two hundred had followed in his wake. Many had set out with less experience than I; some had been complete novices. Though I had long forgotten how to use navigation tables or could no longer make a Double Matthew Walker, I thought that some of the less complex skills of seamanship might still remain.

'But you're still paying off your mortgage,' said the bank manager, stroking his hair, 'on a four-bedroom house. Buying a boat on what's left of your salary is not, don't you see, quite *on*. Look at the sums and you'll see my point. Go home and think about it.'

I left him stroking his hair and did as he told me. The financial figures did not look good but they looked better than my audiograms. Instead of riding the high plateau of normal hearing, my decibels plunged more steeply than the sides of Pieter Both. I wrung my hands and looked at the lines that crossed my palms and wrists. Mum, Gran and Auntie Flo had often disagreed about the messages in the tea-leaves, but they had been unanimous about the importance of those lines. The lines, they said, recorded what I was going to get. The lines prescribed my life before I lived it. It was all there, they said: Head, Heart, Health, Wealth and Happiness, and the longer were the lines, the more I'd get of each commodity. But when that night I wrung my hands and opened them, the creases didn't make sense. One series proclaimed that I had died of a broken heart already, and the other lot prophesied I was going to be a hypochondriac millionaire who snuffed it at fifty. I put the kettle on and made a cup of tea. Those lines, I thought, are a labyrinth of ancient nonsense. Fate was a cop-out. It wasn't the lines in her hands that had killed my wife: Pip had smoked herself to death. Life wasn't what you read in your palm, it was what you made when you closed it in a fist. I drank the tea, pushed aside the dark-brown bottle and went to bed.

The following day I tossed the rest of the pills onto the fire, put my house on the market and biked towards the sea in search of happiness.

*

I had a clear idea of where that elusive quality might lie but I was not altogether sure of what my ideal boat might look like. Multihull enthusiasts like James Wharram and D H Clarke had made strong cases for catamarans and trimarans and the latter craft had begun to scoop the prizes in trans-ocean races, but they were not the kinds of boats for me. For one thing, they were apt to whizz along at a rate that my nerves could not easily cope with; and for another, as far as I knew at that time they were not amenable to single-handed sailing over long distances.

But if shallow-draught multihulls were out of the reckoning, so were many monohulls. The greater the draft of my chosen vessel, the fewer were the bays and coves it could get into. Yet if I settled on, say, a shoal-draught centreboarder, would it survive a mid-ocean roll-over? I rubbed my chin and wondered. I looked at, and almost bought, an impressive 39-foot steel-hulled sloop that had been sailed from Australia by a husband-and-wife team at an average speed of 6.5 knots. For a time I was keen: then I looked at the 400-plus square feet of the foresail and had second thoughts. The foresail had no roller reefing-gear. How the hell was I going to handle *that* on my own in forty knots of wind? And though its hull would see me safely across the Atlantic, what would be the point if its deep keel stopped me from exploring the jewelled shallows of the tropical cays?

It took me a long time to settle on the form and size of my dreamboat. Time and again I was distracted from the contemplation of my ideal single-handed craft by having to defend my desire to sail alone. Friends raised their eyebrows, relations shook their heads, and insurers just didn't want to know about boats that were setting out to cross oceans with fewer than three crew aboard. How, they wondered, could I persist in such folly?

The chief objection to single-handed sailing is that it flouts Article 5 of the International Regulations for the Prevention of Collisions at Sea. I had learnt the 31 articles of the Regulations by heart in my youth and so the stipulation of Article 5 was not unfamiliar: 'Every vessel shall at all times maintain a proper look-out...' I knew that failure to do so was a frequent cause of maritime disasters. How, then, could I possibly justify my desire to sail alone for days and possibly weeks on end? When I had to go below and sleep, wouldn't I be hazarding my own life and the lives of others in a knowing, cold-blooded way that made my shameful failure in Port Louis seem trivial by comparison?

The answer I offered has not changed over the years: if I know that I shall be among shipping routes for more than forty-eight hours after leaving a port, I shall carry another person aboard to act as look-out. On the other hand, if I can be confident of sailing clear of shipping routes before I need to sleep, I shall sail alone. In this way I hoped to reduce the risk of collision to minimal levels even if I could not eliminate it completely.

Sixteen years and more than 50,000 sea-miles later I have learned that although in theory I contravene Article 5 almost every time I put to sea, in practice, single-handed sailors are among the safest on the seas even if they lack electronic 'look-out' equipment. In my view, the complacency induced by electronic aids to navigation poses a far greater threat to safety than does the onset of eyeball fatigue in short-handed sailboats. Many of today's trading-vessels are charging across the seas at 15 or more knots with only one pair of eyes on watch — and for most of the time those eyes are reading the messages of the radar screen, weatherfax machines and satnav computers rather than actually looking at the sea and the sky. Where is the ship-borne radar that can see a wallowing, dismasted hulk, its decks awash among twenty-foot seas? And in 1991 of what use was modern technology to three shipwrecked fishermen in the Gulf of Honduras? Radar-equipped vessels were passing only half a mile away and yet their crews were unaware of the fishermen's plight. After twenty-two hours adrift they were located by the skipper of a chance sailboat using only eyes and ears.

21

In the end, though, the decision to sail by oneself is not the product of rational argument. Sometimes it may seem to be dictated by the circumstances of the moment, such as the unavailability of crew, but at bottom it is to do with the appetites of one's heart. I believe that I sail by myself because I need to. And, taking my cue from Shakespeare's Lear, I tell myself to reason not the need.

Though choosing a lifestyle is a matter for one's heart, before choosing the boat I felt I had to be a little more analytical. I went home from the bank manager's office, took out a sheet of blank paper and closed my eyes. What, I asked myself, must my dreamboat look like?

At first, all I could summon up was an image of my Auntie Flo.

My Great-aunt Florrie Parr had landed on our doorstep in the summer of my ninth year. At that time I had only a vague idea of her identity and no inkling of her talents but I supposed them to be great because of the size of her handbag, which had the weight and girth of a new-born hippopotamus. From it she produced a gaggle of treasures: a magnifying glass, an Eccles cake wrapped in grease-proof paper, a pack of Happy Families, a rare bull's-eye marble, and a brass compendium tool-kit made from the debris of battlefields by German prisoners-of-war. I fingered the tool-kit sceptically, unscrewing its matching cases and examining its contents with wonder. It was the first occasion I can remember handling an object which was doing a job it had not been created for. Until that time I had lived in the belief that people and things had fixed identities that went on for ever. The idea that my father could also be a son was unthinkable. And a screwdriver was always a screwdriver, never a chisel. But now I was fingering an object that had started its life as cartridges attached to bullets, and when the bullets had been fired the cartridges had been given new lives as a tool-holder. It was my first practical introduction to the useful notion of metamorphosis. Suddenly I realised that the very form and nature of creatures and objects could be utterly changed if one worked at it hard enough, and that there was no problem in the world that patience, application and determination could not solve.

Aunt Florrie waited until I had drunk my tea. Then she took the cup and put it to my lips again.

'Come on, now! Every drop!'

When the cup was dry she peered at the tea-leaves through her half-moon spectacles.

'H'm,' she said. 'I see what looks like an... I don't know... from one angle it resembles... what? An aeroplane?' She glanced at me swiftly, and, perceiving no reaction, went on: 'But no! It's not an aeroplane at all, is it? Could it perhaps be a... er... gun?'

'Don't be ridiculous,' said my mother, puffing a Gold Flake. 'There's no soldiers on my side of the family. It looks quite like Big Ben to me.' She prodded my shoulder. 'What did I tell you? You're going to be Prime Minister when you grow up.'

'It's a ship,' I told them.

'So it is!' cried Aunt Florrie. 'How daft I am! I can't see for looking!'

'What sort of ship is it?' I challenged her.

'Wait and see,' said Auntie Flo. 'Wait until tomorrow when we build it.'

We started with a piece of wood about a foot long, four inches wide and an inch-and-a-half deep. I had found it underneath the bath. Sticking to the wood was a slim packet containing a contraceptive sheath. I had no idea of its real purpose but thought that, since it had been found beneath a bath-tub, the sheath must have aquatic uses. I therefore slipped it onto a tap and turned the handle. The sheath had swelled to the size of football before the weight of water dragged its lips from the tap and the water deluged onto my boots. Agreeably mystified by the experience, I added the sheath to my accumulation of bath-toys, dried my boots on a face-flannel and bore the block of wood downstairs to Aunt Florrie. She produced a ruler from her handbag, drew a rectangle on the smoothest surface of the block and sucked her lower lip.

'That's the deck,' she said. 'I would like you to hammer a long nail into each corner of that oblong. Make sure the nails are straight, and that they all stick up the same height from the deck.'

'What are they for?'

She rummaged in her handbag and drew out a pair of scissors, a tangle of cotton-reels and a fistful of coloured rags.

'Flagpoles,' she said.

We carried our creation to the local park in mid-afternoon. It was so hot that the tarred path was like toffee beneath our shoes and people were stretched out asleep in the shade of trees. Even the poplars were dozing, with not a leaf stirring.

I had no doubt that Auntie Flo was a genius. From the most ordinary materials she had built a stout boat that could cross oceans. No important detail had been left out and everything validated the exciting doctrine of metamorphosis. The mast was a turkey-skewer held vertical by unmatched bootlaces and string from my last-year's birthday parcels. Salvaged from worn-out knickers, the hand-sewn sails were of the purest silk, and the shape of their baggy folds could be altered by tweaking the soaped button-thread that ran through deck-leads made from debris we had found beneath a loose floorboard. Most of the foredeck was taken up by an impressive weight of ground tackle. The anchor was two safety-pins lashed back-to-back, and its cable was a Woolworth's chain-necklace that had lost its clasp. The only thing I was unsure of was the bunting. The bunting was adornment without utility. After twining like variegated ivy around the four nails, it criss-crossed the decks at a height that would decapitate the crew and hinder Captain Hook's cutlass.

'It's a pirate ship,' I said.

'What's its name, then?' asked Auntie Flo, getting ready to pencil it onto the bows.

I considered deeply. I didn't want to be a copy-cat. *Jolly Roger* and *Hispaniola* had already been used elsewhere and, anyway, they were old-fashioned. My pirate ship needed a modern-sounding name. I looked at the silken sails and had a sudden inspiration.

'It's called *Durex*,' I told her.

Watched by a sceptical duck, we placed the vessel onto the still waters of the pond and pushed it off on its maiden voyage. For a while nothing much happened. The duck snuggled its beak under a wing and closed its eyes. But eventually a leaf twitched on a poplar and a cat's-paw teetered across the pond. The silken sails shimmered briefly, the masthead bunting flopped to leeward and, watched by its horrified builders, the top-heavy creation turned upside-down.

Forty years after Auntie Flo had led a crest-fallen nephew homeward from the park, I opened my eyes and began to list my requirements for an ideal cruising boat. Not surprisingly, the first was that it should have a substantial keel.

'Watched by a sceptical duck.....we pushed it off on its maiden voyage.'

The Harbour Inn,
Southwold.

2

The Boat

In the lower bar of the *Harbour Inn* at Southwold hangs an old chart of
the British Isles. The chart records the mortality of ships during the year
1868, the heyday of sail, when the tea-clippers were setting new speed
records on their passages from India. In that year alone, says the chart,
2,131 vessels became casualties in UK waters, and it shows the location
of each casualty with a black dot. The thickest clusters of dots are along
the East Anglian coast between Cromer and Orfordness, the stretch that
includes Southwold. Of the 2,131 casualties, 527 were total wrecks, and a
further 841 were so badly damaged that their cargoes had to be
transhipped. Almost all of the wrecks must have been sailing vessels, for
steam power was still in its infancy, and although some of the losses
happened offshore many of them occurred where the sea meets the land.
These vessels had not been sunk fathoms deep by huge waves, they had
been stranded in shallows, driven onto sandbanks and shingle beaches
because, for one reason or another, they couldn't keep away from the
land. Their hatches had been stove in, their masts had snapped, their sails
had blown out or their cargo had shifted so that they had lost the ability to
make headway in a gale of wind. They couldn't, in other words, beat off a
lee shore.

Now although a couple more nails and a lump of lead hammered onto the underside of Auntie Flo's creation might have saved it from capsizing, it could not have sailed to windward of the sceptical duck without a shapelier keel than that. The weight of the keel is vital, of course, but its shape is important too because it enables the hull to grip the water. I looked at the wreck chart and decided that the boat I would buy must have the hull-and-keel shape that would let her heave-to twenty miles off Southwold during a midnight gale without drifting so rapidly to leeward that she would be driven ashore on Benacre Ness before dawn with her sails in tatters. More than that, she would need a keel-shape and sail plan that would enable her to beat out of the Wash or the Orwell estuary in a middling gale of wind. While the modern fin-and-skeg was good for such a task, I believed that such a configuration made downwind sailing more stressful than a single-hander could cope with for long periods. What I needed was a medium-length ballast keel with a cut-away forefoot, a shape that would do quite well upwind and also look after itself downwind; one that, even if it couldn't turn on a pinhead, could go about between the cast-iron thimbles on the Lowestoft pierheads and could run a straight course downwind among twenty-foot waves.

Although safety and seaworthiness were the most important matters, other considerations crept in. I needed a boat small enough for an un-practical person to handle and maintain without rupturing either himself or his purse. Wooden boats looked good and felt even better, but they needed a lot of work, I thought, to keep them up to scratch. Steel boats were stronger than anything else, but good second-hand ones were more expensive than I could afford. Glassfibre boats demanded less maintenance than wooden ones and were less expensive than steel. I therefore cast around for a good, second-hand glassfibre boat, 26 to 30 feet in length. Whatever it was made of, though, I decided that my boat, like the woman I had loved, must look shapely and true.

*

If I ever reach Australia again I'll seek out a certain Mr Playdon in Sydney. According to *Kylie*'s papers, he was the chap who fitted-out the dreamboat I bought twenty years ago.

'You did a good job on *Kylie*,' I'll tell him; 'you did very good job.'

But his skills would have been nowhere without the art of David Sadler, who designed her hull, and Jeremy Rogers who built it. Mr Sadler drew much inspiration from the shapeliness and the sailing qualities of the

Scandinavian Folkboats. Since the early 1940s their clinker-built hulls had been slicing through the grey waters of the North Sea and the Baltic. Whether racing round the buoys or cruising offshore they had performed well under a wide variety of sea and weather conditions. With their seven-eighths rig, low coachroof and narrow beam, they looked as sleek as otters, as powerful as sharks and as true-running as tunny after mackerel.

Unfortunately, in a seaway they were as wet as them as well, and so Mr Sadler drew out the Folkboat shape, added a couple of inches of freeboard, put on a masthead rig, curved and raised the coachroof and offered boatbuilders the Contessa 26 as a drier, cruisable version of a racing dream.

Jeremy Rogers liked the Contessa design, set up a production line and began to mould them in glassfibre. Mr Playdon, who wanted to sail with his wife to Australia and was wary of the size and shape of the waves they might meet on the way, persuaded Mr Rogers to mould him an extra-strong hull with more layers of glass and more stringers than normal. Mindful of pressures that would be imposed if the boat ever suffered a knockdown, he cut out only two cabin windows instead of the usual six. After the hull was delivered he designed a plain, robust interior, with simple facilities for a two-person crew to make long passages safely in reasonable comfort. In the cabin he built two 6-foot-3-inch berths, a fully-gimballed galley stove which was usable in all but a hurricane, and clothes-storage lockers abutting the deckhead. For strength and safety he invested in gear with scantlings heavier than standard, such as a Proctor E50 mast, and a teak rudder with a thicker stock and a blade that had been strengthened with stainless steel rods and hung on 11/16-inch-diameter bronze pintles.

In April 1977 I saw *Kylie* lying on the buoys at Brixham, sold my house in three days and bought her almost on the spot, without a professional survey, 'as seen' and just as she lay. It was her name, I suppose, that really clinched the deal. I opened my *Shorter Oxford English Dictionary* and read: '**Kylie** *(kæ.li) W. Austral.* 1839. *[Native name.] A boomerang*'. In another place I discovered that *Kylie* was also Australian vernacular for 'a pretty girl'. What a good augury, I thought: the boat is a boomerang, but also a pretty girl who, if handled properly, will always return to the place from where she came. The purchase was something I have rarely regretted, for since then she has fulfilled all of my essential requirements for single-handed, long-distance cruising; and, even when mishandled, she has always returned safely.

'Kylie'

Not long after I bought her I was grateful for the heavier scantlings, just as others had been before me. John Campbell, her second owner, had survived an unusually heavy Atlantic gale when she was pitchpoled by breaking seas between Bermuda and the Azores in '73. On that occasion, as on some others that I was to meet with, it is possible that the kettle stayed put on the galley stove, for Mr Playdon had gimballed the two-burner Primus to loop the loop at the drop of a barometer. Outboard of stove he built the snuggest, neatest crockery stowage that I had ever seen.

Following his arrival in the UK, John sold *Kylie* to Simon Hunter. After completing a qualifying Azores-and-Back race in 1975, Simon set out on the *Observer* Trans-Atlantic Race of 1976 but, plagued by weeks of light and adverse winds on the southern route, he had overrun the time-limit of the race and had turned back somewhere north of Bermuda. As soon as he had done so, the wind backed to the east and stayed there, and so Simon did not arrive at the Azores until seventy-two days after he had set out from Plymouth. When I bought her, *Kylie* was therefore already a well-used, much-travelled boat after only five years of life. Jeremy Rogers' strong hull had kept her crews afloat, and Mr Playdon's well designed cabin had kept them and their possessions reasonably dry and comfortable.

Above the foot of each berth he constructed deep lockers that extend downwards for 15 inches from the deckhead. Clothes stowed in these lockers get wet only when enough ocean has got inside to be lapping the cabin clock, by which time it might reasonably be supposed that the occupants will be seeking their life-jackets rather than their cummerbunds.

Forward he built an extra-large forepeak, big enough to house a deflated eight-foot dinghy, forty fathoms of rope and chain and a couple of king-sized fenders. Where other Contessas had their two forward berths, he built capacious sail-bins and stowage for three 5-gallon water containers, while still leaving enough space for a chemical lavatory. Beneath the cabin berths he left room for six months' stores, and abaft the starboard bunk he fitted a permanent chart table to take half-folded Admiralty charts. Immediately below the chart table and well out of reach of all but the most catastrophic inundations, he lodged a 90 amp-hour battery in its own acid-proof box.

I could tell from the cabin layout that Mr Playdon knew a lot about short-handed sailing. Just the fact that the galley was on the port side was enough. Really, there's no better place to put it. In bad weather or in congested shipping-lanes the tired sailor usually lies with his boat hove-to on the starboard tack, with its foresail backed to starboard and mainsail sheeted to port. This assures him of right-of-way over most other craft while he dodges below to cook a stew. The pressure of the wind in the backed headsail will give the boat a port list so that, if the stew-pot does happen to leap off the stove, the scalding liquid will fall away from the cook and not on to his person. A galley that lies to starboard could be a death-trap.

On deck, a 25lb CQR anchor lay in *Kylie*'s bows. After reading Tristan Jones's assertion that he carried a 60lb hurricane-hook aboard a 19-foot boat, I laughed without stint for half an hour. A few years later, when the message had sunk in, I divided Tristan's figure by two and shackled a 33lb Bruce anchor in place of the CQR. Between then and the time it took leave of me when a chain-link parted, *Kylie* dragged only twice, both times on weed. Fathoms of nylon warp and chain sally through a short, 3½inch-diameter pipe instead of the more usual 2-inch elbow. *Kylie*'s anchor cable never jams, and the straight, wide-mouthed pipe gulps it back again without hiccoughs when I weigh. At sea, the navel pipe is stoppered with a teak plug.

The keynotes of *Kylie* are still the same now as when I bought her: strength, simplicity and spareness. Over the years I have more often said, 'What can I get rid of?' than 'What shall I buy next?'

The first item to be jettisoned was the chemical lavatory. I reasoned that the loo occupied valuable space, was unsightly, and was altogether too permanent. Really, it was little more than a jazzed-up bucket without the bucket's unpretentious mobility, and so after the first few months *Kylie*'s forward accommodation lacked the chemical toilet but her cockpit locker contained an extra bucket. The re-arrangement hasn't caused problems for my infrequent guests. In Antigua, for example, the aristocratic nostrils of my crew didn't wrinkle in disdain when she viewed the rest-room arrangements. She used to take the bucket on the foredeck, swathe her lower half in a bath-robe and fix her binoculars on the courtship rites of egrets in the mangroves.

Although *Kylie*'s interior looks rather Spartan, in a seaway it is quite comfortable. Even when the waves are high she responds to conditions without any slams, bangs and jerks. And, until quite recently her hull and gear never complained about the loading.

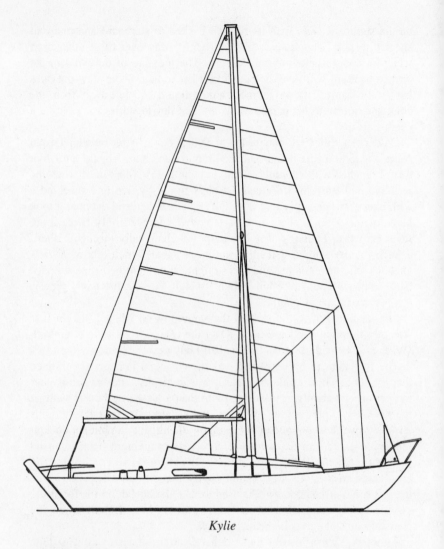

Kylie

Length Overall: 25 ft 8 in
Length on Waterline: 21 ft
Beam: 7 ft 6 in
Draught: 4 ft — 4 ft 4 in, depending on weight of stores
Displacement: 5,400 — 6,000 lbs
Ballast: 2,300 lbs
Sail Area: 304 sq ft

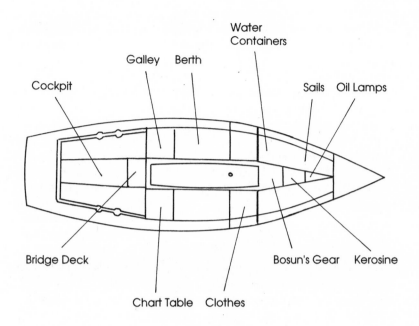

Water
Containers

Galley   Berth

Cockpit   Sails   Oil Lamps

Bridge Deck   Bosun's Gear   Kerosine

Chart Table   Clothes

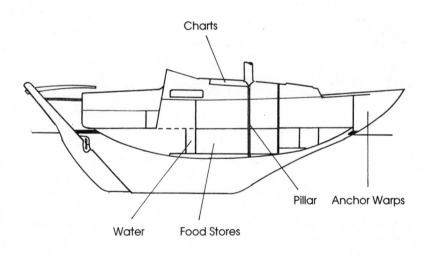

Charts

Pillar   Anchor Warps

Water   Food Stores

Kylie

Interior Layout

A few years ago I noticed that a hairline crack in the gelcoat covering the mainbeam had become wider. My response was to insert a beefy steel pillar between the beam and the sole of the bilge and it seems to have done the trick.

Other alterations have been few in number but large in importance. After the Fastnet Storm I bolted permanent stormboards over the side-windows. On deck, I have rigged twin forestays so that I can go downwind under poled-out headsails rather than under a more troublesome spinnaker which interrupts my cooking or curtails my naps. Between the backstays I used to carry a wind-driven generator but now I have a 33-cell solar panel which so far has provided enough electricity to meet my needs. Below decks, to house the charts I have built a shallow rack beneath the cabin deckhead. They are now more easily accessible than when they lay in their former lodging beneath the bunk-cushions.

Not without shedding a sentimental tear, in 1985 I sold-off the 30-year-old Stuart Turner gasoline engine and installed a famous make of diesel in its place. Life with that diesel became an almost continuous chronicle of disasters, burnt-out alternators or seized-up flywheels being the most common. I thought that the disasters were solely the results of my ineptitude until an American engineer diagnosed some serious shortcomings in its design and told me that the manufacturers had given up marketing their marine engines altogether. So the diesel engine went over the side too. All I have now for propulsion in calms is a two-oarspower wooden engine, but *Kylie* is 300lb lighter, floats higher and sails faster. Moreover, her bilge is a lot cleaner.

Kylie's lack of the more usual mechanical and domestic amenities has the advantage that there are fewer things to go wrong. With no engine, no sink and no lavatory, there are only two holes (the cockpit self-drainers) below the waterline. Though kerosene is dirtier than propane, storing and using it is safer, and the stove is simple to service and maintain. However, though the galley is old-fashioned, the navigation department contains an odd mixture of sophistication and simplicity. Until three years ago my navigation aids were a magnetic compass, a sextant, a radio direction-finder and an electrical depthsounder. When the depthsounder began to suffer from arteriosclerosis I ditched it in favour of a forty-fathom line weighted with a lump of lead. Despite my misgivings about electronics, a few years ago I bought *Kylie* a satnav as a Christmas present, and I'm very glad now that I did so. On a subsequent voyage when neither sun nor stars were visible for five days, the satnav enabled me to skirt a dangerous lee shore. Without the help of the satnav I would have had to lie hove-to in gale-force winds for days until conditions cleared. Either that, or *Kylie* would have become another black dot on a wreck chart.

It used to be said that after his fiftieth birthday a skipper needs to increase the waterline length of his boat by a foot every year. With this adage in mind, over the years I have tried out several larger boats with the idea of selling *Kylie* and moving up-market with my contemporaries. I found that although in theory the larger boats were safer and more comfortable, in practice most of them had crucial shortcomings when compared with the Contessa 26. To mention only two: the larger boats were so spacious down below that I was thrown about and bruised in moderate-to-heavy weather, even when the interior was well padded and had plenty of handholds. Secondly, though some had long keels and 'comfortable' lines, they jerked and slammed so awkwardly in even moderate seas that sailing them was a stressful drain on my stamina. After trips in other boats, I returned each time to *Kylie*'s cramped but cosy cabin, bathed my bruises and said yet again that I was better off with what I'd got.

In 1993 *Kylie* celebrated her 21st birthday. When I bought her in 1977, she had already covered 30,000 miles, having completed an AZAB and a quasi-OSTAR with Simon Hunter, an Atlantic crossing with Mr Playdon and another with John Campbell. During the sixteen years that have elapsed since then, she has sailed another 50,000 miles, venturing as far east as the Black Sea and the Lycian coast of Turkey and as far west as the Mississippi.

In 1976, however, all that was in the future. As I sailed her timidly out of Brixham harbour I was keenly aware of my new responsibilities and painfully aware that I was not particularly competent at boat-handling, let alone cruising.

My first go at sailing had taken place at Mombasa, and it had been a disaster. On the way to Mauritius, Captain Trump had put in at Mombasa to disembark the Coldstream Guards who were bound up-country to the army base at Mackinnon Road. While the soldiers were disembarking I went ashore to post mail and try out some sailing on the sparkling blue waters of the harbour. In the window of the post office was displayed a poster warning of shark attacks and listing the incautious bathers who had lost their limbs and sometimes their lives to the many tiger sharks which cruised that part of the African coast. The list was a long one, but in those days death and injury was something that happened to other people, never to oneself, and so I was not put off.

I persuaded a Chinese businessman to hire me a dinghy and I set out to show my paces to anyone who happened to be watching. I knew the theory of sailing, but during my five years at sea I had never actually sailed a boat. The dinghy was old and heavy and was fitted with a heavy iron centreboard. After half an hour of criss-crossing the harbour and waving to Maureen, I decided to try a gybe. The wind was quite strong and gusty. I failed to shift my weight as the boom crashed over and so the boat flipped, throwing me into the water. I splashed about and tried to right the dinghy, but after a very few minutes I gave up and sat on top of the upturned hull, brandishing the tiller to tap any tiger sharks on their noses. The dinghy's owner had had to come out in a launch and rescue me.

Maureen had been impressed by the capsize but had worried about my safety. Bearing our sunset gin-and-tonics, I escorted her to the boatdeck rail and played down the dangers. I assured her that I hadn't so much as glimpsed a tiddler, let alone a tiger shark. While I was speaking, a pantry-boy had emptied a bucketful of meat bones over the side. Before they could sink out of sight, a huge shape had risen from the depths, opened its jaws and engulfed the lot.

Years later I had bought my own dinghy and, with Pip as crew, had raced at Kessingland and Southwold. Since the spill in Mombasa I had learned how to gybe a dinghy in gusty conditions without capsizing it too often, but I have never been able to sail a boat with the skill of such people as my old friend Syd Brown.

Kylie's first voyage is a case in point. It took me a week to cover the 350 miles from Brixham to Southwold; if Syd had been skipper, he would have made the same passage in under four days. That I did not do so was entirely my fault; I did not sail her to best advantage, even though my friends John and Michael Robbins were a very keen crew.

We left Brixham in an afternoon in late March carried first eastward by a moderate, fifteen-knot westerly wind. Knowing what I know now, I should have told Michael to pole out the largest genoa and, without doubt, we would have made at least a hundred miles a day up-Channel. So ignorant of *Kylie*'s sail wardrobe was I, however, that, in response to Michael's 'What sails d'you want?' my mind worked as follows: 'The wind is Beaufort force four, which means it is average. Therefore, we must, at the most, set only a middling amount of sail. As far as the mainsail is concerned, that means we should take in a reef. And as far the sail forward of the mast is concerned, the number one genoa in the wardrobe sounds like a big fruity cake of the same Italian name: it would be much too rich and showy for lukewarm Protestants. Average conditions are pleasantly economical conditions: obviously, therefore, what is needed is the working jib.'

Apart from the storm jib, the working jib is the smallest foresail of the lot. We set it in Brixham harbour and we did not unhank it until we entered Newhaven three days later, having covered less than 200 miles in the same fair westerly wind. My father-and-son crew differed in their responses to our slow progress. After we had loitered for hours in the middle of Lyme Bay, John, who has a wonderful ability to see promise in the most dismal of performances, patted *Kylie*'s hull and rewarded me with a corned-beef-and-crackers hash. Michael, who knew a thing or three more about getting the best out of boats than I did but who, at sixteen, was too polite to say so, stilled his gnawing irritation by indulging his favourite displacement activity, the constructing of the most enormous sandwiches. Somewhere off St Catherine's, when the wind had dropped to twelve knots and I still hadn't responded to his silent prayers to set just a little more sail, he threw himself below and attacked another loaf. In doing this he disturbed his father, who had composed himself for a nap on the cabin sole. For several minutes John endured the noise of knife sawing through bread, cutlery being clattered, lockers being emptied and jars being rattled. He didn't actually open his eyes and say anything, however, until a dollop of tomato ketchup oozed out of a sandwich the size of a London telephone directory and landed on his chin. John cried out in disgust and crawled back to the cockpit.

'Goodness me,' I exclaimed. 'What a nasty cut you've got!'

John shook his head with the air of an Old Testament prophet who has spent his days framing an eleventh commandment and his nights inscribing it on a tablet of stone.

'Boys', he said, licking the ketchup from his chin, 'are nothing but stomachs surrounded by noise and dirt.'

The light banter, like the light weather, kept up as far as Dover, where things became a little more serious. From what we could work out from the radio, a dangling isobar of high pressure had snagged on *Kylie*'s masthead off the Devonshire coast and had towed us eastward for two hundred miles. An hour after we had anchored, the isobar suddenly twanged free, the weather pattern unravelled and a blast of icy wind roared down from the cliffs. *Kylie* lurched to the blast and Michael paid out another five fathoms of anchor cable. Before nightfall the white cliffs of Dover were themselves covered with a blanket of snow and whirling dervishes were dancing on the castle keep.

'Sorry to have to depart,' said John, 'just when things are beginning to look more interesting, but I've got to get a nature project ready for next term.'

'What's the subject?'

'Trees,' said John, stepping down into the dinghy.

'Not a knotty problem,' said Michael.

When the gale had spent itself Michael and I set off for Southwold, a hundred miles distant. As before, Michael asked me what sails I wanted and, as before, I said we'd set the working jib and a reefed main.

This time it was a wiser choice, for the wind was about twenty knots. We sailed up to the anchor and broke it out.

'Back the jib,' I called, wondering what he might do. I need not have wondered, for Michael got things right first time. He held the clew to windward, *Kylie*'s head paid off and we moved towards the eastern exit. Before we reached it, Michael had lashed down the anchor in its chocks, stoppered the navel pipe and clipped his safety harness to a jack line. Clear of the harbour, I gave him the helm and went below to look at the chart and light a pipe.

I rubbed a palmful of flake tobacco and felt glad that someone like Michael was aboard. Twenty years ago, I reflected, when I myself had first heard the order 'Back the jib' I had not known what to do and, as a result, the bows had swung towards a dangerous shore. We had been anchored off Bournemouth in the old *Airymouse* and a gale had blown in from the west. Torquil Macleod had stood in the cockpit, one hand on the wheel. The main was up, the mast hoops were rattling and the jib was flogging, cutting off my view of his face.

He shouted something I didn't hear.

What?' I yelled above the noise of the rattling gear.

'Pack the fid!' he roared.

'What's that?'

'Bat the blessed chib!'

By the time I had translated the message and backed the jib it was too late for my action to be effective, for by that time the bows had swung to starboard, where the breakers were whitewashing the Boscombe sands, only a hundred yards away. Torquil spun the wheel, and *Airymouse* made a tight loop that brought the breakers abeam to port.

'We're clear!' yelled somebody.

'Down!' roared Torquil. 'She's going to gybe!'

With no time to prepare her by first hauling in the mainsheet, *Airymouse* gybed all standing. The peak of the gaff ripped across the underbelly of clouds and the traveller slammed across the horse faster and more noisily than a steam-hammer onto an anvil. Luckily, the mainsail was loose-footed. Had it been attached to a boom, the mast would have been sprung then and there instead of in the Needles Channel.

In the Needles Channel a westerly gale was blowing against a four-knot ebb and the waves were spiky pyramids. The wind was so strong that the twelve-foot wooden dinghy, which was supposed to trail in our wake, suddenly went berserk and declared unilateral independence. Egged on by the wind, the rebel clambered onto the shoulders of an eight-foot insurgent and started to surf-ride. Had it not been suddenly checked by its tow-rope it would have overtaken us. When it drew alongside and was already making seven knots and trying for ten, the painter had jerked it broadside to a following breaker, which promptly swamped it. In order to get the dinghy aboard we had to heave-to, rig a handy billy to a strop, slip the strop beneath the stern, take up on the purchase, empty the boat of water and manoeuvre it over the gunwales. The operation was neither easy nor pleasant. And after we had swung the dinghy aboard and roped it to the deck we discovered that the mast had sprung.

Under a deeply reefed mainsail and small jib *Airymouse* had limped into Lymington. If the harbour of refuge had been to windward and not to leeward, I doubt that we would have reached it. The sprung mast would have wrecked our chances and, possibly, it would have wrecked the boat.

As *Kylie* rounded the South Foreland and headed north for the Downs and the Gull Stream I double checked that all was well with her mast. With my head against the luff of the mainsail, I shut one eye and squinted aloft. We were on a broad reach, making more than five knots. If the wind held its present strength and direction we would whistle through the Gull Stream at more than seven miles an hour without any problems. However, if the wind should veer sixty or more degrees to the north and strengthen, we would meet waves the size and shape of those *Airymouse* had encountered in the Needles Channel. But, unlike the vessel which had sprung her mast, *Kylie* would then be sailing into the wind and waves instead of running with them, and the strain on her mast would be much the greater. Although a wind-shift seemed unlikely, one could never rule it out. I shut one eye again, and again I squinted aloft.

'No sideways bends?' said Michael.

'No. Just a slight fore-and-aft one.'

'Looks a very good mast, I think.'

'Yes, so do I... Would you like a sandwich?'

'Not at the moment. I'm not hungry.'

'Not hungry? What's happened?' I said.

'Well, for one thing: we're moving.'

The wind held its strength and stayed westerly. We bucketed through the Gull Stream and swooshed northward across the mouth of the Thames as far as the Kentish Knock before the tide turned against us. The early afternoon forecast had spoken of gales to the north and said that more were approaching England from the west. The Thames area, it said, would not be having any full-blown gales just yet awhile; they would come later. For the next twelve hours, it said, we would have to make do with a mixture of light north-westerlies and heavy snow squalls.

We rounded the Long Sand Head and made towards Harwich, hoping to be off the Cork before the wind shifted to the north-west. In the late afternoon I looked at the sails and thought: shall I stick to the textbook or shall I not? With twelve miles to the Cork against the tide in a falling wind and only three-foot seas, we need all the sail we can carry. On the other hand, all the cruising logs I remember reading seemed unanimous on the matter of night-sailing: reduce sail at sunset, they said; take in a reef before you get your head down. Michael looked at the sky and read my thoughts.

'What do you think?' he said.

'Let's set the largest genoa,' I said; 'we've got to keep moving, otherwise you'll be fabricating another of your blessed sandwiches.'

By seven in the evening we were off the Cork and, still wearing the genoa, were abeam of Orfordness just after nine. The wind did not veer to the north-west until gone ten, when the first snow squall came. I eased the sheets while Michael handed the genoa and set the working jib. He was wearing his Canadian parka, and when he returned to the cockpit he looked like a walking snowman.

The ebbing tide took us north quickly, but not quickly enough. We anchored with Southwold light bearing west and waited for the flood stream to carry us over the bar. At about two in the morning we warmed our hands on a mug of coffee, shortened cable and started the engine. It started, but it dot-and-carried in a very feeble way, and so Michael again set the working jib while I set the main.

'Swig her up as hard as you can,' I told him. 'The wind will be coming straight out of the harbour mouth, and perhaps we'll have to luff and pinch a lot.'

In those days the Southwold harbour-mouth was a few feet wider than it now is; for all that, there was only about a hundred feet between the piers, which is less than four of *Kylie*'s boat-lengths. With the wind at twenty knots from the north-west there would be hardly room to gather way on one tack before it was time to go on the other. But with a three or four-knot tide to shove us through the narrows, I thought it could be done.

We did manage to wriggle our way in, but without the searchlight of a homing fisherman to help us we might have failed. Just as we got to the now-or-never spot off the harbour mouth, the place where even the nippiest dinghies sometimes run out of room to turn round, a vicious squall howled down from the north-west and filled the air with snow. I held onto the starboard tack and counted slowly to four. The piers were invisible.

'Lee-oh!' I called. *Kylie* came through the wind and didn't falter. I counted four again and downed the helm. From astern, the night was suddenly filled with brilliant light from the deckhouse of the fishing boat a hundred feet astern. Fifteen feet to starboard of my shoulder, the black stonework of the north pier slid past.

Aided by the searchlight, we made another tack and squeezed past the inner knuckle of the north wall. Abeam of Coronation Creek we luffed and let the fisherman come through.

Then the snow cleared away and some stars winked through a break in the cloud. We moored *Kylie* at her new berth on the Walberswick bank, made a pot of coffee and watched the water running up-river.

'It's late,' I said. 'We'd better get to bed, I suppose.'

'Not yet,' said Michael, fumbling for the last loaf. 'I think I need a sandwich.'

*

Before I could begin to think about sailing *Kylie* to exotic places I knew I must practise shorter trips nearer home. The trips, I thought, might be graded in their levels of difficulty in terms of general navigation, seamanship and weather conditions. For three summers I followed the plan, making coastal and cross-Channel excursions to the Netherlands, to Belgium and, with Michael Robbins, Mark Goldsworthy and my youngest daughter Esther as crew, to the west coast of Scotland via the Caledonian Canal. As I went I ticked off the miles and recorded my slow progress through the list of graded tasks.

By the summer of 1979 I had learned quite a lot, but two areas of essential experience were still blank. Though I had experienced a variety of North Sea conditions, in three years I had never sailed non-stop for more than two hundred miles and I had never coped with a full-blown gale. In the summer of that year I thought the time had come to attempt to make up these deficiencies, so on 11th August 1979, Andrew Grigg and I set out for the Sognefjord, on the western coast of Norway, five hundred miles distant.

Three days later we were struck by the gale of a lifetime.

Kylie's *berth*
on the River Blyth.

3

North Sea Knockdown

The night before we sailed for Norway my bones suggested that something bad was going to happen even though the BBC was saying differently. I had moved into a small house in Reydon, just down the road from Southwold and only a twenty-minute walk from *Kylie*'s stage on the River Blyth. While poaching a tea-time egg I listened to the forecaster prophesying fair weather and moderate winds in all sea areas. It wasn't the sort of forecast I had expected. The egg was holding together nicely in the pan, but the weather, I felt, was on the point of breaking up, for outside my window uneasy cattle were gathering amid long shadows in a corner of the meadow, and bird-flights seemed more urgent, like the scurries of shoppers before the pulling down of blinds.

Andrew Grigg arrived from Norwich, freshly shaved and eager to be off. We shifted *Kylie* from her berth on the west bank of the river and lay alongside Syd Brown's *Damaris* to take on stores and stow his gear. When all was tidy below, at sunset we stood outside the *Harbour Inn*, drinking beer and swatting gnats. In the still and humid air they seemed to be flying lower, and they were more numerous than yesterday's.

'What do you think of it?' Andrew began.

'The weather forecast sounds okay,' I said.

'It was the beer I had in mind,' said Andrew; 'I wasn't meaning the weather.'

I looked at the darkening sky, then I stifled a gasp. The moon was up, veiled by a high gauze and encircled by a halo. What perturbed me was not the halo's shimmering ghostliness but its size. From south to west it encompassed a third of the sky. I had never seen one so large. Despite the warmth of the evening my neck went slightly cool. The bigger the ring, I thought, the worse the coming storm.

'Let's go inside,' I said, 'and talk about tomorrow.'

As openly as I could, I spread my concerns on the table. Here we were, on the eve of a five-hundred-mile open-water voyage from the East Anglian shore of England to the western coast of Norway. The boat was ready, we were ready, and — according to the Met Office — the weather was right. How far should I believe these portents of nature that warned of storms? And even if they turned out to be true, wasn't the prime purpose of the voyage to try ourselves out against a gale so as to learn what gales were really like? Of course, one didn't usually go out searching for bad weather, but that was just what the Hiscocks had done in their shake-down cruise before setting off across the Atlantic. Pip and I had bought Eric Hiscock's classic *Around the World in Wanderer III* even though we couldn't quite pay the gas bill at the time. If the Hiscocks had purposely sought out a gale off Ireland in a new and untried *Wanderer III*, why shouldn't Andrew and I go after our own gale in a well-tried Contessa 26?

We drank our beer, thought about our sturdy boat, nodded our heads, and told ourselves: 'Perhaps it'll be a bit uncomfortable, but it'll be all right.'

Outside, we were pleased to discover that the gnats had gone. The halo, however, was still the same size.

The following morning we tuned in to the early forecast to check that the BBC had not had second thoughts on the matter. They hadn't: the day's weather, they said, would be as comfortable as before. Nature seemed to confirm the good news. In the field behind my house the cattle had forsaken the shelter of the hedges, and above the elms crows were riding thermals, and so we hurried down to *Kylie* and slipped our lines from *Damaris* at noon. Syd Brown blessed our voyage with a half-bottle of best Jamaica rum and against the last of the flood we motored down the half-mile of the Blyth River and into the North Sea.

The wind was light and favourable and the barometer steady at 1014mb. We set the largest genoa and the light mainsail and waited for the ebb to take us north. It caressed us off Southwold, then plucked us up and bore us chuckling past Lowestoft. By tea-time we were still covering four knots over the ground but we knew that in the dying wind such progress could not last much longer, and so off Yarmouth I mobilised the yuloh.

This aid to propulsion was a fourteen-foot spruce oar with a stainless-steel ball-and-socket fitting of my own design mounted about a third of the way along the loom. I was quite proud of my modern improvement to an ancient invention. The idea was that a spike on the ball would rest in a socket at the stern and that one or other of us would scull the boat forward. According to what I'd read, some Chinese junks in Kowloon harbour could make more than two knots with their yulohs even without my stainless-steel improvement.

I think we may have touched all of one-and-a-half knots in the brief time we used it, but I can't refer to any figures of an extended speed-trial because after half an hour the yuloh snapped in two, clean as a whistle, just where the hole of my ball-joint had weakened the spruce.

'Never mind,' we told each other, 'it's going to be a calm night', and so at sunset we anchored off the Norfolk coast at Caister in six fathoms of water and waited for either the wind or the next ebb tide to take us on our way. The wind came from the south just before nine, as light as gossamer and hinting of vineyards. We sniffed it as we set the ghoster and smiled at our perverse desire to journey north-by-west in the moonlight. In three hours we made all of six miles. When the tide was once more flowing against us we anchored again at midnight in a dead-flat calm.

'How's the barometer?' I asked Andrew before turning in.

'One thousand and fifteen.'

'Can't be bad,' I said. 'It's rising. Also — have you noticed? — the halo's gone.'

The slow progress continued for a further forty-six hours. Between midnight and noon on the 12th August we made less than ten miles, anchoring again off the Norfolk coast and listening to the signal of the Haisboro Light Vessel through a mist. It was a totally undramatic, uninteresting and undemanding experience. We scrubbed decks, whipped frayed lanyards and fought against boredom but, however hard we tapped it, the barometer stuck at 1015. We listened to the five-to-two forecast and sighed: there would be no change, it said. The BBC, we decided, didn't only forecast the weather; it manufactured it like muzak to send you to sleep forever.

Five hours later a different scenario altered our mood. Still in light winds, we had ghosted past the Dudgeon Light Vessel, plunging to a heavy swell. The barometer had at last risen, but a buzz of apprehension was tingling my hair. Something was amiss somewhere. Andrew was fiddling with the radio, his forehead creased with concentration. What with the atmospherics and Semprini, I couldn't catch a word.

'The Fastnet race-fleet — it's getting a bashing,' he said.

'How badly?'

'Don't know, but they said that helicopters are out.'

I looked at the compass and bit my lip. We were heading 008° Magnetic, on a course for the Montrose oil-rig, two hundred and forty miles distant. The wind was south-southeast and the barometer was as near as dammit steady. Sea areas Lundy, Fastnet and Irish Sea, said the afternoon forecast, would have south-west winds of 15 to 20 knots. The only hint of gales in the offing lay in the report of a barometer reading of 996mb from an area west of Ireland. Well, 996 millibars was a depression all right, but it was nothing out of the ordinary run of the North Atlantic pattern of August Lows, nothing that would have sent the Hiscocks hurrying for shelter when they were trying out their *Wanderer*. Even so, it would've been nice to have heard the tea-time forecast; it was a pity we had missed it...

The barometer remained steady until two o'clock on the morning of the 13th, and then the needle began a relentless, slow descent, falling only five millibars in twenty-two hours. 'Long forecast, long last,' I murmured to myself, digging out the storm jib from the bottom of the sail bins.

According to dead reckoning, at noon we were some fifty miles east of Flamborough Head, with the wind light from the south-west and making four and a half knots. What Andrew heard of the six o'clock news was distorted by fearful atmospherics, but he gathered that things were going rather badly off Fastnet. Many boats were in trouble, he said, and some had been abandoned...

'Must get the midnight forecast,' I told him.

'Yes,' he said. But he didn't; or rather, he couldn't, because by that time we were both on deck, struggling to deep-reef the main in twenty-five-plus knots of wind.

Wet through but not unhappy, slightly scared and therefore laughing, at two in the morning we consumed a bar of chocolate and reviewed the situation. The wind was from the south, blowing at twenty-five to thirty knots.

'Possibly,' I lied, 'it might blow more — say to forty knots.'

'Feels comfortable,' said Andrew. With the storm boards slotted in and the oil lamp painting everything with a mellow glow, the words 'comfortable' and 'cosy' sounded about right. Since it was our first gale together, I thought I would take my time and try all the options one by one to see how *Kylie* liked them. We'd started off by running before the wind and for a while that had worked well. The only trouble had been that although *Kylie* had liked it her crew had not. Two newly-purchased survival suits — '*As Used*,' according to the advertisement, '*in the North Sea*' — had proved to be as permeable as newspaper. In ten minutes we were soaked to the skin; in twenty we were shivering to the bone. To avoid total hypothermia we had streamed warps from the bows and had gone below to chafe some warmth back into our limbs, leaving *Kylie* to lie with her head between forty-five and sixty degrees off the wind.

Even allowing for my deafness, the gale did not seem to be the furiously shrieking creature of my imagination. It blasted through the rigging with the bearable roar of an Inter-city train careering through Watford Junction at sixty and, like a commuter on the platform, *Kylie* appeared to be quite unconcerned, leaning away from the danger and letting it whoosh harmlessly through. The motion, too, was less upsetting than I imagined it would be. It was regular and predictable: one felt the sharpness of the drops into the troughs and the ascents to the peaks. Each peak was marked by its own percussive sound, sometimes the cymbals of a wave-crest breaking aboard, and sometimes the bass drum of a comber against the hull. It was certainly noisy, but it seemed no more dangerous to life than a playground scuffle between a group of boys acting cops and robbers. If this is a typical gale, I thought, then there's not much terror to it.

And the sights of the gale were no more intimidating than its sounds; in fact they were quite appealing. During the forenoon of the 14th I spent most of my watch in the cockpit on look-out. Clad in a spare wet-suit and secured by a safety harness, I sat on the bridge deck with my back against the storm boards and basked in the fitful sunshine. The sea was the green of Lincoln wolds but was lustrous like ivy and was covered by heaving fields of tattered foam. In the sunlight it looked as if all the detergent vats in England had suddenly blown their valves.

I was not the only one to witness the spectacle. Throughout the morning other ships wallowed past, rolling heavily and with their scuppers streaming. Two of them, both trawlers, came close. From their bridges figures in yellow oilskins peered and pointed at *Kylie*. At times

'pressing Kylie over at a constant angle.....'

only her mast could have been visible among the waves. Waiting until we rose to the top of a big one, I stood upright and waved.

'We're okay!' I sang out into the wind. But nine hours later I was singing a very different tune, for by then the wind had become much stronger, pressing *Kylie* over at a constant angle of about twenty degrees from the vertical, and the Inter-city train had been derailed by the shunting of waggon-loads of chain-linked howler monkeys, most of whom were playing instruments. The cymbal clashings became louder and more frequent, and the thumps and thuds of the bass drum became more violent until it seemed as though the percussion section of the orchestra had mainlined its arteries with several shots of speed.

I wedged myself between the berths, with my legs stretched along the cabin sole and with my back against the engine casing. Andrew tucked himself into the weather berth. The simian orchestra worked itself up to greater frenzies. Although I hadn't seen their concert programme I got the impression that an explosive finale was just about due. My impression was correct.

Kylie rose *fortissimo* on a stupendous wave of sound, there was a two-beat pause — and then she fell.

Although a six-foot tumble may be little to a man, it's a long fall for a boat. *Kylie* landed on her side, with her mast horizontal and her deck vertical. The impact punched a six-inch hole in the leeward window. Andrew was lifted from his bunk, rolled across the deckhead and dumped into the starboard berth just in time to be deluged by the jet of water coming in through the hole. I was not shifted at all, though much else was. Most noteworthy of the articles that flew though the air was a two-pound canister of oatmeal. Somehow or other, in the course of its airborne excursion the canister was able to unscrew its lid so quickly that it had time to deposit all of its contents onto me. The two pounds of oatmeal remained on my head and shoulders for only a couple of microseconds but it was long enough for another gout of water to sluice most of the grains into my hair, my ears, and my eyes before forcing the remainder between my clothing and my skin, where my body heat gradually converted it into porridge.

When a man is being pelted by myriad missiles, which of his vital parts does he instinctively protect? As with soccer, so with boats: my first thought was for my head, the second for the waterworks. In less than five minutes I had pumped *Kylie*'s bilge bone dry. She recovered from the knockdown well enough, springing back against the wind and resuming her former angle without complaint. While I pumped the bilge, Andrew stuffed cushions into the holed window. The shock of the fall had snuffed the cabin oil-lamp but outside in the cockpit the dregs of northern summer still gave us enough light to look around for signs of damage. As far as we could see there was none. The inflatable dinghy was still lashed to the cabin top and the wind vane of the steering-gear was still cocking alertly into the wind. We struggled to the foredeck, wondering what to do for the best. Although *Kylie* had lain-to unharmed for hours, it was likely that sooner or later another brute would come along and knock her flat again. Just then I remembered a lesson I'd learned from the jujitsu of politics: when attacked, one should fall backwards and seemingly agree.

After pulling in the tangle of warps we had streamed from the bow, we turned *Kylie*'s stern to the wind and ran before the gale. At once, most of the monkeys forsook the concert and went off to peel their bananas. The remainder stayed with us, still whooping and howling in the backstays, but without much enthusiasm. However, though the noise lessened, the waves got higher. Their angry heads towered with hissing menace above our fleeing shoulders. We untangled two of the warps and paid them out from the stern. The drag slowed us down only slightly and so we paid out more line. Not until the bights of five warps totalling a hundred fathoms had been streamed astern did *Kylie*'s headlong flight slow down to a controllable four-and-a-half knots.

Under bare pole we ran in a north-easterly direction, bolting down extra protection over the side-windows as we went. Snatches of a forecast told of storm-force fifty knot winds in all areas of UK waters. We pulled the hoods of our jackets tighter and drove on through heavy rain. I tried to work out in my head how long it might take for the front to pass through and when the expected wind-shift might come. At midnight it was blowing an estimated forty-five knots from the south-west and the barometer had fallen fifteen millibars in twenty-four hours. In the thirty-year interval since my previous experience of storms I had forgotten what such a pressure gradient indicated. All I could remember from being two hundred miles from a West Indian hurricane aboard a ten-thousand-ton ship was 'Chunky' Edwards saying that if we got sucked into the eye of the storm we were done for. There would, he said, be a sudden lull, the clouds would part above us and we'd have one last glimpse of the heavens before the grandparent of all winds struck us from the opposite direction and blasted us to eternity.

At two in the morning of the 15th August the barometer rose suddenly to 996. The bottoms of the clouds were about three feet above the masthead and it was raining heavily. I tightened the draw-cords of my

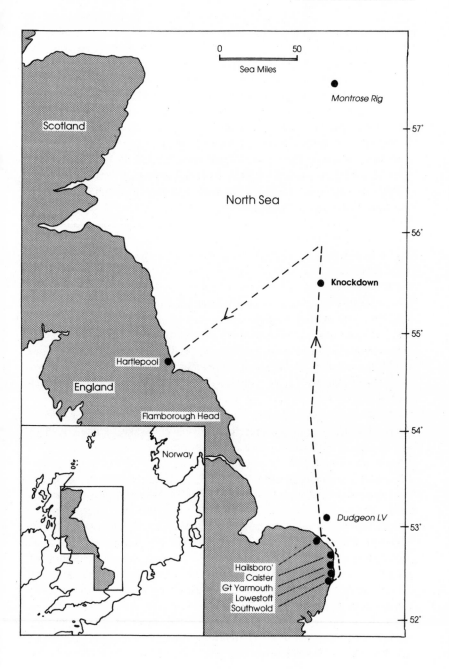

jacket and Andrew went below to dry out. By four o'clock the barometer had climbed to 998 and I was worried. The rain had stopped, but a rise of one millibar per hour seemed a bit steep even for those inflationary days.

'Your watch!' I yelled to Andrew through the storm-boards. 'It's...'

I stopped, astonished. My voice was far louder than necessary. Suddenly, all had fallen silent. The wind had gone in an instant and *Kylie* was now rolling violently, surrounded by black, toppling cliffs.

'What's up?' said Andrew, poking his head on deck.

I didn't answer. I had lashed the useless tiller and wedged myself into of a corner of the cockpit. Head back, I was staring upwards into a huge bright hole. The clouds had opened and I was gazing at a cluster of stars. We were in the eye of the storm.

There was only one thing to be done in such a dangerous situation and we did it. Because of the violent motion it took much longer to do than usual, but somehow we boiled a half-kettleful of water and made two steaming cups of tea.

We sipped the tea and waited. I kept my eyes on the eastern cliffs of waves, trying to see the contrary blasts before they hit us, for there seemed no doubt that we were in the storm's eye and that the new wind when it came would rush at us from the opposite direction to the old one. I wondered how violent the grandparent of all storms could possibly be? Fifty knots would be bad enough; above that figure the wind-speed didn't bear thinking about if forty-five knots of wind had been enough to knock us flat.

We drained the last of the tea and still we waited. Impatience nibbled at the wedge of fear in my stomach. 'For Heaven's sake,' I thought, 'let's get on with it. Let's have it over and done with.'

The new wind caught us napping, blowing gently from the south-west and cooling the stale porridge on the back of my neck. We stood up and prepared against the coming blast, bracing ourselves against the cockpit sides.

The blast never came. Instead there came zephyrs, stealing timidly like kittens through the early-morning air. The prediction had not been fulfilled. It was as if I had ordered a cup of tea, had tasted the liquid and found that it was coffee. My expectation was confounded so suddenly that for an instant I was completely at a loss. I smiled like an idiot at the stars.

We didn't pause to wonder how or why the storm had ended so abruptly, or why such a sudden rise in the barometer had not brought violent wind. We basked in the reality of sunshine and zephyrs, and then we hoisted the main and hanked on the largest genoa.

'Course?' said Andrew, unlashing the tiller.

I looked aloft. There seemed to be no damage there, but on deck there was the holed side-window and the bracket of the patent log had been bent double by the impact. Below, the chart of Norway was invisible, coated by a layer of salt-water porridge.

'Two Four Oh,' I said. 'Let's go to Hartlepool and eat some fish and chips.'

And so although she reached it later, in that year *Kylie* did not get to Norway. I was not too disappointed, for I had done much of what I had intended: I had found a gale and had come through it, and I had re-discovered some old skills that I was going to need when I set out on voyages that were to be solitary, longer, and — in their own ways — just as demanding as this one had been. Perhaps the most important thing I had re-discovered was the primaeval weather-wisdom which lies in the sleeves and pockets of our senses. That some bad weather would come our way I had known in my bones; that the storm would be a severe one I had seen from the size of the halo. That it drowned many people and came to be called the Fastnet Gale is a matter of history.

Fish and chips, Hartlepool

Kylie *ashore*

4

A Norfolk Valentine

*With the experience of the Fastnet gale behind me, I then needed to
acquire the skills of single-handed cruising. From 1980 onwards I began
to cultivate solitude, making weekend solo trips up and down the East
Anglian coast and across the North Sea to Belgium and Holland. All of
them were of immediate practical value in helping me to develop the skills
of one-person boat-handling. But these trips met deeper needs too, for
they confirmed my belief that I could not only cope with solitude but also
enjoy it.*

*By tradition, cruising is a companionable activity, implying that as
every boat must have a skipper, so every skipper shall have a mate.
Single-handed cruising is therefore seen as a paradox. In boating
literature, single-handers often have cranky hang-ups, and in the
commercial world one-person dreams are not very marketable. But
although we never seek loneliness, we sometimes crave solitude.
Loneliness is always painful and is often depressing, but solitude can be
both agreeable and energising. Whether it will be blighted by the pain of
loneliness depends on attitude, self-training and experience.*

*The early solo voyages were rather like riding a tandem as though it
were a uni-cycle. There was much wobbling and many tumbles, which is, I*

suppose, to be expected, for I was trying to do a solo act on a vehicle that had been built on the sensible but erroneous premiss that the number of two is the minimal basis for marketing long-term happiness.

*

She nearly died of the pox in Norfolk. I lifted her out as tenderly as I could on to the bank of the River Yare in Norwich and when I saw the awful state of her skin I almost cried.

'Yes,' they said, lancing the boils, 'she's got it badly.' Some of the boils were as big as pigeon's eggs, while others were only the size of peppercorns, but all of them spurted pus when the lance went in. They wiped their instruments and wrapped them away and then they told me that if I paid them eleven hundred pounds they could cure her. Eleven hundred pounds was seven weeks of my nett salary in 1982, and I could not afford such expensive medication. I looked at her blisters, thanked them for their trouble and said I'd cure her of the osmosis myself. It would be ironic, I thought, if a boat that had survived the Fastnet Gale should perish inland, thirty miles from the sea.

Three of us with angle-grinders and plastering trowels laboured all spring and summer, removing the epidermis and grafting new flesh on her raddled body, and by the time my school re-opened in September *Kylie* was afloat again. When the leaves around the boatyard were beginning to fall, I nursed her gently back down-river to Suffolk to convalesce. In October came the sort of Indian summer that persuades us that life and all we love are renewable for ever. *Kylie* rested quietly at her stage in Southwold, nodding gently in the warm sunshine, and I too drifted into the delusion that pain was infinitely postponable.

It almost is, of course. 'In this hospital,' they had said, 'we do not allow pain,' and they had given Pip the drugs and I believe that even in her last hour of life there was no physical pain. She experienced amazing euphoria and she experienced bouts of distress and bewilderment, but, I kept on telling myself, she had felt no physical pain.

In November the Indian summer ended and the fog rolled in from the sea. I discovered I had overspent wildly and was running out of credit. In January pent-up memories of bereavement sent me into a spiral depression and I was submerged by a wave of influenza which poured liquid concrete into whatever spaces in my ears were not already filled with cotton wool. Before I had fully recovered, a road accident increased my overdraft, and so early in February 1983 I decided that instead of motoring sixty miles a day to and from my school it would be cheaper to lock up the house, sail *Kylie* back to Norwich and live aboard her in the boatyard.

It so happened that the tides were just right for doing the more difficult legs of the forty-mile return passage to Norwich during the daylight hours of February 14th, Valentine's Day. I thought that getting through the Haven Bridge at Great Yarmouth might be tricky, for even high-powered vessels had come to grief against the piers of the Haven Bridge when their pilots had erred. The larger ones had been carried broadside on to the piers by the fierce tides and had been pinned there by the pressures of the water against the hull. Smaller vessels had either been jetted through minus masts, funnels, deckhouses and davits or had suffered more grievous damage that had sunk them on the spot. Because her masthead was thirty-two feet above the water and the bridge when closed had only about fifteen feet clearance, *Kylie*'s safety depended on timing her arrival to accord with the opening of the bridge. I could cope with a twenty-minute wait without too much difficulty, but if the wait was longer than that I'd have problems in stemming the flood. The penalty for tardiness was worse: if I were late and missed the opening I might have to go alongside the high quays and attend to lines and fenders for at least eighteen hours until the bridge lifted again.

After poring over tide-tables I reckoned that given a fair wind I could make the safety of Reedham before dark if the Haven Bridge would open at noon. I telephoned my ETA to the bridge-master, but his reaction was not encouraging.

'We don't open specially for pleasure boats. We're lifting at fourteen hundred for an up-river trader but there's no other commercial movements before then. Call me when you enter the river, old chap, and I'll review the situation and see what can be done.'

'But I don't have a radio,' I told him.

'Then moor up near the Town Hall and walk to my office.'

'I'd rather not,' I said; 'I'm single-handed. I'll come up the river about 11.30 and hang about hopefully. Try to open the bridge at twelve. Please try,' I said before the coins ran out.

In a sullen dawn *Kylie* bore out of the River Blyth at quarter-ebb. The wind was south-by-west at fifteen to twenty knots and there were breakers on the bar, and so she rinsed her decks briskly before making off northwards on a rolling run under single-reefed mainsail and number two genoa. I set the Quartermaster wind-vane gear, scooped a half-panful of water for porridge off Benacre Ness and had fried a two-rasher sandwich

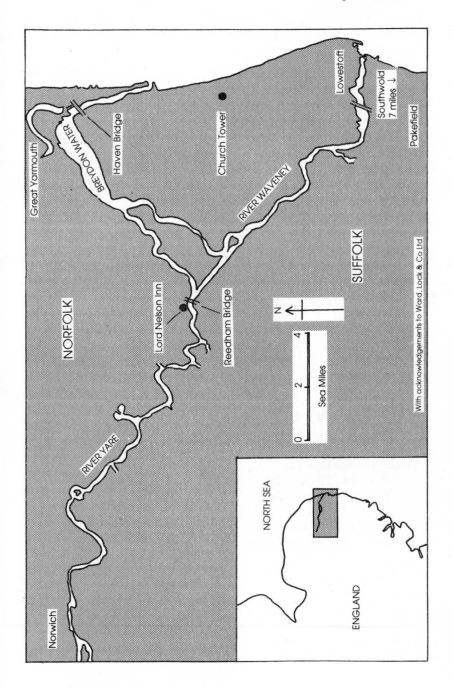

before Pakefield church came abeam. There is no tonic in this world to equal a bacon sandwich when a cold winter's morning and the dregs of influenza are reminding you of mortality. I munched the sandwich in the cockpit, watching the press of the tide against the groynes to port and the dark swirls over the Newcombe Sand to starboard as we swept north with the ebb through Lowestoft Roads. The five-eighth cloud cover had dispersed and bright sunshine sugared the slate roofs of the guest-houses, but it was cold, very cold. I warmed my blue fingers over the Primus and thrust them into a pair of golfing mitts. I thought about how useless they would be when it came to pulling out piston-hanks if I had to change the foresail.

The wind rose to twenty-five knots and veered south-southwest as *Kylie* drove through the tide race off Lowestoft Ness. Before long I could see the chimney of Great Yarmouth power station. Either the chimney was a pink finger testing the wind or it was a one-finger warning, I couldn't decide which. 'We're early,' I thought, and so I hove-to with a ruined church bearing 260°. Although the wind was as keen as a kipper it was coming off the land and the sea was smooth. A spatter of gulls landed nearby and yarped peevishly at *Kylie* as she was borne northwards on the dying ebb. Until the time came to make for the entrance to the Yare I lay hove-to, looking at the roofless church and thinking about the ghosts who had gathered there, all the christenings they had witnessed and all the funerals they had seen. Then I beat the mitts hard to get the lifeblood flowing so I could let draw the jib because I knew that if I lingered longer I'd be chilled bone-deep by graveyard thoughts.

Kylie's single-cylinder Stuart Turner was thirty years older than the hull but it gave her three and a half knots in the slack waters of the Yare against the last dribbles of the ebb. I handed sail as we puttered past oil-rig tenders, a littoral of light-buoys and longshore boats on the strand for caulking. Half a mile from the Haven Bridge I could see that it was still closed, with lunch-hour road traffic dawdling across. Not for the first time I wondered why dealing with British bridges should be such a depressing experience. Everywhere else I have been outside Britain, bridge-openings are done with less fuss and greater consideration for pleasure-boat traffic. In Holland, boats don't just have parity with Porsches, they often have priority. And as for America, why, I'd bet I could go through twenty bridges on the Intracoastal Waterway with less delay and hassle than through any two in Britain.

Three cable-lengths below the bridge I put the engine into neutral, lugged frozen warps on deck, blew on my numbed fingers and howled at the River Commissioners.

'Blast you,' I shouted at their office windows, 'for your boat-baulking bumbledom!'

Greatly touched by my endearments, they at once broke out a boat-friendly flag, halted the road traffic and cranked up the bridge. As *Kylie* inched through, people drew Kilroy pictures on the steamed-up windows of their panting buses or sat stoically on bicycles and ate their cod-and-chips. I waved my thanks to the bridge-master, who said something into his handset and blew a whistle. The bridge swung down behind me as the stroke of noon chimed from a gilt clock on the Town Hall. I stuffed the neckpiece of my balaclava into the throat of my jersey, cut the engine and made out towards Breydon Water under full main and number one genoa.

I encountered the first corpse at about one o'clock. The wind had dropped to eight knots but the air had become even colder. Crusted and layered by a fortnight of Siberian temperatures, the mud-flats of Breydon Water looked like a vast deep-frozen gateau as *Kylie* slid past. She seemed to be the only boat in motion, and I the only living thing. We crackled through a coffee-cream confection against a peacock-blue sky. I looked from the mud-flats to the channel ahead and saw that it was cluttered with chunks of floating ice, each up to four feet square. I unlashed the boathook and stood in the bows. Under a scandalised main *Kylie* was making less than three knots and I wanted to find out if I could deflect the ice-floes before they grazed the hull. I poised the boathook and lunged at a wallowing hunk the size of a two-person fridge. The point sank into the ice and, as *Kylie* moved ahead, the floe overturned. I gasped in dismay. In the ice was a dead tern, killed and entombed by the Arctic weather.

The tern was not an isolated casualty. As we made towards Reedham, Breydon Water became narrower, the ice-floes more numerous and dead birds more frequent. By the time the *Berney Arms* was abeam, death was as familiar as litter is in Liverpool. I counted two more terns and a guillemot completely encased in the ice, and a common gull entrapped by its legs. After the *Berney Arms* I could not keep up the tally for by then the sun was so low that it was a hard job to make out the shape and size of the ice-hazards that lay across our path. Floes were still quite easy to detect because they had an irregular freeboard which cast distinctive shadows on the water several boat-lengths ahead. Their largest dimensions were less than four feet and so it needed only a slight movement of the tiller to avoid them. More worrying were the slabs of sheet-ice, many of which were the thickness of city kerbstones. Formed in the freshwater reaches of the Yare and Bure, they had been set adrift by the wash from the Norwich-bound coasters and had been carried downstream by the current. Unlike the floes, the ice-sheets had no freeboard. I sensed them more nearly than I saw them. Sometimes the merest quarter-inch reduction in the height of the ripples ahead was the only clue to the presence of an ice-sheet fifteen yards square.

Since on the tightest bends the river was less than forty yards wide, in order to skirt around the sheet-ice *Kylie* had to tack and bear away repeatedly even though the slant of both the wind and the river was in her favour. The work on the winches was tiring but necessary, for I could not risk using the engine — one flick of the propeller against a floe or sheet would have torn off the blades.

By four in the afternoon the sun had almost gone from a sky that was Gauloise-blue at zenith and hawberry-red in the west. Reedham bridge was a black lattice among a silvery fretwork of tree-tops, and both wind and tide carried us swiftly towards it. I sucked frost into my lungs and blew three blasts on a platelayer's horn. 'Ice or no ice, if the bridge doesn't open in sixty seconds,' I thought, 'I'll have to swing the engine.'

I had counted to fifty and dug out the starting-handle before the bridge began to pivot. *Kylie* swirled between the piers, the wind giving just enough steerage way. Once clear of the bridge, I rounded up into the wind and tide, tacked twice and moored outside the *Lord Nelson* pub. I lit a pipe and exhaled gratitude and relief: British bridges were treating me better than I had thought they would.

The bar of the *Lord Nelson* looked like a catacomb. It contained nine ghouls and a middle-aged man with an eerily glowing nose and a skeletal dog. The nine ghouls wore identical Lurex tracksuits and sat on a black bench along one wall of the bar. They turned out to be a ladies' darts team practising for next Saturday's match, but at first glance they looked like a burned-out chorus-line auditioning for a fringe production of *Phantom of the Opera*. Perhaps because that comparison was too depressing, I looked again so as to upgrade them into something jollier but the second look didn't make them into anything much better; the second look suggested they were vultures at roost. From time to time one or other of them would descend from her perch and cast a dart at the opposite wall before clucking back to where she'd come from. The cluckings were dark, mysterious and deeply private, and so I tried a greeting on the middle-aged man.

Kylie *approaches Reedham Bridge*

'You wouldn't have got through the bridge yesterday,' he said cheerfully. 'The floes had piled up against the piers and were right across the river. Six foot thick they were.'

Between drams of medicinal whisky I discovered that he was newly widowed too, but bereavement didn't seem to depress him.

'Solitude helps a man become better acquainted with himself,' he explained.

'Samuel Johnson had much the same thought,' I told him; 'but he still turned to Mrs Thrale.'

We finished our whiskies and stood outside together. The stars seemed clearer and brighter and harder than ever before. We listened to the ice-floes grinding and grumbling against *Kylie*'s hull. It was colder than the grave and just as exclusive.

'But isn't your wife's death too steep a price to pay? Just for becoming better acquainted with yourself, I mean?'

'Ah,' he said, 'it might've been if she really did die.'

'What do you mean?' I asked him.

'Nothing dies,' he said. 'Nothing dies... everything grows.'

He clicked his fingers at his dog and they were gone before I could question him further.

I returned aboard *Kylie* with his words on my mind. They were absurd, of course; if he'd seen those birds in the ice he'd have said differently. Nothing could have been deader. I shuttered up the cabin, lit both rings of the Primus and kept them going full blast until I'd made a flask of coffee and the temperature as measured by the cabin thermometer had risen to five degrees below freezing. I hugged the coffee, listened to the rumble of ice along the hull and told myself the engine would be alright. If I ran the Stuart now while the full flood of salt water was going past, the engine-block would be filled with a lovely saline solution of North Sea, and, as every schoolboy knew, the sea round England doesn't freeze...

I ran the Stuart for half an hour, closing the sea-cock three minutes before I cut the engine. Before turning in I set out an empty plastic bottle on the cabin sole, for I had no intention of going out on deck to relieve my bladder if nature were to make one of her insistent calls during the night. I tugged on a second layer of thermal underwear, made sure the bottle was within reach and then I zippered up my sleeping-bag until only my nose-tip was showing.

It was the coldest night I can ever remember. It was so cold that I could not trawl up even the first wisps of sleep. At one in the morning the cabin temperature was seventeen degrees below freezing, and so I lit the Primus and ran the engine again for thirty minutes. Fortified by rum and coffee, I fell into a restless doze. Images of the dead guillemots ran through my brain. That bloke in the bar was a loon; if I didn't watch it I could die from hypothermia; or, like Dr Johnson, from melancholia.

At eight o'clock daylight crept through the curtains and prised me out of my doze. I had to ease my feet by slow degrees to the cabin sole. The statistic about temperature decreasing one degree Fahrenheit with every three hundred feet of altitude needs an addendum: if you sleep aboard an unheated boat during an East Anglian winter, temperature also decreases one degree ditto for every inch between bunk and cabin sole.

My toes took two minutes to penetrate sixteen inch-thick layers of invisible ice, each layer colder than the ones above it. Other evidence of the sub-zero temperature was close at hand: the plastic bottle now contained what looked like frozen-solid sherry, and the seacock could only be eased open after an half-hour session with candles and flaming bandages.

By nine-thirty I had succoured the Stuart. The wind filled from the west and I cast off at ten. Under a bright sun and cobalt sky, *Kylie* creamed up-river towards Norwich, zigzagging to avoid the ice. There were no more dead birds, everything was vibrantly alive. Lapwing, mallard and a solitary heron rose briskly from the reeds as our displacement waves set them nodding to the sun.

I glimpsed the man I had met in the bar plying a scythe in a bed of newly cut reeds. When he saw me coming he stood in the shelter of a five-foot stook and called something to his dog. He was clad in a sheepskin jacket that covered him from shoulder to knee. Around his middle was knotted a rope to hold the sheepskin in place, and his calves and ankles were swathed in sacking cross-gartered with string. On his head was an over-large trilby bowsed down by a red plaid scarf tied beneath the chin.

As we slipped past the reed-cutter I flailed my arms against my body and breathed bouts of steam. He did the same at once, imitating my movements exactly. Nothing could have been more explicit: 'You're right,' said his mimicry; 'it's crucifyingly cold, but it's bloody good to be alive!'

What with the bitter weather, his red nose, the symbolic scythe, the sheepskin and rough sacking, he looked like a figure in an old Flemish painting. And from that ancient canvas he seemed to be signalling a timeless cheer that centuries could not dim.

The dog bounded from the stooked reeds, sensing our risen pleasure. I shook off my mitten and waved to his master. With fifty yards between us he waved back, and through my cotton wool ears I heard him call again: 'Nothing dies! Everything grows!'

The dog barked a deep endorsement, the heron rose higher than the sun, and *Kylie* sped on. I reached for the tiller and began to believe him.

5
Round A World in Forty Days

After she had recuperated from her surgery, Kylie made a 2,000-mile circuit of the British Isles. Its purpose was two-fold: I wanted the experience of planning and making a voyage that was longer in time and distance than anything I had previously attempted, and I wanted to savour in advance the thrill of sailing round the world.

To derive so large a thrill from such a small adventure may seem childishly pretentious, but to some island-dwellers it is not. Even today, many Britons still feel as my mother felt: that the world ends rather than begins at the white cliffs of Dover. Logic argues in vain against the errors of the islander's heart and the beliefs that are in his bone. Looking at a school-room globe, my eyes tell me that my round-Britain cruise was about as impressive as the perambulation of an ant round an oak-leaf. At the time, however, my heart felt that it was a voyage that had taken me to Ultima Thule, the uttermost bounds of the world.

Because parts of the voyage were to be made among busy shipping-lanes, it seemed essential to provide a continuous look-out. I therefore recruited three friends to accompany me, one for each of the three legs of the circuit: Bob Telford from Southwold would sail to the west of Ireland,

John Grix crewed from Ireland to the northern coast of Scotland, and Martin Dyer crewed from there back to Southwold.

*

If you were to tell me that the average height of Irishmen is less than six feet three inches I'd say you had fiddled the figures. At two in the morning the pub on Cape Clear was still crowded with giants and one of them had got me into a corner.

'What are you at?' he asked me.

'I'm sailing round the British Isles,' I told him.

'You are not,' he said, wagging a fist the size of a mace. 'Your boat is lying in Cape Clear, which is part of the Republic of Ireland, which is not British at all.'

I drew myself up to my full height, something that heroes used to do quite frequently in novels. Even then my eyes were only level with his chin and so I decided not to argue.

'Nevertheless,' he continued, 'let me buy you a drink.'

The offer cost him expensive. I asked for a glass of white Jamaica rum, explaining that, since the time when John Robbins had introduced me to it, slipping me a thimbleful between — of all curious accompaniments — tomatoed slices of his home-baked loaves, I had become addicted to the stuff during the graveyard watches when assailed by doubts about my own sanity.

The idea for the round-Britain voyage had started with Barbara Keay's telling me that Cape Clear seaweed was something special and my saying that seaweed was just seaweed anywhere in the world and then her saying, through her witching-hour smile that she had possibly learned during her childhood among the Yoruba, 'Well, why not come here and see it for yourself?'

One thought had led to another, so with Bob Telford as the first of my three crews I set out to see not only Cape Clear but a few other English, Irish and Scottish headlands as well. Like other people with limited holidays, I had to go round them with one eye on the clock. From Southwold it is about 560 miles to Cape Clear, which lies off the south-western tip of the Irish mainland. But that distance was only as the fly crows, and I knew I'd got just forty days in which to make the round trip back to Southwold. Even if I cheated by not passing outside Rockall and the Shetlands, and went, instead, via the Outer Hebrides and the Pentland Firth, it would be a tightish race against time.

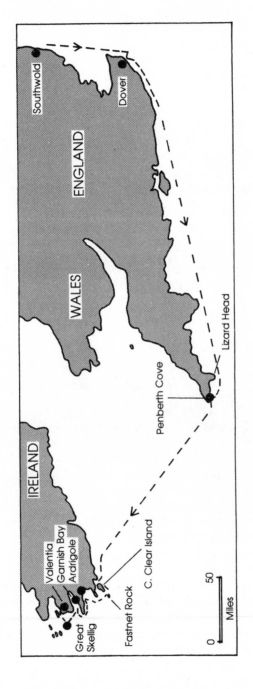

Bob and I left Southwold before sunrise on a July morning, with the wind light from the south-southwest — almost a header. It seemed a pity to start the voyage under engine but I wanted to make sure we caught the tide through the Gull Stream off the Kentish coast and so the old Stuart Turner was running for several hours until the wind backed to a more helpful south-southeast. Our spirits rose with the sun and as usual the wind did the same and so by half past ten that night we were through the Gull and off the South Foreland. I broke out the chocolate and white rum but the mini-celebration was premature because by midnight we were just drifting.

'Where's all those easterlies you talked about?' said Bob as we flopped around off Dover.

'Captain Cook once took three weeks to get down the English Channel,' I said, reaching for the starting-handle, 'but he didn't have an engine to help him.'

'Nor will we much longer,' said Bob, dipping the tank and looking towards Dover, ' 'cos the fuel tank is almost dry.'

The previous time I had tried to enter Dover they had kept me waiting for hours. I'd flashed about a hundred 'W's at them before they had Morsed 'OK' back at me and let me slip into harbour between two ferries, but this time it was easier than playing a one-armed bandit on your saint's day: I just punched twice at the eastern breakwater with a flashlight and Bingo! three green gooseberries spun up on the signal-tower and we were berthed and fuelled in minutes.

Seven hours later we hummed out of the western exit in bright sunshine. A light north-easterly tickled us for seventeen hours, increasing to twenty-four knots and backing north at dawn on the following day. Carrying the smaller genoa and reefed main, *Kylie* surged past Sussex and our hopes for a fast passage rose, but two hours later we were wallowing and woeful off the Owers light-float. This pattern of wind and calms carried on for days. We cursed the calms and were thrown into frantic activity by the merest whiff of wind. During one watch I set and handed the ghoster and main five times and each dousing was followed by the swinging of the Stuart's starting-handle. By midnight I was glad to see my bunk.

The light weather frayed our nerves. Britain simmered through the hottest summer of the century and beaches were thronged with visitors. The bosoms of seaside landladies were heaving with pleasure and their purses were bulging with profit. Aboard *Kylie* it was different. We drifted dolefully past Dorset, buffing the brightwork and fretting at our poor progress and the frequency of fog. The diaphonic moans from Portland Bill sounded as cheerful as an ox in an abattoir and did nothing to soften the hard news that we'd averaged only two point seven knots that day. It seemed as though we were in for a slow passage to Cape Clear. But before the moans of Portland had died astern a comely breeze lifted its skirts and waltzed girlishly in from the north. Two hours later it was doing some livelier capers and by evening it had matured into a double-breasted breeze and *Kylie* was making five and a half knots by the Heinz log.

Owing to persistent neglect, the Walker log had succumbed to a terminal palsy off Folkestone. When neither proddings nor paraffin could revive it, we pacified its demented rotator, interred its warm but untwitching corpse in the bilge and opened a brand-new Heinz log. The Heinz log is a wonderful device. Although it is not widely advertised, the Heinz log is infallible. Moreover, it is easy to make, it gives no mechanical problems and it costs next to nothing.

To make it, one must first consume a fifteen-ounce canful of baked beans. Next, punch a hole in the base of the can and another near the top to take a long, light string-line. For best results, the base hole should be one twentieth of the area of the base. The Heinz log is now ready for ballasting. In British waters the usual ballast comprises three tablespoonfuls of cold porridge, but I am told by American boaters that a couple of Aunt Jemima's time-expired pancakes will do just as well.

Before using the log you must work out your boat-length factor, which is simply three-fifths of the distance between the bows and your usual steering position in the cockpit.

Operating the Heinz log is simplicity itself. Depending on the state of wind and sea, all you have to do is get your crew to throw it, lob it or just drop it ahead of the boat. When your crew cries that the boat's bows are abreast the floating can, begin counting off the seconds, preferably in a mellow, even voice. Cease your counting when the can is abeam of you. Then, divide your boat-length factor by the number of elapsed seconds and you will then have your boat-speed in knots. Finally, retrieve the log by means of the string-line.

All of which explains why I could say 'Five and a half knots' to Bob so firmly when he came back from the bows a-dripping doubts and damns as we crashed across Lyme Bay in a twenty-knot wind against a flooding tide. We thought that *Kylie* was going quite fast but that night we were overtaken by a forty-footer. With her spinnaker quivering in the moonlight she sliced past only sixty feet away. The two figures in her cockpit glowed with an eerie red light, like Martians who were sitting-out a necromantic disco. When they were forward of our beam I saw that the radiance came from a cluster of dials above the companionway. We bade them goodnight but they did not shift their eyes from the dials or make a reply so I eased the genoa sheet a whisker and sought the consolation of a pipe.

Four and a half days out from Southwold we were loafing in light north-westerlies near Lizard Point and eating corned-beef sandwiches in the cockpit. I set a course for Land's End. We had come 346 miles. With more than 200 still to go, I doubted that we could make Cape Clear against such light winds in less than two and a half days.

The tranquillity didn't last. By early afternoon *Kylie* was down to a double-reefed main off the Runnelstone rocks, bucking seas that barged at us from both the north and the west together. They crashed aboard like bailiffs and tried to make off with all our movable assets, fisting at the dinghy and rattling the anchors in their chocks. Bob tightened the cord of his hood and grimaced.

'Ready about,' I said; 'we'll head for the land.' The jib clattered sharply as we came through the wind and made for the Tater Du lighthouse and shelter.

I bent over the chart. Penzance looked inviting but it could be gained only with difficulty and even to lay the course to Newlyn would be hard. Was there, I wondered, no nearer haven? I buttoned my oilskin and went up to scan the shore. Bob pointed ahead.

'Fishermen,' he said. 'They'll know of somewhere safe.'

I eased the jibsheet, put the helm down and *Kylie* came up into the wind, twenty yards from a sixteen-foot boat that was going round in small circles like a terrier chasing its tail. A man stood in the bows paying out codline.

'Any good anchorage around?' yelled Bob, pointing towards a sandy cove.

'Not there,' said the fisherman; 'it's all rocks in there.' He gestured north-east at another boat a hundred yards away. 'Ask 'im. He'll show 'ee.'

From the sternsheets of the other boat two small girls in red life-jackets squinted into the sunshine and inspected us. Their guardian pointed to where the fantastic peaks of Castle Treveen were sawing the skyline. 'You c'n anchor on sand less than a hundred yards offshore in Penberth Cove. Follow me in and I'll show you the best holding.' We handed sail, started the engine and did just that, casting anchor seventy yards off a stone slipway.

Penberth Cove is wedge-shaped, with cliffy sides that are steeper to the west than to the east. Although wide open to the south, it gave superb protection from the northerly gale that howled through our rigging for the next seven hours. The local people were protective too. They threw enough mackerel into our cockpit to feed us for two days, they ferried us ashore in their own boats to drink beer in their pub and they kept a watchful eye on us far into the night while the gale roared through the trees. By the early hours its fury had abated and by the time I was stirring the breakfast porridge the wind had subsided to sighs. We idled for hours in the warmth of the pretty cove but a cheerful teatime forecast on the radio got us going again. Made timid by the gale, we put a reef in the main, edged out from under the lee of Land's End and found that yesterday's bad seas had quite gone. In the sunset, with the wind just east of north we set a rhumb-line course for Cape Clear, shook out the reef and drove towards a coppery sky.

Pendeen, Longships and Seven Stones started winking, the sepia land turned black and *Kylie* scattered diamonds as she left it. By midnight the humps of the higher swells were blotting out Pendeen, and so I took a dipping bearing of the light. It was likely to be my last glimpse of England for a month. What lay ahead, I wondered? I had never visited Ireland, although I had long wanted to do so. Ireland had always sung its own distinctive poetry. It had first electrified me when, during the slump of the Thirties, our house had been filled with Irish workmen. They were not, I found out, just common navvies from Dublin. As my mother told Ma Mason between pegging-out their underwear, they were 'paying guests from over the water'. Even at nine I thought this euphemism a slander, for in my eyes they were joking, gentle giants who had stridden down from the Mountains of Mourne to fill our rooms with chuckling laughter and gently mock my flat Brummagem speech with their hummocky inversions of syntax.

'Is it hraining, it is?'

'Eh? What yow say, Sean?'

'Phwaht? You're not after understanding me? The divil! Ye've been to the pictures, ye have, I'm thinking, and filled your head with nonsense, and it's happened because of that half-penny I gave ye, at all!'

'Whaddya yow *say-ingg*?'

'It's a darling of a day!'

'Yow tipsy agin?' I said, for Mum had found four empty Guinness bottles under his bed.

'O, *usquebaugh*! I'm a fierce man for the drink. '

Bob and I slipped easily into the routine of night watches. When conditions allow I like to work my watches so that every task is followed by a sort of reward. At one o'clock in the morning I check the foot of the genoa for chafe, sliding the clip of my safety-harness gently along the lifeline on the side-deck so that the noise doesn't disturb Bob in his bunk below. Then I slacken the upper guard-rope through its stanchions so that the foot of the genoa does not bear upon it. That done, I reward myself with a pipe in the lee of the spray-hood. My next task at two o'clock involves less exertion but more irk. I squat like a soothsayer and peer into the crystal ball of the radio direction-finder. Round Island is loud and South Bishop is clear, but Mizen Head, 150 miles distant, has a null that is wider than the bogs of Killarney. I pencil a huge cocked hat on the chart, sigh at the size of it and pour a poteen of twelve-year-old whiskey, Sean's *usquebaugh*, 'the waters of life'. This and a Mars Bar syrups me into a better humour. An hour later the whiskey has evaporated but I pump the bilge and write up the log, glad of the warmth of the cabin. At a quarter to four I pour methylated spirits onto the Primus and watch the blue flame creep down the stem into the bowl. When the flame is roaring softly I wake Bob. He sits on the edge of his bunk rubbing resentment out of his beard. I put a mug of coffee into his hands.

'Had a good sleep?' I say, savouring his withdrawal symptoms and looking fondly at my sleeping-bag.

At four in the morning a sleeping-bag is the best reward of all.

*

Thirty-two hours after leaving Penberth we entered Irish waters, with the light of the Old Head of Kinsale rising on our starboard beam. In northerly airs we ghosted westwards until at three o'clock on a blazing July afternoon we entered Gascanane Sound, which separates Cape Clear Island from its neighbour.

'I want to arrive all clean and tidy, like the Hiscocks do,' I'd said, and so we'd washed and shaved and had scrubbed the teak long before we'd got to the sound. I also wanted to arrive under sail, but with the wind in the north I thought it prudent to use the engine in the narrows. My borrowed chart was small-scale and elderly, and many of the soundings in the area had been rubbed out by its owner's wet cuffs on wild days.

The ferry thudded past, on its way from Baltimore to Clear's North Harbour. With its green hull and a snarling wave beneath the bow, it looked like an angry cucumber. It ploughed ahead of us, up Gascanane

Sound, and then veered left, across a stretch of water where my magnifying glass showed rocks and shoals to be as plentiful as dimples in crumpets. I didn't follow in its wake. Instead, I started the engine and crept up the main channel, intending to make dog-legs into Roaringwater Bay. We crawled up the first of the limbs.

'When the summit of Cape Clear bears 215° we'll ease to the west, set the genoa, stop the engine and make into North Harbour under sail,' I said, feeling rather grand in a clean blue shirt. It didn't happen like that at all. In the narrowest part of Gascanane Sound the engine stopped of its own volition. There passed a stressful half-hour. We re-set the main and genoa, and while Bob jilled about I fiddled with the engine. After twenty sweaty minutes my oily fingers grasped the starting-handle and swung it. The engine fired at once.

When an ailing engine is going again, who has the nerve to stop it? So we entered Ireland sheepishly, under engine after all. Also, I thought, looking at my oil-stained shirt and the cabin strewn with spanners and damp rags, we were not even clean and couth down below.

'It's not much better aloft,' said Bob, eyeing the flags. Our circlings had rolled them into tubes round the halyards. I stumped on deck and shook at the halyards until the yellow 'Q' flag and the Irish ensign had unwound themselves. Only when that had been done did I feel I could point *Kylie* towards our first Irish port and prepare my documents to meet its officials.

It turned out that I needn't have bothered, because there weren't any officials.

'The *garda*?' said a skein of jerseyed idlers on the quay. 'Oh, he's gone to watch the Roaringwater regattas.'

But, I said to them, if I couldn't actually *meet* an official perhaps I might speak to one?

'Yes,' they said, 'and so you may. You'll find a telephone alongside the third house up the hill.' It took a few minutes for them to dig into their pockets and lend me coins for the phone. I had got twenty paces on my way when they called me back.

'We forgot to tell you that you won't be able to use the telephone at the moment,' they smiled, 'because Paddy at the exchange won't be on duty till tonight.'

Forty-one hours after setting foot on Irish soil I at last got through to the Customs in Bantry. One reason for the delay was that it took me a long time to find the telephone box, for it was surrounded by luxuriant bushes and it was painted the same green as their leaves. The other reason was that Paddy had forsaken his telephonist's duty-roster and taken upon himself the more pleasurable task of watching over the *garda* at the Roaringwater regattas, which regattas went on for a week.

Chance rather than choice seemed to govern the lives of the islanders, but when your island is only three miles long and a mile broad, and only two hundred and fifty people live there, the chances of meeting so-and-so or of finding such-and-such are closer to being certainties than in most other places. So when in my search for the telephone I came upon my friend Barbara from Norfolk, what I hailed as a marvellous coincidence seemed quite unremarkable to her. We stood in her cottage at Comillane, looking down on Gascanane Sound. The inside walls of the cottage were warmly clad in tongued-and-grooved pinewood. A chance wreck rather than an expedition to the mainland sawmills would have provided that wood, for there are few trees on the island and imports are very expensive.

It is a place where the seasons ebb and flow, and each season brings its own chance of profit: wrecks in winter, herring in the spring, tourists in the summer: that was the way things went. Time passed, of course, but there seemed to be more of it about, and it came along in larger units. Minutes and seconds were never mentioned, and even hours were less important than elsewhere — there were no clocks in Barbara's cottage — and so life went on at a less urgent, less mechanical pace, one which allowed people to bathe forever in warm oases of conversation. Unhurried, unflustered and always smiling, they gossiped in doorways, on hillsides, and over walls in the daytime, and at evening they did the same in O'Driscoll's bar, where no-one, I told Barbara, ever seemed to think of calling 'Time!'.

Bubbling with laughter, she listened to my words and as soon as I had finished she told me of an event that confirmed my view. During the previous summer, she said, a visiting yacht had moored alongside the quay in the small inner harbour. After taking the bottom on an ebbing tide it had listed the wrong way and had fallen onto its side. The anxious skipper had sought local help to right his vessel before the flooding tide could fill the hull with water. Of course, said the islanders, help would be coming immediately, for the harbourmaster had already sent word for Michael on his tractor to proceed forthwith and lead a salvage operation. And how far away, enquired the skipper, with one eye on the now rising tide, would Michael be? The harbourmaster was pleased to set the skipper's mind at rest by pointing out the tractor, clearly visible in a field only three quarters of a mile distant up the hill overlooking the harbour. The relieved skipper returned to his vessel and began to lay out ropes in preparation for the imminent arrival of his salvor.

Barbara's cottage at Comillane

'In fact,' said Barbara, 'Michael didn't get to the harbour until an hour after he had received the urgent summons.' He had come as quickly as he could, of course, but it seemed that conditions that morning had not been conducive to a speedy passage. No, he hadn't got stuck in a soft patch, and no again, the tractor's engine had not been misbehaving. The problem had been that every hundred yards or so Michael had come across several of his many friends and neighbours and had temporarily stopped his tractor to inform them of the reason for his abrupt and unexpected departure from his field. After expressing their vigorous interest in the errand of mercy, each of his audience had volunteered a detailed analysis of the reasons for the accident and had followed it up with equally detailed advice on how best Michael could assist in this grave emergency. Since his route to the harbour passed among so many separate and often contradictory advisers, Michael had been obliged to repeat this procedure four times before he could reach the quayside and start the salvage operation, by which time the tide was lapping the cockpit coamings and the skipper was frantic.

*

After lying for two days in crowded North Harbour I looked at the calendar and decided that *Kylie* had better be getting a move on. With Cape Clear regatta due to be held on the following day, another fifty boats would try to squeeze in, trapping those of us already alongside.

'South Harbour is quieter,' said Barbara. 'You could anchor there and our friends at the youth hostel would ferry us ashore in their boat.'

And so at eleven that morning, when Barbara and her son Tom had come aboard with freshly-baked bread, cheese and beer, we eased *Kylie* out of her berth and at Barbara's request I headed for the Fastnet Rock, four miles to the south-west. Every morning as she walked from her house at Comillane to the pottery at North Harbour, Barbara would see the rock and its lighthouse.

'...and sometimes, walking back in the evening, I stop at the crest of the hill and watch the splayed fingers of light stroke the sea. Sometimes I wonder about the lives of the men cooped up in their little rooms, and I think of how weak their legs would get with nowhere to walk for months on end.'

We moved across a smooth sea towards the rock, and Barbara lifted the binoculars. '...but now I can see that they *do* have a place to stretch their legs,' she said. 'There's three of them in red boiler-suits simply *scampering* around that landing-pad next to the lighthouse tower.'

Kylie approached the pinnacled Fastnet Rock from the north-east and circled it clockwise, about a quarter of a mile distant. A black-hulled steamship with a white superstructure and yellow funnel came up and anchored nearby. Then a helicopter sped out from the mainland, hung above the tower for an instant and dropped onto the concrete pad, buzzing loudly.

'Like a bee onto a flower,' said Barbara. It stayed just long enough for two teams of keepers to swap places and then it rose suddenly, tilted sideways and buzzed back to the land. We freed-off the mainsheet and followed.

Over hot buttered scones we listened to children singing Gaelic songs and afterwards we stood together on the pebbled shore. The wind was light, the stars were bright and I was tempted to stay a few days more. But I knew that I must press on, for *Kylie* had covered less than six hundred miles in ten days. It wasn't at all bad, really, but it left little enough margin if we were to be storm-bound later.

'Goodbye,' said Barbara as I pushed off in the dinghy. 'And be sure to go to Berehaven and Skellig Michael on your way.'

'I shall,' I said. 'And if there's time I could look in on Rathlin O'Birne.'

'Who's he?'

'A notable Irish luminary.'

She laughed, and I laughed too, but for a different reason. For Rathlin O'Birne is a lighthouse.

*

Although she was no sailor, Grandma Hancock was very thoughtful about wind. Whenever a steady, twelve-knot, self-generated belch failed to ease her indigestion she would rise from the table and fiddle with her corsets.

'Moderation is all right,' she would say, 'in owt except wind. A body can enjoy its pudding only after gales of wind or none at all; little burps get your guts nowhere.'

Entirely unstayed, Gran passed away more than forty years ago, but I'd have taken issue with her ghost if I'd met it when I was trying to sail the western edges of Ultima Thule. Off Ireland and the Hebrides the lack of steady, moderate wind disrupted a vital crew-change and messed-up my cruising schedule. Between leaving Cape Clear and arriving at Scrabster sixteen days later we had only ten hours of winds that were more than 24 knots — and most of them came while we were anchored off Barra, in the

Outer Hebrides. On the other hand, one hundred and fifty two log-entries recorded winds of less than seven knots. For only one quarter of our working hours did it blow in the moderate, acceptable twelve to twenty-knot bracket.

'Be sure to visit Berehaven, Great Skellig, the Blaskets and the Aran Islands,' Barbara had said when I left Cape Clear. Bob and I tried hard, but the wind let us reach only two of them.

We started quite well; five hours after leaving Cape Clear *Kylie* was off Mizen Head in a twelve-knot breeze, making for Ardnakinna lighthouse to enter Berehaven. In the funnel between Bere Island and the mainland hills the wind rose to twenty knots, and so we looked again at the aged chart and sped on happily past Castletown, spreading *Kylie*'s white embroidery on the green waves as we went.

Old charts are lovely things, and not only for navigation. My borrowed chart of Bantry Bay had been drawn in 1850. Folded once, it was an accurate gauge for setting the spark-plug gap. Bob liked this built-in engineering feature but he was less enthusiastic about its accuracy as a map. He thought that even Ireland would have changed a little over the centuries.

'Don't worry,' I said. 'The basic data are reliable enough. A rock with two fathoms above it in 1850 won't have grown any taller since then... Besides,' I enthused, 'just think of all the history that chart gives us! Just look at those ancient pictures on its surface: a place called Brandy Hall is next door to the Union Workhouse. With a bit of imagination, one could write a pseudo-Victorian pamphlet entitled 'From Drink To Destitution In One Short Step'. And that *View Of Hungry Hill* is absolutely quivering with history! Can't you see it? O'Sullevan Bere and his tattered army must've scrambled those very slopes to make their last desperate stand against the Tudor generals while the equally desperate galleons of the Spanish Armada were banging themselves to bits on the Ducalia Rocks.'

'Did Spanish galleons have funnels?' sniffed Bob. 'If so, we'll soon be running into a somewhat ancient monument.'

Still bearing my tot of White Jamaica, I clambered to the cockpit and peered forwards. Only half a mile ahead the wreck of a steamship lay across the channel, its superstructure high out of the water. Of course, the wreck wasn't shown on our 1850 chart.

Silent and thoughtful, we forsook the chart and ran between the rusting relic and the shore, and at five in the afternoon we nosed into Ardrigole, a couple of miles east of Hungry Hill. I tidied the deck and set an anchor light. From the shore came tardy replies, hanging their reflections in the still water as we ate our meal and made plans for Bob's remaining days in *Kylie*.

On paper the plans looked quite straightforward: we would start very early tomorrow, sail the thirty-eight miles to Great Skellig and spend a couple of hours on the island before making for an anchorage in Ventry Bay or Dingle, twenty miles away. On the following day we'd cover the seven miles to the Blasket in the forenoon and after a picnic we'd depart before sunset to sail seventy miles to Inishmore, the largest of the Aran Islands. From there it was only twenty-three miles to Galway, where Bob's berth would be filled by my next crew. One hundred and thirty-five miles in two-and-a-half days seemed a realistic target, especially as fifteen knot westerlies had been forecast.

The plan went awry from the start. The fifteen-knot winds never came, and it was not until early afternoon that we were again off the western entrance to Berehaven. With twenty-eight miles still to go, we couldn't make Great Skellig in daylight and so we used the tide to shoot the narrows of Dursey Sound and soon we were among fishermen's buoys off Garinish Bay. Between the buoys lay webs of fine-filament nets, hanging from the top-ropes that went on for miles, stitching the swells and hindering our passage.

We eyed the setting sun and thought about anchoring. While Bob handed the main, *Kylie* puttered away from the nets. To starboard were rocks and high, grey cliffs. I wondered whether the nets were for salmon. We had seen the boats of Cape Clear after hake, and another Irish boat had shouted of mackerel and had pitched a bucketful into our cockpit, but even in *O'Driscoll's* bar, pints of Smithers hadn't loosened any talk about fishing for salmon.

'Tis illegal in July,' they'd said with a sigh.

At half-past seven, with the sun quite gone, we brought up in three fathoms on sand. I tidied the cockpit and lit a pipe. Garinish Bay is a silent, brooding place; moreover, I reminded myself, it was a *foreign* place. Something about the light and the landscape was subtly different from England...

A crescent of beach stretched from our starboard beam to broad on our port bow, while a cable's length away on our port hand was a steep cliff. Astern of us lay more rocks, with a narrow channel between. On the beach stood a man, and he was watching us.

Why was it that I reached into the cabin, studied the chart, pulled out a compass and took a bearing of that channel, our sole exit? It wasn't only that the cliff looked oppressive, almost threatening. It wasn't just that those rocks were rather close. I took the bearing because of the way that man was watching us. He was watching us intently; and, I thought, he was watching with secret purpose...

Bob was amused to see me taking bearings. 'Surely we'll not need to get out of here quickly?' He tapped the barometer. 'It's still at 1030 millibars and there's no sign of wind.'

I looked again at the chart to make sure. The west coast of Ireland abounded with bays; in one of them, not too many miles from this one and not so long ago, hadn't our Queen Elizabeth's uncle Lord Louis Mountbatten been bombed to bits under the gaze of secret watchers from the shore?

I noted the bearing and said nothing. I glanced out of the hatchway. Bob was right: the weather showed no sign of change, but I sensed that *something* was different. Slowly, I allowed my eyes to look at the shore. I saw at once what had altered.

The watcher had been joined by another. They stood together, hands in pockets, looking fixedly at me.

'Sun's gone,' I said, turning my back on them. I set about lowering our flags: first the Irish ensign from the spreaders, and then the red ensign of Great Britain at the stern. It seemed important to fold and roll them neatly; it was as though I was wrapping-up the vibes that were homing-in on me from the shore.

'Where is it you're going?' they'd ask me for sure, more roughly than my friend at Cape Clear.

'Just sailing round the British Isles,' I'd say.

'You're *not*!' they'd say, priming the fuse. 'This is *Ireland*, it's not bloody British at all...'

As though they had heard my thoughts, the watchers moved to action, pulling a small black boat to the water's edge. While one readied the oars the other strode to a nearby car and lifted something out of its boot. He cradled the thing in his arms and carried it to the waiting craft. In seconds they were afloat, the oarsman rowing in regular, unhurried sweeps towards me.

At ten yards distance the oarsman stopped rowing and growled something to his tall companion who stood in the sternsheets, his arms hanging loosely at his sides. It wasn't a very seamanlike stance, but it was curiously familiar. It was the way John Wayne had often stood, just before whipping out his Colt 45. The man was the same build as John Wayne, too...

The boat came on, its bows creasing the dark waters. The feeling of unease, which had grown to one of prickly menace at the approach of the black skiff with its grim crew and unknown cargo, now became one of full-blown fear. I felt that a smile of welcome would have been as misplaced as confetti on a coffin. Instead, I wanted to scream 'For God's sake pass me the Very pistol!'

Unfortunately we had no pistol, Very or otherwise. Also unfortunately, it was now too late to do anything, for the boat was alongside.

The cargo lay between John Wayne's feet. The assassins had tried to conceal its true character by covering it with a piece of torn sacking, but through the holes I glimpsed something that had the sheen of steel.

John Wayne was so tall that his eyes were level with mine, even though he stood a foot lower. I felt for the backstay to brace myself against whatever might come.

Keeping his eyes fixed on mine, the big man reached under the sacking.

I couldn't move.

He leaned forward, grabbed me roughly by the shoulder and thrust something under my nose.

Then his face split into a wide smile, and his voice when it came was soft as Irish moss.

'Do ye fancy a fresh salmon?' he said.

*

We made out of Garinish Bay under ghoster, using the early-morning zephyrs to thread our way between fleets of nets that snaked offshore. By ten o'clock even the zephyrs had disappeared, and so we dropped the sails. Two dolphins idled past and a flotilla of Portuguese men o' war drifted by under their purple spinnakers. Sighing, we started the engine and five hours later arrived off the sheer cliffs of Great Skellig.

The cliffs rise straight from the sea and are topped by a 700-foot pinnacle. Near the top of the eastern cliffs are the beehive-shaped cells in which monks had lived fifteen centuries ago. Outside one of the beehives I came across an archaeologist eating a tomato sandwich. In girth and demeanour he resembled Buddha except that his legs were not in the lotus position; they were extended straight out and were clad in corduroy. Beside him was a blank notebook. An aeroplane flew in noisy circles overhead and waggled its wings, at which the archaeologist waved a response and shut his notebook.

'Hot,' he said, composing himself for a nap.

Below me others were sleeping too. Arms wide, a brace of lighthouse-keepers sprawled cruciform in the sunshine. Near them a crane poked out from the cliff, a hundred feet above the sea. Every so often a launch darted away from an anchored ship with another boat-load of stores and chivvied the sleeping men into silent activity.

'We should be moving as well,' I said to Bob when he got back to *Kylie*. She lay alongside the stone quay of a 60-foot gut called Blind Man's Cove, her bows nestling in a deep fissure in the rock. Less than twenty feet to starboard a sheer cliff hung above the truck of the mast, while between the quay and the cliff filtered the surge and heave of the long Atlantic swells. *Kylie* snickered uneasily at her fenders and snapped at her lines.

We cast off and motored stern-first out of the cove. I dipped the fuel tank and saw from the marks on the stick that only a gallon remained — enough for about three hours at half throttle. From Great Skellig it was twenty miles to the Blasket, eighty to the Aran Isles and one hundred and six to Galway. Made optimistic by an early tot of rum, I wrote in the log, *Going Aran tomorrow to replenish tank. Also, need more tobacco.*

During the ensuing three hours we made only four and a half miles, and so Bob's patience wore thin.

'Aran? Tomorrow? You must be joking.'

'Valentia, then?' I offered. 'It's only ten miles to Fort Cromwell.'

To cover those ten miles took ten hours. Not wanting to enter a strange harbour in darkness, I was content to curry faint airs and creep along the shore, but before dawn the fog which had been hanging in the valleys all night seeped out to sea and swallowed us. I snatched a bearing of Fort Cromwell light before it was hidden and then headed towards it. An hour and a half later, when visibility was down to a hundred yards, Bob heard breakers ahead and at the same time I glimpsed the white body and red eye of the lighthouse. No longer needing to navigate by Bob's ears, we started the engine and at breakfast-time brought up in two fathoms near the Knightstown lifeboat.

Years ago it was common knowledge that when you said into an English telephone 'Please send reinforcements, we are going to advance', the chap at the other end heard it as 'Please send three-and-fourpence, we are going to a dance'. These days, what is not quite so widely known is that when your crew says into an Irish telephone 'Please tell John to join *Kylie* at Valentia', the message is received as 'Please tell John to laze for two days in a Galway bed-and-breakfast while the skipper washes his socks'.

Actually, I'm not being truthful. While waiting for John I washed not only my socks but all my other clothing as well. After that I went on to scrub the waterline, repair the Primus, air the sails, renew frayed yoke-lines, make up six reef-points and re-read a back number of *Punch* till I knew four jokes by heart.

Bob's successor John Grix arrived by taxi from Tralee just in time for tea. Forty minutes later, while he was still stowing his gear, I edged *Kylie* out of her berth and set off for the Outer Hebrides, 320 miles away. I think my haste was excusable, for with three-eighths of my holiday gone I still had three-fifths of the distance to cover. Had the forecasters been talking about moderate winds I'd have gone to all the other places we wanted to visit, but they said the high pressure was intensifying, from which it seemed to me that light winds and slow progress were to be with us for a long time yet.

Off Valentia we counted ourselves lucky to find a force two northerly as we headed for the Blaskets. Although going through Blasket Sound would have saved twelve miles, the absence of shore lights, the strong tides and the litter of rocks in the area persuaded me that a night passage would be too perilous, and so all night long we pressed westward in a fading wind. At three in the morning we were clear of the Blaskets and had reached the most westerly point of my round-Britain circuit. I bit into a Mars Bar and pointed for Achill Head, 115 miles distant.

It took two days eight hours to cover that 115 miles. At first the wind freshened a little and veered north-east, so that we made good twenty-three miles in six hours, but by noon on the following day it had backed to the north and dropped to six knots so that we were beating limply towards the Mayo coast. To purge my frustration I washed a bucketful of dirty clothes, using bilge-cleaner and salt water. The results felt and smelt surprisingly clean.

They were not the only surprise: for three days we hadn't seen a ship. During my North Sea and English Channel passages, sightings of other vessels had been so frequent as to be unremarkable, but between Valentia and our landfall on the Outer Hebrides we sighted only two other ships. The first, a coaster, overtook us off Eagle Island. The second, a handsome 15-ton cutter, met us on a reciprocal course twenty-five miles west of the Bloody Foreland when *Kylie* was pitching towards Barra Head.

Her motion was easy and comfortable. I washed and shaved in half a pint of hot water in a nine-inch bowl which sat on the lee-side of the cockpit. Another cupful of hot water poured onto a rough flannel was enough for a head-to-toe rub-down. A freshwater flannel-bathe after a long night watch lifts your spirits almost as much as when you make a landfall exactly when you said you would.

Good landfalls are not windfalls; you have to work for them. For seventy-two days Simon Hunter had to work himself and *Kylie* tremendously hard before he sighted the Azores, and that must have been a very good and welcome landfall. A good landfall may not be spectacular; indeed, it may be a rather drab thing, just a smudge seen through rain. Sometimes, a landfall may not really be a landfall at all; it may be only a tree-top that is glimpsed above a wave's crest. But when a landfall appears on the bearing and at the time that you said it would, when your concoction of arithmetic and hunches produces actuality for once, and when the glorious vision reveals itself as it does at the rise of a theatre curtain, why, then you are back again with Jim Hawkins in the *Hispaniola*, borne upwards and onwards forever by the notion that some of life's voyages can, after all, end in a right and fitting way. Even more than that, making a good landfall is like discovering one of the eternal verities: one feels as Archimedes felt on discovering his Principle, and if, at his moment of truth, he could be so moved as to cry 'Eureka!' after a few minutes in a mere bath, what more tremendous noise might not come from the throat of a mariner after weeks on an ocean?

There was a pressing need to make a good landfall on Barra Head. It was a Saturday, we had only two potatoes left in the bin, and we supposed the Castlebay shop would shut for the weekend at five thirty. But again the wind was much lighter than predicted and so we did not sight Barra Head until mid-afternoon. Swathed in summery mist, it shone at us suddenly, its sheep-grey cliffs capped with grass so vividly green that we shouted with delight and surprise. In the lee of the island the wind fell away still more but we did not care, for we had made a wonderful landfall. By then, glimpses of Berneray, Mingulay and Pabbay had opened a Hebridean heaven that wiped all thoughts of potato-famine quite out of our minds. And so, though I glanced at the starting-handle I could not bring myself to use it. Instead, we put up the ghoster and trickled with the tide to Castlebay, anchoring two hours after the shop had closed.

A forecast of gales and thoughts about slippery kelp prompted me to put down two anchors. At the time *Kylie* was carrying a 25lb CQR, a 15lb fisherman and a 10lb Danforth. In average weather, and when anchoring in sand or mud, I used only the CQR. But when anchoring for overnight stays, or when the weather or sea-bed seemed to be

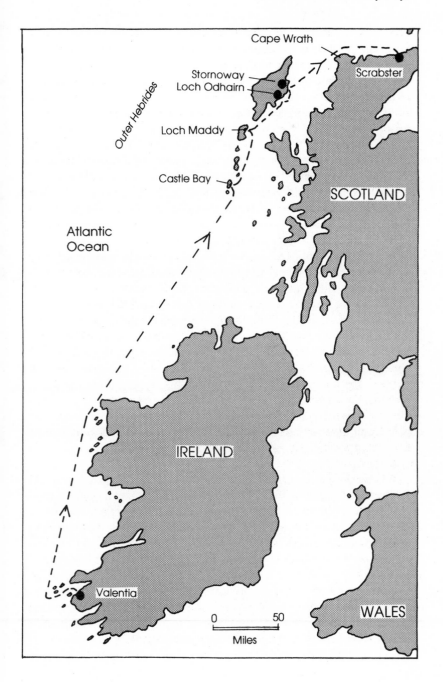

unhelpful, I liked to back-up the CQR by adding the fisherman or Danforth in tandem. Because *Kylie*'s low profile and fine hull offered below-average resistance to wind and waves, I was using only quarter-inch chain as her main cable. I would perhaps have been happier with five-sixteenths, but the safe working load of the quarter-inch tested chain met all my foreseeable needs and had the great advantage of lesser weight.

At Castlebay I lugged the fisherman anchor from below and shackled the end of its two-and-a-half-fathom chain onto the crown of the CQR. When the western church tower was almost in transit with the corner of a manse I swung the fisherman over the bow and paid out its cable until the weight was taken by the CQR, whose upper shank was wedged in the cheeks of the bow-roller. As we started to make sternway I tipped the CQR off the roller and paid out the cable round the deck-cleat until we were lying to twenty fathoms of chain in five fathoms of water. The following night it blew at thirty five-knots from the south-west but we slept soundly and *Kylie* didn't move an inch.

By then we had made 1,100 miles in twenty-one days and I was not unhappy. Before setting out I'd reckoned we needed to average fifty miles a day every day if I were to do the clockwise circuit of Britain in forty days, allowing time to shelter from storms and see something of about a dozen stop-over places. So far, *Kylie* had averaged fifty-two miles a day and had spent eight out of twenty-one nights in seven harbours or anchorages. With eight hundred miles still to go, I had nineteen days remaining. We could have afforded to cruise at a leisurely pace along the length of the Hebrides if John had not had to be back in Norwich a week hence. To meet his deadline we had to get to Scrabster in six days.

With fresh potatoes in the bin we set off before the gale had spent itself. Once clear of Barra the wind got at us cleanly, gusting hard from the west, but in the flat sea we held onto the genoa until the lee rail was burying itself too often and for too long. John plied his camera at the mountains and at the cloud-wracks of the sky. I changed down the headsail. Almost at once the wind dropped away and so it was not until nine at night that we crept into Loch Maddy, anchoring near the pier in a rain-storm which so darkened the sky that we lit the cabin lamp early.

The following day saw us surging past the hills of Harris and Loch Seaforth. It is a gem I'd want to see again before I die. We glimpsed its beauty only briefly, but the sight was unforgettable. Near to was the sugar-candy lighthouse of Eilean Glas on Scalpay. Behind it, dappled in sunshine, rose steep mountains, their peaks less than two miles apart. Between the mountains the bright shaft of Loch Seaforth lanced for miles into the green heart of Lewis. The forms and colours were so dramatic and so fitted our mood that the spectacle quite dimmed all the later sights. When we ghosted up Loch Odhairn to a silken evening anchorage it was the images of Loch Seaforth that still crowded our mind.

But soon the pretty pictures were ousted by practicalities. It is fifty-four miles from Stornoway to Cape Wrath and another forty-six to Scrabster. We left Stornoway with plenty of time in hand, we thought, to reach Scrabster and John's homeward transport by Saturday morning at the latest. But Thursday's early-morning forecast of fifteen-knot winds again fell short of the mark. *Kylie* dawdled across the North Minch, making only three knots through a drear sea and cold drizzle. By mid-afternoon we were in mist, listening to Tiumpan Head fog-signals twenty miles distant and admiring the flight of some gannets with yellow-tinged necks. Through midnight rain we picked up the light of Cape Wrath at ten miles, but then the wind died completely and so we started the engine. The rain thickened and we went by dead reckoning until through a sudden hole in the curtain the light gleamed briefly down on our deck. It looked much too close for comfort so I turned sharply away and opened the throttle.

The result was alarming. The engine noise, usually a busy chatter, rose at once to an outraged roar. I eased back to slow speed, telling myself that the carburation had gone haywire. But after I'd checked the engine and found nothing amiss I began to think the problem was more serious. Each time I gave her more than half-throttle the cockpit-slats would tingle through my trousers. At full revs the compass card was spinning like a roulette wheel.

Brooding, I settled for slow revs and nursed us past Strathy Point. At nine on Friday evening we entered Thurso Bay. Scrabster lay before us, its green harbour light winking enticingly. The lure of a quiet haven was more than the engine could stand. It gulped the last of the fuel, emitted a scream and died.

We paddled *Kylie* into the harbour, watched by a line of late-night fishermen on the breakwater.

'What do you reckon the matter is?' asked John as he caught the last 'plane to Wick.

'Probably lost the tip of one of the blades,' I said.

'That's a serious problem.'

'In Scotland it isn't,' I said easily. 'Why, Scotland practically *invented* the propeller. Don't you worry; someone here will fix it.'

Someone did, but not in Scrabster.

*

Scrabster's only hotel is snug and pleasant, and when Martin Dyer arrived to replace John Grix as *Kylie*'s crew, we went into the bar to celebrate his safe coming and to drink some local advice from a member of the lifeboat crew.

'Don't on any account leave here,' the lifeboatman warned us, 'until the men out there have stopped their jig.'

Martin Dyer looked at me and I looked back at him. Both of us wondered if the lifeboatman had heard my question.

'Better still,' continued the lifeboatman, 'wait until they're fast asleep.'

As I said to Martin later, we had only done what all the cruising handbooks told us to do: we'd talked to the locals. And if the local advice was different from our own reasoning, the sensible thing to do was to follow the local advice, especially when it came from a lifeboatman and we were about to go through the Pentland Firth, where the tides could run at more than ten knots.

With the charts spread out in *Kylie*'s cabin I went through it all again.

'Here's the Merry Men of Mey.' I pointed to the tide-race symbols extending the full width of the Pentland Firth. '*He* said that the race is only there on the ebb. I didn't know that, but I believe him. He also said — and this I find hard to believe — that we shouldn't leave Scrabster until an hour and a half before high water, when the Merry Men have gone to sleep.' I rubbed another palmful of flake. 'That's four hours later than I'd calculated. I'd thought to set out with the first of the flood so as to carry the whole of the tide past Dunnet Head,' my finger wended eastwards, 'past Stroma and the Pentland Skerries and halfway across the Moray Firth.'

'Let's do that then,' said Martin.

'No,' I said, folding away the chart. 'The books say we should follow local advice. We'd better let the tide-race go to sleep.'

'Four and a half hours after the end of the ebb the Merry Men won't be just asleep,' scoffed Martin; 'they'll be dead.'

'All right,' I said. 'I take your point.'

'So we stick to our original plan?'

'No,' I said. 'We'll do what the English so often do when they're in a dilemma.'

Holborn Head Lighthouse, near Scrabster

'What's that?' said Martin.

'We'll compromise.'

'Oh, dear,' he said, turning down the lamp.

*

We got under way at a quarter to seven, two hours earlier than the lifeboatman had advised but two hours later than I had originally planned.

The barometer had stood at 1017mb for seven hours. The early-morning forecast had said that a force three north-westerly would later veer south. I didn't have much faith in those predicted force threes. During the previous weeks all the force threes had turned out to be force twos or less. Off Dover, off St Catherine's, off Cape Clear and Great Skellig, off Barra and Cape Wrath they had forecast their ten-knot winds, and always, in the end, we'd had to use the engine. 'An engine in a sailing craft should be merely a bit of help on the side; an engine should *not* be the sole source of power,' I told myself, echoing the sentiments of the pre-1960 textbooks. But now, with time running out, I could wait for wind no longer, and we used the engine yet again to get out into Thurso Bay.

I kept the revs to slow speed, for I knew that to widen the throttle would bring on another attack of the frenzied vibrations that had started off Cape Wrath. We had lain alongside at Scrabster for two days, waiting for wind. At each high water I had considered whether to shift to a shallow corner of the harbour to examine the propeller but each time I had decided against doing so. If the propeller did need repair, I told myself, the tides wouldn't let us hang around the western end of the Pentland Firth to do the job. On that point the pilot books were unanimous: avoid spring tides when transiting the Pentland Firth, they said, for at springs the current runs at twelve knots off Muckle Skerry. No sailboat I know could cope with a twelve knot tide, even if it had a big engine and a brace of propellers. Every day we remained at Scrabster brought us another day closer to springs. Today was almost our last chance to get through, for today the tides were between neaps and springs and they would run at about six knots. I stopped worrying about the propeller and prayed for wind.

In Thurso Bay there was little enough of it, and already it had begun to veer. We beat slowly up to Dunnet Head on port tack, tending the genoa sheet to catch every breath. I looked again at the courses. The first was to a point a mile off Dunnet Head, and the next was to a position two miles north of Stroma, from where we'd go midway between Duncansby Head

90

and Muckle Skerry before sliding out across the Moray Firth '...with about three knots of tide beneath us,' I told Martin, 'plus what we make with the wind.'

'If we still have any,' said Martin; 'it's getting lighter and shifting more to the east — we'll have to go about.'

The windshifts squeezed us into a series of tacks, and it was not until half-past eight that we brought Dunnet Head abeam. Then the flood stream gripped us and we covered the next twelve miles to Duncansby at six knots, through occasional patches of boiling water that shook the wind out of the sails. Coming towards Stroma the wind headed us, and so we forsook the charted track, steering instead for the narrower Inner Sound between Stroma and the mainland. *Kylie* plunged through acres of seething cauliflowers.

'That looks like the worst of it over,' I said as we crashed through.

'If that is so,' said Martin, 'then what's this up front of us?'

I looked ahead and blinked. Then I jumped onto the coachroof and looked again. The line of the eastern horizon was not black, but white. It was not distant but ever-nearing; it was not a remote ocular phenomenon but a writhing, spitting, living thing. It was a monstrous white serpent, ten miles long and three feet thick, thrashing in acid.

It was the resurrected Men of Mey, thought Martin, doing a merry, endless conga.

It was the Race of Duncansby, stretching from the headland as far as my eyes could see, and there was no way we could miss it.

The tide bore us onwards at umpteen knots. I held my breath. There was the sudden noise of a thousand saucepans boiling over, *Kylie*'s bows lifted sharply and she trod the serpent underfoot without even wetting her decks.

Aware of a certain dryness in our throats, we made a cup of tea.

Beyond Duncansby the tide slackened and petered out, but astern of us the rocks of Muckle Flugga still lay flat on the water, like fallen skittles at the end of an alley. Soon the ebb would be setting against us, bowling us back into the mouth of the Firth at an increasing rate of knots. Like so many other compromises, mine had almost failed, but I could console myself with the thought that had I followed local advice and left Scrabster two hours later, *Kylie* would not have got through. Even now, success was touch-and-go.

'We should be all right for crossing the Moray Firth,' I told Martin, 'if the wind doesn't fail.'

But, of course, the wind did just that. Force two at noon, it was force

91

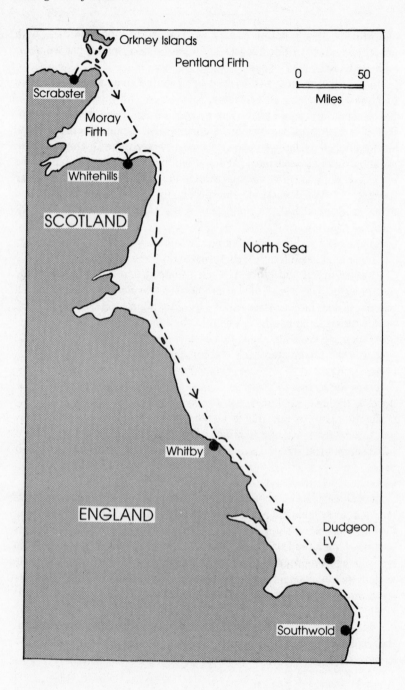

one at midnight, and in the dawn it died altogether. At sunrise *Kylie* lay on still waters, her mainsail trussed like Auntie Flo's umbrella, surrounded by a fleet of fulmars arguing about the whereabouts of fish, but for Martin and I there was no arguing with the tide and the weather. The tide dribbled us back and forth, twelve miles off the invisible coast. The needle of the barometer was still glued on 1017mb and there was no sign of wind. We stuck it out, hoping for a breeze when the land warmed, but at one in the afternoon we gave up and worked our way into Whitehills, three miles west of Banff.

The sight of a yacht leaning against their quay brought the villagers out in force.

'Och, ye've got problems,' they said, wagging their heads gloomily when the falling tide revealed that *Kylie* had lost an entire propeller blade. Most of them turned discreetly away, as though strangers at a graveside, but one man refused to bury all hope.

'There's a propeller factor at Buckie,' he said. 'Take the keys of my van and drive there straight away before he closes.'

Then he thought again about his offer and bit his lip. 'No,' he said. 'On second thoughts I'll drive you there myself.'

His kind act cheered us greatly, but in Buckie we were cast into gloom again.

'Electrolysis,' they murmured, 'and broken off near the boss, too. We can't do anything with that.' But surely they could find us a complete replacement? The shop-floor was strewn with propellers, their bronze blades as thick as leaves in Birnam Woods. They pursed their lips and shook their heads: 'We doubt there's anything as small as this.'

Nor was there. They riffled through drawers and cabinets and they poked into dark and dusty corners, but in the end all they had to offer was the address of a place which would certainly have one of our size.

'Where is it?' we said, thanking them for their trouble.

'London,' they said, handing us a slip of paper.

It was out of the question, of course. We went into Banff and telephoned. 'Five or six days,' they said, 'by express delivery.' And so we went the rounds of the local boatyards. In one of them we found David Mackie, who collected propellers as assiduously as some people collect teaspoons.

'No,' he said at first, shaking his head as gloomily as all the rest. By now the head-wagging had become a national trait, like wearing kilts and playing bagpipes. 'Eleven-by-six, two-bladed, left-handed ones are hard to come by.'

93

We waited for another thought to strike him. It did.

'Just a minute,' he said. 'I may have one underneath my rowan tree.'

He came back with a soil-encrusted antique, but it was of the right pitch and diameter. By the next low-water Martin had beaten out two little copper collars that ensured the propeller fitted snugly on the shaft. With the tide lapping his knees he tightened the castellated nut on the end of the shaft and we prepared for a trial run.

The replacement had three blades, whereas the original had only two. The extra blade would impose a greater load on the engine and transmission, and so, fearful of damaging the clutch, we again ran it at no more than half-throttle. Even so, it pushed *Kylie* through flat water at a steady three knots. Most importantly, there was no vibration.

We left Whitehills at one in the morning. With 450 miles still to go and only six days of holiday left, we were anxious to make progress, but for the next sixty hours the winds were as light as ever and, worse still, were always in our faces. The easterly that met us as we half-beat, half-motored the twenty miles to Kinnairds Head became a southerly when we turned the corner and headed south. But off the Firth of Forth it strengthened, and for the first time in a fortnight *Kylie* was heeling ten degrees as we beat towards the Northumbrian coast. Because of the light winds we had scotched an earlier plan to put in at St Abb's, but we still thought it prudent to keep in sight of land in case the engine gave more problems.

It was fortunate that we did so, for that evening Martin fell ill. Pale and wan, he rigged the lee-cloth and lay shivering in his bunk. We ran through the night before a freshening north-easterly. Although the seas were only moderate they came jumping at me from the backs of the swells, setting *Kylie* rolling heavily and dumping green water on deck. In such conditions I thought that entering Tynemouth or Sunderland at night would be uncomfortable if not foolhardy and so at midnight I altered course for Whitby and raised it in the morning.

Martin struggled into the cockpit as we approached the piers. The clouds were low, the wind strong, the waves steep, and his face grey. He looked pretty ill, and I was anxious to get him to a doctor.

We shuttered the hatchway, clipped on our harnesses and shot between the piers. I handed sail, Martin took the helm and we motored through the unfamiliar harbour towards a marina. It was crowded, with boats three deep on most of the pontoons. But at one spot a forty-footer lay singly. We edged alongside, and a bristly face emerged from the deckhouse.

'ere!' it yelled. 'Yer can't come 'ere! This place is taken!'

We were in no mood to argue. I cast a bight over his cleats and asked about doctors.

The hospital diagnosed gastroenteritis and ordered Martin to his bunk with a large bottle of pills.

'Stop apologising,' I said as he crawled back into his sleeping-bag. 'It's probably my cooking that's to blame. Besides, I've always wanted to come into Whitby and sample its seafood.' I unrolled a clean shirt and laced-up my shoes. 'Shall I find you,' I said, 'a nice line in eels?'

By the following morning he was feeling much stronger and so we decided to press on. Our leave-taking was happier than our arrival, for the owner of the sloop *Bluefin*, learning that our clutch was slipping, towed us out to sea.

When we had gained an offing *Bluefin* cast off the tow-line and we wallowed for a long time until a light north-easterly came along to waft us languidly down the coast. We hoped always for better, but all day the winds remained light and soon they became adverse again. As we neared the Dudgeon lightship two of the crew were rod-fishing from the helicopter deck. We called to them, asking if they'd like any mail posted, and they swung us a bucketful of mackerel with their letters. With a farewell wave, we beat towards the Norfolk coast, leaving them sunbathing under a sugar-dusted sky. It was so hot in the cockpit that I stripped off too, while Martin sang songs about sheep-shearers and I sang the Birmingham University undergraduates' anthem. Somehow, it summarised things neatly, placing my college prize and my old troopship and my early seafaring ambitions in the centre of England, just about as far away from the sea as my father, mother and Auntie Flo had really wanted them to be:

> 'My old man's a fi-i-ireman,
> Now what d'you think of that?
> He wears gorblimey trousers
> And a little gorblimey hat.
> He wears a something muffler
> Ahra-ahnd his something throat
> O, my old man's a fireman
> On an Elder Dempster boat....A-a-a-men.'

Southwold was still simmering in the same heat-wave when we got back. We crossed the bar of the Blyth at half-flood and moored outside the *Harbour of Refuge Inn*. I went ashore, carrying the letters from the crew of the Dudgeon lightship. On the flap of one of the envelopes had been written 'S.W.A.L.K.' Takes me back a few years, I thought.

'Smashing weather,' said the landlord. 'Wonderful for trade.'

'Could do with some wind,' I told him.

He frowned, and then he pulled me a pint of Broadside ale. 'The trouble with you sailing people is,' he said, 'that you're never bloody satisfied.'

6

Five-handed Solo

Jennie Cooke disappeared from the cockpit on the afternoon of Friday the thirteenth, four days out from Falmouth on passage to Gibraltar. The wind was north-northeast, about twenty-five knots and rising. She was wearing yellow oilies and pink carpet-slippers. I did not try to get her back.

I recollect that shortly before she vanished I was on deck, tying down a second reef in the main and setting a Yankee in place of the number two genoa. It was wettish work but it wasn't cold, and to conserve my dry clothing I was wearing only swimming-trunks and safety harness.

'Why do you bother with the swimming-trunks?' she called as I towelled myself in the cabin. 'A small boat is no place for prudery. Let go... just let it go.'

'Together with your pink slippers,' I muttered. Because the knot in the waist-cord had contracted I was having difficulty untying it, and so when *Kylie* yawed and lurched, I was pitched into the starboard bunk, with the trunks halfway down my thighs and with my right hand doubled under my left shoulder.

'Not a lot of help, are you, telling me to let go when I needed to hang on?' I called, but there was no reply.

I looked out. The cockpit was empty. Astern were heaving grey hills, but there were also some very rumpled plateaux the colour and texture of baize. Some of the plateaux were spread with tatty white doilies. I thought how untidy they looked in the slant of the afternoon sunshine: tatty white doilies on crumpled green baize table-cloths... At four o'clock, I remember thinking, Jennie's mother will be along. She will smooth the untidy table-cloths and she will set out tea and Maid-of-Honour cakes. However, I did not think of throwing a life-belt overside or retracing my course to search for her daughter. Out there, amidst the watery hills plodded a couple of size five pink slippers. And they were made — for Heaven's sake! — of satin. They were not quite the proper footwear for a swim in the ocean, I thought; or, come to that, for a tea-party. That was why I left her to it: because the slippers were definitely out of place. 'Let go', she had said, and so I did. Jennie had gone.

I dribbled fresh water onto a flannel, bathed the salt from my eyes and nursed my sore wrist. I took down the cutting-board, opened my knife and divided the daily Mars Bar into four portions. I inspected them critically. The farthest left-hand piece seemed fractionally smaller than the others.

'I'll have *you*, I will, at two in the morning with coffee and rum,' I promised it. Then I sighed, thinking that if the wind strengthened I'd have to set the storm jib in place of the Yankee. Wouldn't it be wonderful thing if somebody else would help me? Jennie would have done it... And Mark Goldsworthy would have *leapt* to do it. 'Jennie...!' I called. 'Mark...' I called. But there was no reply.

I sighed again. Things were uncommonly difficult to work out. I had never imagined that a straightforward passage to the Mediterranean could involve such utter confusion. Despite my declared intention of sailing solo once the English Channel was behind me, while preparing for the voyage my iron resolve had been melted down by the worries of my daughters and the flickers of my own fear. When I looked at the modern charts I was astonished to find that since my days in the troopship with Captain Trump, Gibraltar had drifted a couple of hundred miles farther from England than it ever used to be. In the end I had come to the tacit agreement that single-handed sailing was a postponable luxury, to be indulged in only after one or other of my friends had crewed me to Gibraltar. My friends were fine, capable people, but their present rate of comings and goings was upsetting. Would none stay aboard longer than an hour or two?

The comings and goings had started in Falmouth. Mark and I had set out from Southwold, hoping to sail *Kylie* to Falmouth in less than a week, and to Gibraltar in four. It wouldn't be difficult, we thought, to sail from Southwold to Falmouth in under a week, but it had taken us much longer, for we had been held up by westerly gales and engine problems.

'At this rate we'll be only half-way across Biscay by the time my month is up,' had said Mark, worrying about a backlog of work. We agreed that work must take priority, and so, regretfully, he had left. He had been the first to go. Although the sailing season was ending, we had told each other it would be easy to find another crew, and we had believed it.

I had asked around, had advertised on the marina notice-board, in the local press and in tobacconists' windows. By the end of a week there'd been four applicants.

The first had phoned to say that he'd broken an arm and would I wait a month for it to heal? The second, a nurse, had declared that she'd *love* to see Gibraltar or wherever, but could I put the departure on hold for twenty-eight days while she worked out her notice? The third, an end-of-season beach-boy trailing the sun, had looked at *Kylie*'s 26-foot length and said, 'Sorry, friend, but there's nowhere to stow my surf-board.'

An ex-bo'sun of an *America*'s Cup competitor was the fourth. He had inspected me and *Kylie* closely, and then he had nodded his head. Delighted, I had curried some chicken and opened a bottle of *Entre Deux Mers*.

'Morning tide?' I had suggested as he selected one of my King Edward Invincibles.

'Ah,' he'd said, blowing a smoke-ring, 'that might be a bit difficult. Can't be aboard till twelve. Have to pick up my gear, like.'

'Never mind,' I'd said, inhaling the heady aroma. 'We'll take the evening tide instead. Down past the Lizard and away...'

'Tomorrow at twelve, then,' he'd said, draining his glass.

But he hadn't turned up on the morrow... Nor on the next day. I had worried. He had seemed such a solid, healthy person, the sort of oak-hewn yeoman to whom Nelson would have entrusted his 'England expects...' signal off Trafalgar. Perhaps he'd met with an accident? After thirty-six hours I had dialled a contact-number and got through to a pleasant voice who'd said he was my crew's brother. No, he said, he hadn't seen my crew for months. And no, he said, my crew wasn't accident-prone, nor had ever suffered from any recurrent disease that might have struck him down on platform eight at Paddington. So he must have met with an accident, I'd thought. Even as we were speaking, perhaps they were plugging him into a life-support machine at St Bart's... Unless, of course, I had completely misread the grain of his English oak...

'Er... May I ask you a rather delicate question? I know he's your brother and all that, but would you say he's... er... er... reliable?'

I had expected a pause. I mean, a brother is family and all that; not the sort of subject to be discussed with strangers. But the answer had come back almost before I had finished the question.

'*My* brother, my *bloody* brother,' choked the voice, 'is about as reliable as an ice-cream in Vesuvius!'

I had returned aboard, tapped the barometer and written a postcard to my daughters: 'Seems I'm jinxed,' I wrote. 'Haven't found a crew, but must get away before equinoctial gales start. Am leaving Falmouth today.'

Jinxed? Had I said 'jinxed'? I dabbed more fresh water on my eyes and studied the logbook. There was no evidence of black magic in there. In fact, it said that in the four days since leaving Falmouth things had gone quite smoothly. It assured me that we were steering 206°, that our latitude by observation at noon was 44° 51'N, and that our estimated longitude was 10° 10'W. The only bug in the system was among the food stores: I'd opened two tins coded *tomato soup* to find that they contained rice pudding.

I paused in my reading. If tomato soup is rice pudding, and if pink carpet-slippers are worn in wet cockpits, where was reality? Was I *really* sailing alone? Or had Jennie been a flesh-and-blood crew and not a phantom? The nape of my neck went suddenly cold and my mind wouldn't answer.

Kylie gave another heave and lurch, and a dozen doilies wafted aboard. I took the duckboard below, opened the self-drainers and squeezed a bathplug into the hole in the cockpit sole. There came a loud, hard thump on the port quarter. *Kylie* yawed the wrong way, leaned over and stayed there. The mainsail was aback, held by the preventer. I buckled into the safety harness, tugged at a pair of floppy wellies, pulled a storm jib out of the starboard bin and clambered into a half-filled cockpit.

'About time,' grumbled Syd Brown, his face like un-wrung chamois-leather. 'I'm just about holding her, but you've too much sail up.'

The situation was uncomfortable rather than serious, but it could become serious if I didn't do something. I slithered to the foredeck and set about lowering the Yankee and slacking the preventer. With her head nearer the wind, *Kylie* came upright. I hanked on the storm jib, tied down a third reef, set the main on the opposite side and let her go onto a broad reach. Then I bundled the Yankee into the cockpit and waited for a lull before removing the boards to go below. I noticed that Syd had gone and

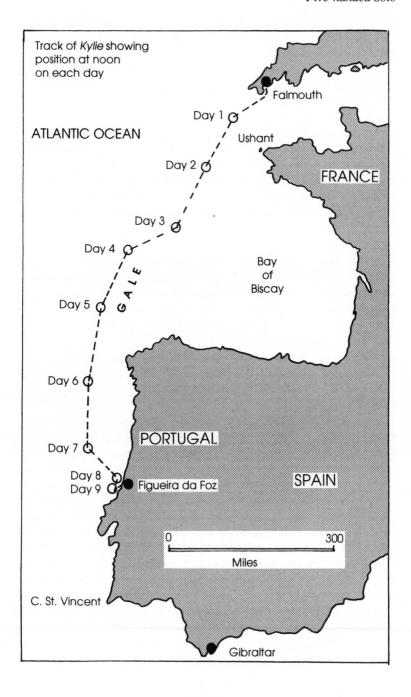

Track of *Kylie* showing
position at noon
on each day

ATLANTIC OCEAN

FRANCE

Falmouth

Day 1

Ushant

Day 2

Day 3

Day 4

GALE

Bay
of
Biscay

Day 5

Day 6

PORTUGAL

SPAIN

Day 7

Day 8

Day 9 Figueira da Foz

0   300
Miles

C. St. Vincent

Gibraltar

that John Leach was sitting in his place. He was wearing the khaki drill uniform of the Malay police and was measuring the angular height of the nearest wave with his swagger stick.

'Kuala Lumpur was never like this,' he said, a shade grimly I thought.

I decided to humour him.

'You are looking very cheerful,' I said.

'On account of my feet being wet. This cockpit is damp,' he replied, paddling in a foot of water and unwinding his puttees. 'We're about eighty miles west of Finisterre, so we can steer 175°. That'll edge us towards the coast a bit. If you'd like to take a breather, I'll manage on my own.'

When a smoother patch came along I removed the upper boards and prepared to go below. Then I withdrew my head quickly.

'No wonder you're wet,' I said. 'We're half-full of water; the cabin's awash.'

Had *Kylie* been holed? The memory of that thump on the port quarter suggested we'd hit something. Bucket in hand, I plunged into a slopping mess of cushions, charts and unbagged sails. After twenty bucketfuls had been decanted into the cockpit, the water-level had fallen, but only a little. For a while I scrabbled about, searching for the leak, but nowhere could I find it. Then I stood up and looked at John.

'Hell!' I said. 'Where's it coming from?'

'Plughole?' mouthed John silently. And when I didn't react he said loudly, 'You know...the hole what my baby went down.'

He was right, of course. From the swirling waters in the cockpit I fished out the bathplug I'd dislodged when I'd staggered out there in my floppy wellies...

Soon the cabin was empty of water. I pumped the bilge dry and slumped onto the cabin sole feeling very tired. 'Don't worry,' someone was saying, 'I'll look after her...'

Seven hours later a tinkerbell of sunshine prised my eyelids open. The wind was north-east, about thirty knots, with a moderate-to-heavy sea and swell. *Kylie* was over-canvassed, lurching along on a very broad reach, spluttering water from her toe-holes. A lanyard had come adrift from its cleat on the tiller, and the boat was yawing thirty degrees each side of her set course. The cockpit was deserted again, but a khaki puttee was battering the sprayhood.

'Bloody crew!' I shouted. Had she heard my swearing, Mum would have clouted me with a dishcloth, Aunt Flo would have frowned and Gran would have thrown me out of the back door, along with certain photos she had found while going through my wallet.

But where *was* my confounded crew? I tore off my clothes and hauled myself to the bows, where I was beaten on the head by a gaggle of demented geese. I pacified the foresail and cried: 'Call yourselves crew? You are nothing but lazy skivers, leaving me to do all the work...'

The logbook said that radio bearings at ten o'clock put me fifty miles offshore in 42°N, making gradually towards the distant lee of the Portuguese coast. By eight in the evening the swell had lessened, and by four o'clock the following morning the wind had decreased to twelve knots.

The seas went down and conditions became idyllic. I treated myself to a flannel bath and a clean shirt. All that I needed otherwise was more sleep, but I daren't risk another seven-hour stretch because we were crossing the busy shipping-lane between northern Europe and all places south and east of Gibraltar. I set the clockwork timer to twenty-minute intervals and stuffed it into my jacket between collarbone and neck, where the alarm would bell me into wakefulness.

Between coffee and rum, an hour after sunrise a new voice came from the cockpit.

'I c'n smell Portugal. It smells like ambrosia... or maybe nectar...'

'The only smell *you* react to is grass, *smouldering* grass, ' I said, glad that Simon Lofting had joined me. 'Are you really at sea-level? Not your usual altitude, is it? You're usually transcendental.'

'No horizon...' crooned Simon happily. 'Everything's insubstantial and vague... I know not which is air and which water.'

'Nor which is tomato soup and which rice pudding,' I said severely; 'you ballsed the coding again.'

'Sorry...,' said Simon. '...but it's only food... mere bodily fuel.'

We sailed on, closing the land, and seven and a half days out from Falmouth we sighted Cabo Mondego at two miles, swathed in mist. We approached the port of Figuera da Foz, eighty miles north of Lisbon. I sprawled in the cockpit, trying for *Lillibulero* on the mouth organ. A fishing-boat thundered towards us, carrying a name I translated as *Saint Mary And All The Angels* on the bows. I relaxed and waved my hand. From a boat with such an exalted name one would certainly get a prodigal welcome...

'Go away!' shouted its crew, making rude gestures. 'We don't want English boats here!'

Simon saw my bewilderment and pulled a face.

'Remember what happened at the Heysel Stadium a couple of months ago?' he said. 'When our yobbos kicked a few foreigners until they were dead? As far as those chaps in the fishing-boat are concerned, it was you an' me who were the yobbos on those terraces.' Then he nodded towards mainland Europe and said, 'Why go in? It's lovely out here.'

I put the helm over, heading us away from the unforgiving shore. I told myself we should not have closed the coast so soon, that we should have kept our distance off and steered for Cape St Vincent, where Captain Trump's brother might still be waiting for investment tips. Foreign ports meant hostile people, dirty decks and scummy topsides.

Cabo Mondego disappeared into the haze, but Simon did not disappear as quickly. He stayed aboard for longer than the others had done, discussing metaphysics in the cockpit, while *Kylie*, being of a more practical nature, argued against the light headwinds. I did not have her stamina. After eight days at sea, the tiredness was so deep it was etching my bones.

What eventually persuaded me to put into Portugal was that I opened a tin coded *minced beef* and found it was peaches, but by then I was too tired to kick up another fuss with Simon. While he ambled off for a word with Descartes, I switched on the motor and headed for the coast.

'*Das pesoas embarcadas?*' enquired the port captain when I got there.

I hesitated, considered deeply, and began to tick them off on my fingers: Jennie...Syd...John...Simon... That made five, including myself. But would he believe me, even after a largish tot of Glenlivet? I dropped my fingers and spread my hands wide, palms upwards.

'*Ninguno mas*. Am solo,' I told him.

He accepted my words, but his eyes flicked in disbelief around *Kylie*'s seven-foot-wide cabin. He also inspected the bilge and discovered that it contained a very squashed Mars Bar, at which he wrinkled his nose, shook his head and grimaced.

'This situation, it is inhuman,' he said. 'Don't it drive you crazy? Don't it give you bad dreams?'

'Oh, it gives me plenty of dreams,' I said, 'but they're usually nice ones.'

When I looked into it later, the logbook made curious reading. It told me that since we left Falmouth, my crews and I had sailed 797 miles, had met with gale-force winds for thirty-seven hours, had lain hove-to for eight hours, and that in nine days the skipper had slept for precisely twenty-three hours and eight minutes. On some of the pages it mentioned Jennie, Syd, John and Simon by name.

But the logbook said nothing whatever about dreams.

*

I had been to Iberia before, puzzling about dreams. The summer after I left the Merchant Navy I had hitched through France and bussed through the Pyrenees to Roncesvalles in Spain, my mind buzzing with a book about dreams and their connection with our waking lives. J W Dunne's *Experiment With Time* said not only that we foresaw the future but also that we pre-experienced it. All we had to do was to record our dreams in the notebook we took to bed and lodged beneath our pillow, and behold!, various parts of our dreams would crop up in our waking life during the days that followed. The trouble was, the clues to the future were mixed up with all the clutter from the past, and it was difficult to sort out which was which. But it could be done, I was sure, and in the space of a few weeks I had proved it to my entire satisfaction by studying the *Daily Mirror* and the Prime Minister, who at that time happened to be Winston Churchill. I dreamt I was flying a Tiger Moth aeroplane which was being pursued by a Bristol Blenheim piloted by Auntie Flo, who, for a reason I could not quite work out, had defected to Hitler and had painted-over the RAF roundels with Nazi swastikas. Her rear gunner was none other than the Prime Minister himself. I could see him clearly, glowering at me out of the dome of his gun turret, puffing a cigar and taking occasional swigs from a Thermos until the trembling yellow fuselage of my Tiger Moth should come into his gun-sights. 'Left!' he bellowed to Auntie Flo. Then 'Up a bit!', and then, just as he was about to press the trigger and shoot me down in flames, he roared 'BAKELITE!' I was so startled by the mismatch of the word to the circumstance that I woke up in a cold sweat, plunging earthwards onto Mauritius again, not knowing which way to push the telegraph-handle, thinking that yet again my ears had got it wrong.

Bakelite? Churchill would never have said 'Bakelite'. But, when I had thought more about it, I said to myself: 'Wouldn't he? Whoever would have guessed he drunk his whisky from a Thermos flask?'

Four days later the *Daily Mirror* front-paged a Churchillian broadside on, I think, the future of the British Empire. As reported by the *Mirror*, the Prime Minister had gone on for hours but, to my dismay, not once had he alluded to the proprietary name of the synthetic resin formed by the condensation of phenols and formaldehyde, used for years as a plastic in the manufacture of, for example, ashtrays that you could float in your bath. Bakelite wasn't mentioned anywhere on the front page; nor, to my mounting concern, did it come in on page two, where the Churchillian phrases had rumbled to a stop. It seemed that Dunne's theory had flopped. Dreams didn't foretell the future after all. I mean, the probability that Churchill would work his way into the dream about the future was statistically quite high; he showed every sign of being in the newspapers for ever. Churchill on the front page was commonplace; it didn't prove anything for or against Dunne's theory. No, Churchill by himself was worthless; it had to be Churchill *and* Bakelite. But *Bakelite*? How statistically likely was it that the future of the British Empire turned upon a chemical process perfected by Leo Hendrik Baekeland in 1913?

It didn't, of course. But, tucked away somewhere between Cassandra and the Blondie cartoon I found it at last: incontrovertible proof that Dunne's theory was right. Not quite pushed out by Churchill, someone was offering to sell me cigarette boxes. Like the ashtrays, they would float in the bath, and they were made — would I believe it? — from Bakelite.

That time in Iberia I stayed first in Pamplona, where I forsook Dunne and for three days tried to write like Hemingway about real bulls knocking flat real men. On the fourth day, David Wright and I moved on to Madrid, where I was knocked flat one morning in the Prado by Goya's nightmares and in the afternoon rented a room on Calle Atocha, where I drank a skinful of wine to shake off the faces that were chasing me from his *Horrors of War* and *Saturn Eating His Sons*. I did not succeed. Life kept on imitating art in the way that Wilde had said it did. Before sunset someone murdered someone else on the sidewalk beneath our window. After the water carts had hosed the blood away we escaped to a café, but Goya was still there in the Civil War cripples and in the bullet-pocked walls.

Then we journeyed far beyond Madrid, travelling to the Atlantic coast of Portugal, where the past and the future, real life and dreams, became so interwoven that even now I cannot with certainty pick out the warp of the one from the weft of the other. For a start, the bulls in Portugal had little balls stuck onto the tips of their horns, and so I thought that, unlike Spain, Portugal was not real life. And if the prettified bulls were not evidence enough, one only had to look at the house-chimneys: they were not grimed with soot and pitted by sulphur. Without exception, they were so icing-smooth and white that even if you weren't trying to look at the place through Hemingway's eyes, Portugal looked and felt like dreamland. You felt that if you so much as licked it, the country would dissolve.   David and I stayed in the *quinta* of the Rego family at Ericeira, on the coast north of Lisbon. I was borne open-mouthed between servants, fed on oysters and confections that raised my palate to the clouds, and I was given glimpses of a culture that raised my spirits to the skies. We were chauffeured round in a Jaguar for weeks and, still in a dream, wafted back across Biscay, fares-paid in a queenly ocean liner, with our names printed on the passenger list in royal-blue letters of the same case as those used to inform everyone who hadn't yet noticed it that Baroness Bogarde was sitting at almost the same table as two callow and quite ignoble young Englishmen.

*

'In light winds, I dawdled down the coast.'

Kylie and I didn't leave Figuera da Foz until a Saturday. The weather had been good on the Friday, but I had agreed with Jennie that I would live up to our superstitions and never leave port on a Friday, and so I sat aboard *Kylie* and watched another boat leave harbour and hare away southwards under a good strong Portuguese trade-wind. When Saturday came the wind had fallen light, and while weighing anchor I had daubed a dollop of harbour mud on the foot of the number one genoa, and so I left Figuera da Foz in a bad mood.

In light winds I dawdled down the coast, and found myself in a theatrical sort of fog off the village of Ericeira. The fog was shallow and billowy. It looked like manufactured stuff, puffing from the stage-wings as it had done in the theatre at Stratford-upon-Avon, where I had seen Peter Pan cross swords with Captain Hook so many years ago.

Shall I go in and anchor off Ericeira, I wondered? Shall I venture in through that mist, which is dispersing even as I look at it, and find an anchorage in the Never Land? I could have done it. I believed it would not be too risky an undertaking for *Kylie*, but it would, I thought, be too risky for me. Thirty years previously, I had dwelt for a month at the Rego *quinta* above the cliffs. We had swum from the beach and picnicked among the rocks, and Paula's father had chaffed David and me. '*Arcades ambo!*' he had laughed as we brushed sand from our hair before venturing to taste the wine. 'And in Arcadia I...' David had sung back at all of us. At that time I had not known what *Arcades ambo* meant, nor had I the faintest notion of where Arcadia lay. But since then I had grasped some idea of the meaning of the one and the direction of the other. A few months later Paula Rego had attended the wedding of Pip and myself, but since then time and circumstance had separated both the principals and the wedding guests... and, besides, the wedding had been in another country... and besides again, the bride herself was now dead...

I backed the jib and hove-to... and wondered. After picnicking in Ericeira I had returned to England, where I had been obliged for a while to familiarise myself with Greek oracles. 'You cannot step into the same river twice,' went one of them, and over the years I had committed it to memory. Through the mist I thought I could make out the hinterland of Ericeira and — between the screeches from Semprini — my ears fancied the boom of Atlantic surf breaking against cliffs. And standing in *Kylie*'s cockpit, with my eyes straining through the mist, the words of the ancient oracle waylaid my intentions. Truly, one could not step into the same river twice... Both Paula's father and David had uttered their antique words too long ago, it seemed to me, for either the meaning or the sentiment to be of any present consequence. It was possible that Paula's parents were still alive, of course, but the dictator Salazar had been ousted by a revolution, and I thought it only too likely that the servants had become masters.

And so, thirty years after I had last set foot in that delightful place, I put the tiller upwind and headed away again from Ericeira, too frightened by thoughts of what I might find to step ashore.

Two days later and in a more optimistic frame of mind, I did steer *Kylie* close inshore, passing less than half a mile off Cape St Vincent. The weather was fine and warm, and the visibility good, but I did not see Captain Trump's brother, and no girls waved from the lighthouse. This time I saw nobody.

*'My body was found
at half-past six...'*

7

Treading Water in Majorca

When other senses give out, it's as well to follow your nose. Deafened by
the buffetings of Biscay and fuddled by the fog off Ericeira, *Kylie* scented
something delicious, an aroma between popcorn and cinnamon, and was
so besotted with it that she sniffed her way through the Strait of Gibraltar
and into the Mediterranean, whereupon a burly *Levanter* slapped her on
the nose and booted her in the ribs. Hurt by this unkindly welcome, she
scampered into Almeria, a hot and airless kennel on the Costa del Sol, to
pant beneath a skimpy awning until her owner's bruises had either faded
or been dissolved in the local wine. When both she and he felt a little
better and the *Levanter* had blown itself out, she snuffled to the south-
eastern corner of Iberia, anchoring in a cindery cove under the lighthouse
on Cabo da Gata while the skipper wondered where to go next.

Although the sun was still toasting her decks, the years in East Anglia
had fixed the notion that October was the time to think of hibernation, and
so I mulled over the charts of the Balearic Islands, looking for a winter
haven. There were lots on offer. According to the guidebooks, Ibiza had a
pleasant climate and its harbour was hugely protected, but when I saw
how the mellow charm of the old town had been poxed by eruptions of

raw concrete I looked for places elsewhere.   Mahon in Menorca was said to be one of the best harbours in the world, but the island often bore the brunt of long and severe gales. Nelson complained bitterly of the strength and duration of the winter storms he met while lying-to off Menorca; he wrote that he had never met savagery to match them, and so on the strength of his testimony I decided to steer clear of Menorca, at least until the following spring.

The sister island of Majorca, lying thirty miles off the track of the Menorcan storms, seemed to be less nakedly exposed. It possessed several good harbours, it seemed large enough to offer interesting mixes of scenery, lifestyles and culture, and its people were said to be hospitable to visitors. After weighing all the pros and cons, I headed for Puerto Pollensa, a harbour lying under the island's north-eastern tip. I went there mainly because my daughter Sarah had vouched for the attractiveness of the Formentor peninsula but also because it seemed to me that its mountains would protect *Kylie* from the sort of storms that had battered Nelson's ships.

I anchored for the first time in Pollensa Bay at half-past eight on an October evening, tired but content after a twelve-hour passage along the rugged north-western coast. All day I had struggled to make progress in light winds, pestered from all directions by vagrant waves rebounding from the cliffy shore. At last, at six in the evening *Kylie* had rounded the bony finger of Cape Formentor and entered flatter waters. We had not got there before time, I thought, for the barometer had been falling for hours, and the skyline was jagged and purple against a livid sky. I looked at the protective mountains, set an anchor and felt altogether safe.

By the middle of the following morning I had some doubts about the safety. Having rowed ashore to stretch my legs, I came across the wreck of a fifty-foot Scottish fishing boat, laid over in the shallows at the head of the bay. At first I thought her derelict. Atlantic barnacles pimpled her bottom, blocks and frayed ropes'-ends hung like discarded sporrans in the rigging and the topside paint was scabby and flaked, like a haggis with eczema. Nobody seemed to be aboard, but a cat lay asleep outside a deck-house.

Before rowing back to *Kylie* I went into a bayside bar to ask about the wreck and the security of my anchorage.

My worries were diagnosed by Katy, whose needle-sharp Catalan eyes mainlined my sclerotic arteries with shots of undiluted amity spangled with glittering anger that tingled my veins. Her lips discharged a bewildering mixture of vocal missiles and emollients that could blast holes in a starched shirt-front, pacify Rottweilers or charm twittering officials from their perches. Best of all, even her whispers were loud enough to penetrate my cotton wool.

Her life had been riven by tragedies. On the eve of her wedding her Swedish fiancé had died of a heart attack while awaiting an underground train. Later she had married a Majorcan businessman, but after a few happy years he had suffered a stroke that deprived him of speech and mobility. The tragedies had made her a woman of burning compassion. Most of her days were spent in fighting battles against the gigantic ogres of illness and misfortune that stalked the earth. By day, no creature was too small to be denied a vibrant crusade for its welfare, and no task too large to defeat her imagination. At nights she went into town and played bingo.

'BOWAT?' she boomed, pointing a quivering finger at the wreck and rattling her keys. 'That boat is a BRITISH BOWAT. A giant Tramontana wind roared down from Puig Major last winter. He picked up the bowat and POUF! he flinged it on the beach, and - LET ME TELL YOU SOMETHING! — that bowat don't get away from here very quickly. The mayor, he try all ways he can think of to get it off — his tractors digging channels and putting out anchors and everything but, I AM TELLING YOU!, the mayor need more than tractors to get THAT bowat away from THIS bay. ISN'T THAT RIGHT, TOMÉO? 'Use the helicopters!' I tell him. 'If helicopters can put mansions on top of mountains for Generalissimo Franco, helicopters can put bowats back in the water for mayors.' And Toméo! DON'T let the mayor tell ME that he is hiring more tractors when THIS moon is full! I tell him he don't try moving that bowat again at full moon because that is when the cat will be having her kittens and — SAN IGNACIO BE MY WITNESS! — NOBODY disturbs that cat except over my dead body!'

Her eyes glistened and she whirled the keys above the table. 'Isn't that RIGHT, Toméo? Don't I say that?'

Two dogs ran in from the beach and nuzzled her quivering thighs. Toméo looked into his coffee and nodded. She glared at the sea.

'That your bowat out there? You sail THAT all the way from England? YOU HEAR THAT, TOMÉO? He sail that LEEDLE BOWAT all the way from England and now he is drinking only coffee. *MADRÉ DE DIOS*! you need something stronger! Have a *Cienta y Treis* on me! And yes, I will find you a better place to keep your bowat! One English wreck is more than enough! The winter, he will be long and dark — much rain, and much, much wind. I tell you, THE WIND HERE IS

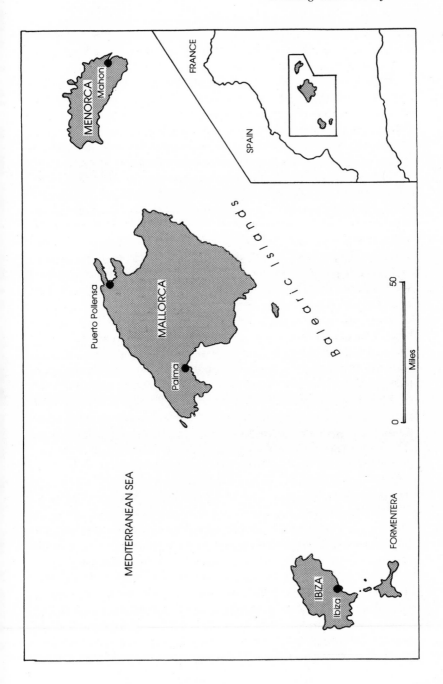

ESTUPENDISSIMO! But, don't you worry, I will find a place for your bowat... I will find you anything you want... ISN'T THAT RIGHT, TOMÉO? For sailors I will find anything!'

She was as good as her word. Six hours later *Kylie* was fastened to the beefiest mooring I have ever used. It comprised two gigantic anchors, either of which could have moored an ocean-going tugboat. The anchors were joined by ten fathoms of hefty chain attached to a swivel. Above the swivel rose two more fathoms of chain shackled to a nine-inch hawser. The mooring had been laid by its British owner for his 35-foot cruiser, but since his boat would be spending the winter in another part of the Mediterranean, he obligingly agreed that *Kylie* should use it.

As I cleated down the mooring pendant the first of the storm clouds muzzled the jaw of Puig Major. *Kylie* whipped round sharply to the new wind, straining backwards at her tether like a startled whippet. I looked into the ruffled waters, along the line of the bottom-chain. It stretched in a northwest to southeast direction, in line with a cleft in the mountains. I secured the pendant to the horn of the cleat and swigged it very tight, for I knew that through the cleft would come the strongest gusts.

Nelson would have said it was not a strong blow, but it lasted three days. *Kylie* was moored seventy-two dinghy-strokes from the shore in six and a half feet of water. Toméo said that the mooring was as near to the shore as was possible, but before the gale was an hour old I was wondering if *Kylie* were not too close, for thirty yards ahead the water was only five feet deep. I watched the build of the waves astern. Even in gusts of twenty-five knots, a boat moored a hundred yards to seaward was plunging heavily, and plumes of spray were spattering her foredeck. When the wind got stronger, wouldn't *Kylie* be plunging that much too? And with her four feet three inches of draught, wouldn't she be bumping the hard, sandy bottom? I lashed down the dinghy on the coachroof and stayed aboard to find out.

Although the early gusts swung uncertainly between the west-southwest and north-northwest, after a few hours the gale settled down to blow in earnest from the north-west, straight through the cleft in the mountains. I made a cup of tea and waited to see what would happen.

By early evening the wind was gusting more than thirty knots. *Kylie* lay far enough offshore to be outside the protection of the buildings along the waterfront. Twenty yards in their lee the water was barely ruffled, at fifty yards the white wavelets were six inches high, but where *Kylie* lay — a hundred and fifty yards distant — they were more than two feet from trough to crest. Her situation was less than perfect, but as far as comfort was concerned, being aboard *Kylie* was better than being aboard the other boat, which by then was bucking and plunging wildly. However, comfort was one thing; whether *Kylie* was in a safer situation was quite another. A mile away lay the wreck of another British vessel which had thought itself safe in such a wind.

I lit the cabin lamp, parcelled the hawser, tapped the barometer and tried not to be anxious.

After twenty-four hours I felt better about the safety angle but less happy about the comfort. Although the noise in the rigging had risen to shrieks and *Kylie*'s plunges had sometimes left my stomach in mid-air, she had not bumped the bottom. During the morning I watched Katy walk along the promenade beneath the palms, trailed by a string of ecstatic dogs. I sighed, and made a cup of coffee. In the early evening I watched the people gathering in the cafés, bright with yellow lights and busy with movement. I sighed again, more heavily this time, and tried to concentrate on Volume 1 of the Admiralty's *Mediterranean Pilot*.

I was unable to get ashore until two days later, when the gale had blown itself out. Although I had settled the question of *Kylie*'s safety by then, the matter of my own comfort was filling my mind. According to the Admiralty, I could expect to be isolated from shore by similar gales for three days in every twenty I was on that mooring. It was, I thought, a bit much. I rowed ashore, hoping to find a more comfortable berth in the harbour, but discovered that such a berth was not to be had; all the yacht-club slots were taken, and at the only available public berth the skipper of a French sloop told me he had to keep his engine running at half ahead for two days and nights to stop his boat's stern from smashing against the quayside.

I came away from the harbour feeling low. The prospect of spending days alone in *Kylie* at sea does not alarm me — indeed, solitude was an important attraction of my cruises — but I was less happy about spending hours watching other people enjoy vices I was denying myself. So again I headed for Katy's bar in an attempt to solve a problem, and again, of course, Katy came up with a solution.

'No,' she said, 'I don't have no ROOM to rent you for the winter, but — you know something? — I do have an *apartment*. It is the best in Puerto Pollensa and in the summer it is VERY EXPENSIVE...'

I fed some biscuits to the dogs and it was not long before we agreed that, since summer seemed to be on its way out and the dogs had not objected, it would be mutually helpful if I were to rent the apartment at one third of its usual rate...

A few minutes later I had paid the first instalment of my rent and was standing on the balcony of my winter home. The gale had gone, *Kylie* lay directly before me, her trim shape reflected in the still waters. She would be always under my eye and barely more than a good stone's-throw away. Things, I thought, could not be nicer. Two dogs were polishing the terrazo with their tails and Katy had presented me with a bottle of brandy. It looked as though I had fallen on my feet in Majorca.

For three months things did go very well indeed. On every morning of fine weather I rowed out to *Kylie* to ply the varnish brush, whip ropes' ends or grease the winches. In the afternoons I wrote stories for my family or I walked through the mountains to the western coast. In the evenings I went downstairs to Katy's bar to be inspected by her dogs and to stir a broth of conversation with new friends from widely different backgrounds: her brother Toméo the fisherman, his wife Margharita, Pepper from California, Veronica from Scotland and Tom and Mary Winters, who had settled in the island from England. On market days we would be joined by Mrs Ezra, who always seemed to be carrying packets of broken biscuits and dented tins of soup. She was a woman of restricted means but great energy, who trawled for knowledge with nets of rather small mesh. Having discovered the notebooks of an uncle who had accompanied Younghusband into Tibet, she had compiled a colourful street-guide to Lhasa and had been so gripped by the magic of the place that she had campaigned for the annexation of the entire country. When the Foreign and Colonial Office had remained indifferent to her pleas, she had retired to Majorca and vowed to follow up the street-guide with either a compendious revelation of how Queen Victoria was descended from the tenth Dalai Lama or — if that failed to move things — an inflammatory history of the Brahmaputra river. Thirty years later she was still researching both works and not quite sure where to begin. Most of the rooms of her house in the hills were filled with snippets on the utility of yaks, the properties of the Tibetan ragwort and the incidence of derailments on the Trans-Siberian railway between Tomsk and Omsk. In the course of her research she had come across and married a man who had given up a promising career in fertilisers to fortify her against creeping malapropitis. He bobbed along in her broad wake like a small dinghy after a factory-ship.

'Coming along nicely, aren't we, my sweet?' he murmured, his eyes glazing.

Mrs Ezra lowered her bust to the table and rolled a brandy. 'Just between ourselves,' she said, 'what think you of the ampersand?'

'Hadn't thought about it,' I said.

'You use ampersands? In manuscript, I mean.'

'Not in formal letters, no; but in notes to friends I do.'

'Ah!' said Mrs Ezra. 'Just as you thought, Wilf: the ampersand is out. It's a shame, though. Squiggles are easier for me, you know. My alleys in Lhasa went on for miles. It's the same with words, too. Don't stop once I've started, do I, Wilf? Get into spate too quickly, I suppose. My imagination takes over, doesn't it, Wilf?'

'Like a dream, dear.'

'Yes... Sometimes I think Lhasa was a just a dream, you know; just a pigment of my imagination...'

*

At Christmas my children flew out to celebrate. After brisk sails in *Kylie* across the bay and back, in the evenings we sang Catalan songs in front of Katy's roaring fire. Behind the shuttered windows of the bar, all was cosy. Outside, *Kylie* still lay on quiet waters. The October gale had not been repeated, and serenity, like the dozing dogs, seemed to be a permanent part of the scene.

On Twelfth Night everything changed. With my daughters returned to Britain I spent part of the morning working on *Kylie*'s engine. The barometer, I noticed, had fallen. At eleven I rowed ashore and at midday I cycled four miles inland to the old town of Pollensa for lunch with Tom and Mary Winters. It was, I recollect, a quite excellent loin of lamb. At five o'clock I cradled my second brandy and enquired why it was that Mary is so insistent on closing the windows.

'Tramontana's coming,' said Tommy.

I raced back to Pollensa Bay in less than half my usual time. The sky was six-eighths cloud, the air restless, and the beach deserted. Although on the way back I had felt several side-gusts from the mountains, the gale itself had not yet arrived. On her mooring *Kylie* looked at ease, but I was struck by a sudden concern. Had I remembered to switch off the battery before I left her? I dragged the dinghy to the water's edge, threw in the oars and rowed fast towards her. It took me less than two minutes to reach her, another two to secure the dinghy and verify that the battery was switched off, and a further three to check that the parcelling on her mooring was in place. In that short interval the first hard gusts swept up the western cliffs of the island, were squeezed by the cleft in the mountains and descended with greatly increased force on Pollensa Bay below.

Kylie was lying almost broadside to the cleft. At the sudden impact of the wind she lurched ten degrees to starboard, sprang quickly upright and faced the oncoming storm. I stood in the cockpit and tried to make a decision. There was ample food and water aboard: either I could stay in *Kylie* for three days of discomfort, or, before the full weight of the gale arrived, I could chance it and row back to my comfortable bed. I looked at the hard and narrow berth, dragged my life-jacket from its locker and began to uncleat the painter of the dinghy.

I stood on the capping, both legs outboard of the guard-rail, waiting for a gust to die. Ashore, Katy's windows were already lit and the last dog had left the beach. Below my heels, for the moment the dinghy was still. I took my left foot from the capping and stepped backwards. Simultaneously, another gust descended, stronger than any before. The dinghy took off, wrenching the painter from my hand and pulling me into the water.

My first reaction was not of alarm but of relief, for the sea was much warmer than I had expected it to be. Really, I thought, it was rather awkward to have lost the dinghy, but even if I couldn't swim into the wind I could surely swim across it, and so there would be no problem about getting ashore.

For the first five minutes the swim was agreeable. The buoyancy of the life-jacket kept my head above all but the largest waves, and although the water seemed to have become colder, my breast-strokes were taking me steadily nearer the dainty flickerings from the shore. After ten minutes I trod water and revised my opinion. The exercise was not merely agreeable, it was an unique and wonderful experience, filled with blissful feelings of featherdown and immortality.

I lay backwards in the waves and, smiling, went to sleep. I dreamt of rolling pneumatically in the lee of Mrs Ezra, of Captain Hook, Wendy, and Peter's lost shadow, and how remarkable it was that, of the fifteen hundred lighthouses on the eastern side of the Atlantic, only seven per cent of them bore the names of saints...

My body was found at half past six by Alfonso Jaumé, who had come out of his villa for a walk along the darkening beach before dinner, just as far as two concrete blocks that lay half-buried in sand at the water's edge. When he approached them, however, he saw that there were not two objects at the water's edge but three.

Alfonso summoned his friend Claudio and they carried me into the villa, stripped off my clothing, swathed me in blue blankets and propped me up before a blazing hearth of pine logs. It is not the recommended treatment for acute hypothermia but, to my regret, it worked.

I came back to this life reluctantly, detained among velvet draperies by lissom figures in lustrous robes. Behind an arras I spotted my grandfather James Edwards, plying his trade as a journeyman shipwright building the Pier Head landing-stage. In marbled palaces I stroked the jewelled hands of princesses from Aquitaine, Acre and, I think, Peru. They were taking tea with Emma Edwards, née Welch, who had popped up from below stairs wearing a floral apron. I begged the princesses' smiling pardons for the breach of taste and implored them to sing madrigals to the music of their lutes.

The response I eventually heard was unmelodious and puzzlingly hostile.

'*Como se llama usted?*' barked a voice. It issued from a dark cave, stinking of nicotine and garlic.

I shook my head, smiled and passed out. In death I had all the answers; it was only the right questions that I needed.

At half-past eight the following morning I awoke in a cell of Pollensa police station. Why I had been transported to a police station and not to a hospital I was not at the time sure. Looking back now, I think they suspected I was a terrorist. It is not a far-fetched idea. I had met and spoken with a young man from Menorca who had been overheard speaking Catalan to a friend while in Castile and, as a result, so his story went, had been thrown into jail.

'*Solian cantar,*' he had sung in *Kylie*'s cabin.

'*Visca Catalunya!*

Visca el Catalya!'

'Hurrah for Catalonia!' I had echoed outside Katy's bar that night and I murmured the translation again under the blue blanket in the prison cell: 'Hurrah for Catalonia! Hurrah for the *Catalya!*'

The Catalans had been simmering with unrest in mainland Spain. Who knows what I might not have been up to in Pollensa Bay? Planting bombs or laying mines, perhaps? There were a number of prime targets within a mile of where I was found: a hotel where Prince Rainier and Grace Kelly had stayed, a summer residence of Juan Carlos, a naval seaplane base... Surely, I thought, it could not have been forty years since I had seen the headline 'BARCELONA FALLS' in the *Birmingham Mail*, and, in the middle of eating a slice of bread-and-dripping had said, 'Mum, what's a Fifth Column?'

I rattled the door handle of my locked cell. It was half-past nine and I was hungry. When were they going to let me out? What was holding things up?

They were waiting, of course, for Katy.

She burst into the police station with her eyes full of indignant tears, her face a mixture of operatic horror and pity, and her arms embracing twelve bottles of brandy. Her words ricochetted around the interior of the police station with a fusillade of quivering questions, accusatory statements and piteous exclamations.

'Are you English all the same? When you is not wrecking your bowats you are drowning yourselfs! But, *Madre mia*!, that bump on your head, IT IS BIGGER THAN AN EGG! Where was you *been*? Las' night when you wasn't come in I don't know what to think! An' the dogs don't sleep neither — they is WHINING ALL THE NIGHT outside your apartment!'

I try to offer an explanation. While I am doing so she sets down the bottles on the sergeant's desk. The sergeant counts them and raises an eyebrow.

'Thirteen?' booms Katy. 'I thought there was only twelve of you here.'

She drove me back to my apartment, put me to bed and prescribed a lavish invalid diet. Between bowlfuls of Catalan broth she fixed me sternly with her dark eyes, clacked her tongue and berated my foolishness. Her ministrations had me on my feet in no time, but although I soon recovered my composure, it seemed that my reputation had blown away with the dinghy.

In the early days of spring the clouds disappeared from Puig Major and *Kylie* was lifted from the water for a coat of anti-fouling. Soon afterwards, the first of the Easter visitors arrived, I gave up my apartment and prepared to set off for the Eastern Mediterranean.

But I could not go without first expressing my gratitude to Alfonso Jaumé and his friend Claudio for saving my life, and so before leaving Majorca I took them on a four-day 'thank-you' cruise, intending to sail the coast from Puerto Pollensa to Palma, but when we arrived off the south-eastern tip of the island the wind suddenly veered to west-northwest, which meant that if we were to continue towards Palma it would be a hard beat all the way.

'Let's go to Isla Cabrera,' said Alfonso.

'Is possible I take pill?' said Claudio, eyeing the sea and dabbing Nivea cream on his nose. Claudio is an actor, the son of Fernando Colorio, who is also an actor, and so using skin creams was a perfectly normal routine. Skin cream to Claudio was like barrier cream had been for the mechanics who, yet again, I had to employ on *Kylie*'s engine.

'Okay, Alfonso,' I said. 'Let's look at Cabrera.' Then, 'Pill will no help you now,' I said to Claudio. It was Claudio's first-ever sail, and he had already sacrificed his breakfast.

This rugged and hilly island, said the pilot-book, is *some 3 miles long by 2 miles wide with several deep bays. The only inhabitants are a small military garrison...*

We covered the ten miles from the Majorcan coast in two hours, during which time Claudio went very pale indeed and was sick many times.

'I think your next part will be Hamlet's father's ghost,' I told him, hardening the sheets.

'No. My next play is Strindberg's *The Father* at the *Teatro Principal*. The first night will be on 2 May, and I think you will not be invited.'

In the lee of an ochreous cliff we beat into the harbour under a storm jib and double-reefed main, watched by some soldiers sitting outside a *Refugio de Pescadores* at the foot of the cliff. On top of the cliff was a castle, and from the battlements a big red-and-yellow Spanish flag cracked and rattled in the strong wind. The soldiers smoked cigarettes and drank *San Miguel* beer from the bottle and watched us make fast to the small stone pier. A very smart Dutch sloop was lying the other side of the pier and so I told Alfonso to make up the falls of the halyards extra neatly.

It took us all of ten minutes to bag the headsails and tidy the decks and cockpit, and another ten before we had hung our wet oilskins in the rigging and Alfonso and I had combed our hair and yet another five before Claudio had cleaned his teeth and bathed his face and applied fresh Nivea cream to his nose and cheeks and lips. All this time the soldiers outside the *Refugio* did not move. They drank their beer and smoked cigarettes until we were about ready to step ashore and then a sergeant put on his olive-green cap and walked over to where we lay alongside the jetty. Alfonso greeted him with smiling courtesy and the sergeant replied with equal civility. They talked rapidly for several minutes, by the end of which time Alfonso was not smiling. The sergeant was still half-smiling, but Alfonso was looking grim and several times he jerked his arms up and down, as though his fingers had been burnt.

'No', said the sergeant in the end. He smiled, shook his head and walked back to his *San Miguel*.

'It's no good,' said Alfonso. 'We cannot stay. He will not let us stay. We have to depart in one hour.'

'Bloody hell.'

'Cabrera is *una zona militar*. No-one can land without a certificate from *El Commandante* in Palma. We do not have a certificate and so we cannot stay.' He shrugged his shoulders. 'It is a strict rule.'

'But it must be blowing thirty knots outside.' I looked at the way the flag was cracking, and the way the tops were being whipped off the wave

121

Outside the Refugio de Pescadores, *Isla Cabrera.*

crests between the ochreous cliffs. 'Does he expect us to go out of here is this strength of wind?'

'No,' said Alfonso. 'He does not make us to go outside the bay. But we cannot stay at the pier. We can walk ashore, the sergeant said, for one hour, and then we must leave the pier and anchor between the jetty and the cliff.'

So we walked ashore on Cabrera for just one hour. I took a camera and as we passed the sergeant I held it up and said '*Permiso fotografía?*' and he smiled agreeably, and so I photographed the castle with its flag. Then I photographed Alfonso with Claudio and the *Refugio* with its soldiers, and then Claudio took the camera and photographed Alfonso and me standing outside the soldiers' café-bar. We bought three *San Miguels* there, but we did not stay inside to drink them. The place was swarming with big flies which were so numerous and active in the still air of the bar that I had to keep one hand busy all the time, brushing the flies away from my nose and eyes and ears and the top of the opened *San Miguel*. We carried the beers outside, into the wind again.

'The flies did not go near you,' I remarked to Claudio. 'That Nivea on your nose must be toxic stuff.'

'Was not the Nivea on the nose,' said Claudio. 'Was the Strindberg under the skin. What was you been reading lately?'

'*Johnathan Livingstone Seagull.*'

'That book is shit, is romantic shit, is why you had more flies around you than anybody.'

We sat down, still carefully in the wind, next to the people off the Dutch boat.

'You have a *certificado*?' I asked the skipper.

'No,' he said, 'we have to leave too.'

We finished our beers and I made sure we were back aboard *Kylie* before the hour had passed so that we could leave the jetty before the Dutchman and choose the best place to anchor.

We anchored in one and a half fathoms on sand, a cable distant from four military huts built around another flagstaff which carried another, smaller Spanish flag. Twenty minutes later the big Dutch yacht chugged slowly round the bay and then it motored round a second and third time, but because the bay was small the big yacht could not find an anchorage where he could lay out enough scope of cable. After the third circuit the Dutchman gave up and motored back to the jetty. I watched him and felt smug.

'He cannot stay at the jetty,' said Alfonso,

'No,' I agreed. 'He has no *certificado*. The soldiers will not believe he cannot anchor. Why should they? What do soldiers know about winds and anchors?'

'The sergeant will think the Dutchman is trying,' said Alfonso. '*Es correcto*, "trying"?'

'No,' I said. 'The sergeant will think the Dutchman is not trying at all. But, if he has run out of patience, it could be that the sergeant will think the Dutchman is very trying, in which case the sergeant may tell the Dutchman that he, the Dutchman, is, as we say, "Trying it on".'

' "Very trying" is "not trying"? And "trying it on" is... what? I do not understand.   What is "it"?   What means the expression?'

'It is an idiom. It means, like, to do something cheekily in order to find out if you can get away with... er... overcome any objections.'

Alfonso photographed sea-birds heeling and diving and braking in the wind. It was a sunny afternoon but it was very cold. Claudio lay in the cabin under a blanket, learning his Strindberg part. I stuck it out in the cockpit. Between reading pages of *Jonathan Livingstone Seagull* I trained the binoculars on the Dutch yacht. I sat in the cockpit all afternoon, expecting all the time that the Dutch yacht would have to come out into the bay again. By sunset our anchorage had been two hours in shadow and it was bitterly cold. I watched three soldiers lower the Spanish flag. While one of them lowered the flag and another saluted it, the third blew Taps on a bugle. Then the bugler and the saluting soldier went back to the hut, leaving the third soldier to fold up the flag. He tried to fold it, but in that wind it was impossible for one person to make a neat job of it. After several attempts got nowhere, he bundled it under one arm and walked to join the others in the hut. I put a matchstalk at the page I had read to and went into the cabin myself, but still the Dutch yacht had not moved from the jetty.

'Is trying?' asked Claudio.

'Very,' I said.

'Cabrera is a terrible place,' said Alfonso. 'During a war between France and Spain ten thousand French prisoners were sent here. It was very bad for them. There was no food. Things were so bad that they had to eat dirt, and so more than half of them died. That happened in 1809, but Cabrera is still a terrible place.'

Before sunrise the next morning the wind had died down to twelve knots. We got under way before the sun rose and I thought how odd it was that the larger flag had been left flying above the castle all night, while the smaller flag had been taken down at the previous sunset. I pointed out the inconsistency to Alfonso, adding that it seemed that the left hand of *El Commandante* did not know what the right hand was doing.

'You are angry about it?' said Alfonso.

'No, of course not.'

'Yes, I think you are angry. I think you are trying it on against the soldiers because...'

'I am not trying it on!' I said, but, of course, Alfonso was right, for out of the corner of both our eyes we could see that the large Dutch yacht, like the large Spanish flag, had not moved an inch.

*

Four days later I moored *Kylie* alongside an arm of the *muelle* at Puerto Pollensa and invited everyone to drop by for wine and pastries. There was cloud on the mountains and rain in the valleys and there were rainbows in between them. It was a warm and emotional occasion, and I was surprised and honoured by the numbers who turned up. Not only were the mechanics who had repaired *Kylie*'s engine there, but also their wives and children, as were the families of the four ambulance men who each and severally claimed to have conveyed my lifeless body to the police station. Also, at Katy's insistence, there were eight of the thirteen policeman and as many of their families who were not otherwise occupied with a seasonable flurry of baptisms and funerals. Katy, for once unattended by her dogs, presided over it all, booming good humour, swinging her keys and commenting scathingly on the mayor's ineptitude. Mrs Ezra, too, dropped by on her way back from the market, laden with broken biscuits and towing her husband,

'It is going to be a good year,' he said. 'She has started the first chapter.'

'On Queen Victoria or the Brahmaputra?'

'Neither. It is to be a history of the ampersand.'

I replenished his wife's glass and wished her book well.

'It will be multitudinous and many-fauceted, won't it, Wilf?'

'It will be good, I'm sure, my sweet.'

'Not just "good", Wilf. Think of what I did for Lhasa!' She lifted her glass in the direction of a rainbow. 'The rise of the ampersand, Wilf, will outshine all the colours of the rectum.'

My final memory of Puerto Pollensa was of Katy, standing as tall as the Statue of Liberty on the sunny strip of beach in front of the bar. She was surrounded by a vibrating mass of adulatory dogs, feeding them tit-bits with one hand and pointing upwards with the other. She looked a goddess triumphant. It was understandable, for at last one heavy Brittanic responsibility was departing; now only one remained. The wreck was still on the beach, but hovering above Katy's pointing finger were two very large helicopters.

*'They pressed me
to eat my fill...'*

8

Working Towards Serendip

It was time to tack. I put aside the galley knife, uncleated the genoa sheet and put the helm down much too quickly. *Kylie* hung in stays. Menorca tumbled from between the starboard guard-rails and huddled in prayer above the pulpit before disassembling itself again among the waves beyond the galley vent. The coast was still miles away but it was closer.

I went back to sharpening the knife, a Taiwanese product to which neither I nor its manufacturers had been able to put a lasting edge. If the wind held for another hour and I paid greater attention to the mechanics of tacking, I might soon reach Serendip, which was the name I had given to an unlabelled dent in the coastline of Menorca. 'Serendip' had been an ancient name for Sri Lanka, and 'serendipity' has come to mean the knack of discovering happiness by accident. From meeting voyagers who had set out from their homelands without any clear notion of their destination but who nevertheless had somehow found an island paradise, I suspected that it might be possible to come across happiness in this way, even though I had been brought up in the belief that happiness wasn't something that could be left to chance. Like other commodities in this life, said my father, happiness must be ordered in advance. As proof of this, holidays at New Brighton had been sandcastled with bliss, but only, I was made to understand, because the boarding-house had been booked months ahead. If you went there on spec, my dad said from the depths of his deck chair, you would end up in a dump in the back-streets, where they had neither sing-songs round the piano nor a view of the sea. This incontrovertible truth outlasted the British Empire.

Never had I chanced upon happiness; I had always calculated its whereabouts and headed for it. Jennie said it was silly to do so, that I should just lie back and let the wind take me wherever it blew. As a piece of advice to long-distance cruising sailors, her words had value, but as a philosophy of life they seemed like dangerous nonsense. If you went downwind through life you were in perpetual danger; you could be pitchpoled by the mountainous emotions that overtook you. And anyway, it was often more satisfying to a nominal Protestant to make for a place that lay up-wind. I had been beating for two hours up-wind towards Menorca, and even if I didn't stumble upon serendipity there, it would be pleasant contrast to anchor in a smaller, quieter place than the bay of Pollensa. However, serendipity had to be silent. It may seem odd that a deaf person should crave silence, but I do. That's a curious thing about being rather deaf: silence becomes even more valuable. I seem less able than others to tolerate noise. I couldn't stand discos, over-revved engines and amplified parties. During the previous weeks there had been a lot of those sorts of noises penetrating my cotton wool at all hours of night.

While I was philosophising, bits of Menorca had sneaked westward and were teetering above the weather-side winch. It was time to tack again. This time I would have to be more careful. Last time I had not been watching the wave-shapes and had almost muffed the tack. Last time I had gone about too quickly; this time I would have to watch the waves and tack slowly.

I waited for an awkward-looking hummock to pass, put the helm down slowly, came through the wind's eye and gathered way on the starboard tack. Menorca slid smoothly across the bows, slung itself between the guard-rails and stayed there, just where it should be. That tack had been a better one; *Kylie* hadn't lost any way at all on that one. Tack slowly, I thought, and in less than an hour's time I might be serendipitous.

With the wind-vane latched in, I picked up another knife and tested its edge against my thumb, and then the words sank in. *Tack slowly...?* I let fall the knife and laughed. Tack-Slowboys had been *their* name. Wasn't that odd? Here I was, trying to beat against the wind towards a serendipital future, and it turns out that all the time I am somehow sailing backwards. I tack slowly towards a futuristic destination and suddenly I am sailing forty years down-wind and am with the Tack-Slowboys again.

Dining with the Tack-Slowboys in Port Louis, the evening after I had so nearly wrecked Captain Trump's ship, had been another disaster. I had not sought them out. Somehow, *they* had found *me*, and had despatched a note to the wardroom, 'By Hand' and via the steward, to inform me that Mrs Bernard St J Tack-Slowboys would be pleased, etc, to stand me a dinner. The invitation was not addressed to me by name, but to 'The Fourth Officer'. And who, I asked the steward, had delivered it? He didn't know; it had been among a bundle of mail cast aboard by the shipping agents.

I had attired myself in a white mess-jacket and had gone by taxi to what I imagined would be at least a mansion. After a ten-minute drive I was set down among puddles, before a shack of rusting corrugated iron in which dwelt a woman and her three daughters. Their table had been spread with a cloth of damask linen patterned in whorls. Though spotless and uncreased, the cloth was fragile with age and in places it had been darned. The crockery was a mixture; few pieces matched. Above our heads hung a naked electric bulb which cast fitful light on walls painted the shade of green found in school halls and money-lenders' offices, but it also illuminated aids to higher thoughts. Throughout the meal, Their Majesties King George V and Queen Mary gazed down on us from the howdahs of the Delhi Durbar and, although dressed in Brownie uniform, the Princesses Elizabeth and Margaret Rose waved at us quite cheerfully from the balcony of Buckingham Palace. Despite these encouragements, our conversation had not prospered. I had not been able to hear the lady's questions, and her daughters had hardly spoken at all. I had found their Mauritian accent strange and had not felt like trading compliments. They had eaten little, but whenever my own plate had been near to empty they had pressed me to eat my fill, glancing at me throughout the evening with beautiful dark eyes. We had not touched on the lady's marital state, but I formed the impression that she was a widow. I had accepted their kindness gracelessly, and I had been so preoccupied by my mistake with the engine-room telegraph that on my return aboard I had not even bothered to write my hostess a letter of thanks.

Not until years later, when I was hard up myself, did the purpose of the invitation dawn upon me. I realised with disquiet that the crockery had been the best she had, and that the darned table-cloth was a priceless heirloom, to be taken out of the bottom drawer only on important occasions. On the brink of middle age I conceded at last that the dark-eyed daughters had been Cinderellas in a show-case, and that I had been invited into their colonial home to assess their suitability for marriage. Mrs Tack-Slowboys had been hoping that her daughters would do better in the world than she had done, and that they would find a wealthy English suitor, perhaps even a prince, who would bear them away from the sugar-caned poverty of Mauritius to the rustless homes of England.

And there the matter had rested for years, although it had not rested easily. From time to time I had thought about my ungracious behaviour and had felt ashamed. I wondered what had become of the Tack-Slowboys. In my scheme of morality, they had deserved a reward. God knows, they had worked hard enough for happiness. Serendipity happened, I supposed, but only to princes who had money in their purse.

A mile or so from the island, I engaged the wind-vane and considered what to do. The cliffy entrance to the cove was about sixty feet wide, with rocks jutting into the narrow channel, beyond which the cove branched into two. Each branch was less than a hundred yards long, and even at its widest was no more than fifty yards across. Now that *Kylie* was in the lee of the island the seas were smoother, and no lop would jostle her in the entrance. On the other hand, the wind had gone down too, and was fluctuating in its direction. It looked as though I would need the engine to get into Serendip. I dodged below, switched on the fuel and pressed the starter button. The starter motor whirred but the engine did not fire. I lifted the casing and tried to bring the motor to life by cranking it with a handle, but without success. Breathing hard, I went to the cockpit, disengaged the wind-vane and hove-to. *Kylie* lay half a mile from the entrance to the cove, with the genoa backed and her bows pointing away from the land. This, I thought, was a fine state of affairs. Only a month since its last service and the engine was playing up again. While waiting for my heart to get back to its normal rhythm, I looked eastwards towards a headland. Beyond it lay Mahon, the finest harbour in the Mediterranean. What I ought to do was let draw the genoa and make for Mahon. I could enter the harbour easily under sail, I could have the engine put to rights there and be back at Serendip in a couple of days without any difficulty at all. Then I looked towards the cove. There would be lots of noisy people in Mahon; the cove, on the other hand, was silent and deserted.

When my breath had returned I let draw the genoa and headed for the entrance to the cove.

Two hundred yards from the shore the wind became very light and fluky. I eased the genoa sheet a fraction and sailed by the luff. Fifty yards from the land a deflected puff came off the starboard-hand cliff and wafted *Kylie* into the entrance, where a truer breeze caught the port side of the genoa, carried her clear of the rocks and into the basin. I spotted a patch of sand among the weed, luffed up and tipped the anchor over the bows. In a matter of minutes I had swum a sternline ashore, made a fisherman's bend around a pinnacle of rock and was back in the cockpit opening a beer.

It was a beautiful spot, with steep cliffs on two sides and pinewood slopes on the others. In the cliffs, prehistoric man had carved out his cave dwellings. Beneath me was clear, unchlorinated water, and around me was unleaded air. Even better than that, the air carried no noise. Quite alone, I settled down to wait for serendipity. Soon, the pine-trees would decorate the sunset, and later perhaps I would glimpse an owl in the moonlight. I supposed it couldn't be called serendipity because I had not been carried there by chance, I had worked upwind to get there; but for all that, I certainly knew happiness for a while.

About five minutes before the sun was due to impale itself on the topmost pine branch, a thirty-foot power-boat zoomed into the cove and whirled around it like a zapped wasp. I clapped my hands over my ears and screwed up my eyes. When I opened them again, the power-boat had throttled-back its engine, had cast its anchor over mine and was panting amorously towards *Kylie*'s backsides, twenty feet from my trembling beer. The sunset was probably beautiful, but I was too busy putting out fenders to a watch it. While the sunset was happening, the younger members of the power-boat's crew draped themselves in the mouth of the nearest prehistoric cave, switched on their ghetto-blasters and repaired their lipstick. And although some of their elders pottered off to hunt for squid, mum and dad hauled a sulky television on deck and spent the rest of the evening watching a soap opera.

It seemed that Jennie was right: serendipity lay downwind, somewhere you didn't have to work yourself silly to wiggle into. Also, I thought, 'serendipity' has got to have an antonym; there must be a word of opposite meaning. 'Hedonism' meant the pursuit of happiness, but surely there was also a word for the habit of falling into accidental unhappiness?

They kept the television going until gone one o'clock. I lay awake with my eyes shut for a long time, but I could not think of the word.

The following morning I disentangled my anchor, ghosted out of Serendip and sailed into Mahon, where a mechanic dropped ash into my coffee and said that the engine had ricked an important part of its anatomy. Because of a thirty-per cent tax, buying a replacement in Spain would be much more expensive than buying the part in the UK. I worked out that the difference between the two prices was more than the cost of a return fare to Gatwick, and so I left *Kylie* in Mahon and flew back to England, where I lodged with Sarah among the Dengie Hundreds of Essex.

The Dengie Hundreds are very unreliable acres of the realm. Despite their seeming numeracy, they don't seem to know whether they are integers of England or decimalised left-overs from an historic division sum. Nine hundred years after the Battle of Maldon had thought it had settled things for ever, the Dengie Hundreds are still lying around like homework waiting to be marked. Their seaward boundaries are elusive, and they quiver with furtive activity which ought to be locked up or, at the very least, kept down, but which somehow never is. The water and the land both have indecent tendencies, but they indulge them without much conviction. The watery fingers slip into the pockets of the land and the land sneaks into the sea, sliding its fingers under the skirts of the water, but neither is ever seen doing anything to the other that could strictly be called criminal. That gungey creek has been loitering with intent perhaps, but there has been no hint of a chargeable offence; neither nothing nor nobody has actually been caught doing anything culpable or getting anywhere important. The ambiguities of the Essex coastline would have had my gran fiddling with her corsets.

I obtained the engine-part quickly, but before I could return to *Kylie* I was waylaid into playing Captain Smollett in a production of *Treasure Island*. I set about learning the lines. When Sarah had left for work, I sat down every morning in her living-room at Steeple, going over my lines with Transom for as long as he could bear it. At twelve o'clock I would put away the text, pull on a pair of boots and take him for a walk along the banks of the Blackwater. Transom liked romping through the muddy fields, the ooze-filled creeks and the cattle plasters. I much preferred to clomp along pavements but, since he had been good enough to listen to my lines, I agreed to these one-hour walks on condition that they ended up in places where they sold strong ale.

One Wednesday morning Transom had been standing in for Long John Silver, parleying with me for an hour outside the blockhouse on Treasure Island. I had worked hard, but I couldn't get the lines right. It was important to get the lines exactly right because if I muffed them in performance I'd never be able to hear the prompter, who had a high-pitched voice that tangled among Semprini's pizzicatos. I said the lines to Transom over and over again, but always with some mistake or other. By twelve o'clock Transom had had enough. He looked at the clock, shook himself and stared intently at his lead. Although I still couldn't remember all my lines, I honoured my promise, pulled on the boots and took him for his walk. As he slurped through creeks, mud up to his ears, I persevered with Captain Smollett. *'You can't find the treasure!'* I roared at a mudhopper. *'You can't sail the ship - there's not a man among you fit to sail her. You're in irons, Mister Silver, you're on a lee shore!'*

Transom lolloped out of the creek and offered a supportive growl.

But at the rehearsal that evening I found that I still hadn't got the lines right. It was a lighting rehearsal and, blinded by the spotlights, I couldn't see the lips of either the prompter or the producer, only twenty feet away in the stalls. Every time the producer shouted advice, I had to break off, walk downstage, shade my eyes from the spotlights and ask him what he'd said. Although I'd prepared myself in advance against this kind of happening, the frequency of the hearing-failures shocked and depressed me. Lying in bed that night, I felt I had allowed myself to drift onto *Treasure Island* and had found only misery. Chance happiness was impossible; serendipity was a fiction. If 'serendipity' did have an antonym, it would have to centre on the fact of being born. I thought that 'nativity' might fill the bill.

The following day, instead of learning my lines I pulled on whatever clothes were nearest to hand, caught the early bus into Chelmsford and went in unshaven despair to the hearing-clinic, where was told that my audiograms were unchanged but wouldn't I like to attend a local support group to exchange problems with other deaf people? The weather, too, was unsettling, with flurries of sleet one minute and sunshine the next. Hemmed in by umbrellas, I stood on a pavement, waiting for the traffic light to change. I felt the strength of the wind on my back suddenly increase: another flurry was sure to follow soon. I pulled up the collar of my salt-stained jacket against the wind and stared at the crossing-light, which was still red. Then, out of focus at first, I saw something in a window across the street that rushed a sudden warmth to my neck. The traffic-light changed from red to green but I did not hurry forward. A cavalcade of desperate umbrellas swept across the street, but I was not among them. Transfixed, I gazed at the first-floor window of a late-Victorian building. Its ground floor had been done up by a building society in plate glass, stainless steel and strip lighting, but the upper floors had not been modernised. Above the illuminated mortgage-rate figures the rooms were small, and were lit by single electric bulbs. On one of the higher windows had been etched, with late-Victorian floridity, the name of the room's occupants:

TACK-SLOWBOYS & Co.

And, as if that were not shocking enough, they had added beneath:

Commissioners for Oaths.

The lights had changed to red again, but I dodged through the traffic and ran up worn stairs to a thinly carpeted anteroom. Hardly pausing to knock, I requested a pen and scribbled: 'Mauritius, 1951? If so, I would appreciate a word.'

The note was borne through a green baize door. I stared at an unfamiliar hollow-cheeked and unshaven face in a mirror and thought: I should have written more... Or perhaps not mentioned Mauritius at all... Others could have had their cover blown in Mauritius too... As it stands, the note could evoke unhelpful feelings...

After a couple of minutes, during which I supposed questions were being asked about my clothing, deportment and mien, the door swung open and I was handed back my piece of paper. I glanced at it and saw that my question had been answered. Underneath the enquiry had been written:

It was an uncle. He is dead.

I returned to Steeple morosely. It seemed that dark-skinned Cinderellas could be an embarrassment, even to princes. When the ashes were cold after midnight, Cinderellas were kept below stairs... And perhaps their bones were interred there too...

Transom had been puzzled by my absence and was so overjoyed by my return that he pinned me to the cottage wall, both paws against my chest, wagging the stump of his tail. Although it was much later than usual, I took down his lead and said, 'Alright then, let's go.'

He plunged ahead, nose to the ground, heading for the river. I followed him along what looked like firm ground, but was soon deep in mud, and — even more distastefully — my left boot was filling with water. I struggled to a tussock, where I emptied my boot and swore at the awfulness of the Dengie Hundreds. Captain Bloody Smollett, I decided, must have been a Dengie man. *Smollett*? Like 'Dengie', the name was neither one thing nor the other. Either 'Smollett' slithered penuriously between 'Small' and 'Wallet', or — when one had drunk a bit too deeply in the *Sun and Anchor* and it came out as 'Shmollett'— it floundered piscatorially between 'Shoal' and 'Mullet'. But what could you expect in this phlegmy labium of England? *Dengie*? What was 'Dengie' but a squidgy conflation of 'Dense' and 'Gungey'?

'Transom!' I shouted angrily towards the Blackwater.

And then the sun came out and made the state of things clearer.

Osea Island was a dismal smudge and stayed so. To the north the cloud was leaden, but low in the west the sky had opened, and the sunlight streamed through, turning the river to puckered gold. But the beams fell on something more valuable than that. A gaff-rigged cutter was coming down-river from Maldon, beating past the Barnacle against a stiff wind. With the ebb weakening and the afternoon far gone, the cutter would need to hurry if she was to make a haven by nightfall. The seams of her mainsail were ochred by the sun and pulse of foam gleamed beneath her bowsprit. Two figures were at the mast, oilskins shining yellow as they sweated taut the halyards.

A sudden white ferret raced upwards from the jaws of the gaff, was plucked by its tail and transformed itself into a topsail. The cutter heeled a plank to port and the pulse of foam became a tumbling breaker.

Transom emerged backwards from a swamp, dragging a three-foot log. When he reached firm ground he shifted his jaws to the middle of the burden, lifted it clear and lurched towards me. Two feet away, he opened his mouth and dropped the log at my feet. From paws to haunches he was plastered with Dengie mud. The wind was cold and his belly was unfilled, but his stump was wagging, and beyond his tousled head the cutter was making for the Mersea Quarters, her sails varnished with spray and sunlight.

The dog's paws were daubing mud on my trousers, but I did not push him away. I glanced from the urgent sails to the hope-filled eyes and back again.

O, Transom, I thought. O, serendipity.

'There's a good dog,' I told him. 'There's a good *boy*!'

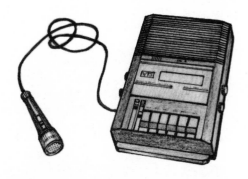

9

Bulgaria Untaped

At the root of most failures is a failure of understanding. Whether the scenario is the divorce court or a maritime shipwreck tribunal, somewhere along the line messages were not understood.

Since my deafness causes me to misunderstand spoken messages, I give more weight to those received through my other senses, especially if the words are coming at me in an unfamiliar rhythm. Until I could pick up British or US short-wave broadcasts, I almost always read the weather from what I saw in the sky and the barometer rather than from what I heard on the foreign radio-bands. And on entering each new country I drew evidence of its character more from what I saw and touched and smelt than from what I heard from the lips of its people. In Majorca I responded to the smell of the pinewoods and the sight of Katy's fingers stroking the ears of abandoned dogs. Later in Greece, my eyes took in the classical architecture but also saw the carpet of cigarette butts in the streets. Later again in Turkey it was eyes and nose together: sunset over the Blue Mosque and the smell of the world's best bread,

Sometimes what I saw was rich and appealing; at other times, as in Bulgaria, it was distressing. I had wanted to sail across the Black Sea to

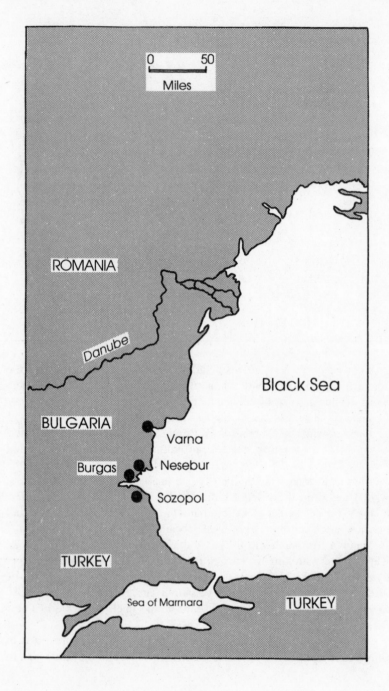

Russia, but I could not obtain a Russian visa, although I could get visas for Romania and Bulgaria. I did not apply for a Romanian visa because I had been there before and on the whole I had not enjoyed it. I had been there in 1948, aboard the first British vessel to enter the country since before the Second World War. Before we sailed from Liverpool someone had come aboard with a miniature camera and told the captain how to take pictures from his cabin scuttle, out of sight of the Romanian pilot, pictures of anything that might interest our Secret Service. When we had berthed at Constanza we found that everybody was hungry, and the only taxi in town was still having to pick its way down streets which were cratered from the bombing by what the Romanians had been told were American Flying Fortresses. Despite the hunger and the bomb-damage, we thought the people would be glad to see us. After all, we had helped them to win a war which had saved them from being kicked to death by the Nazi jackboot. It soon became clear, however, that they were not at all pleased to see us.

A beautiful blue-eyed girl had crossed the main street and climbed a pile of bomb debris just to tell me so.

'Are you British?'

I had tightened the knot of my tie. My uniform cap, I already knew, was at the angle that had turned a few heads, even on Lime Street.

'Yeah,' I had said. Of course, Noël Coward and Jack Hawkins pronounced the word differently in their films, but they were always at sea on the bridges of destroyers or corvettes, having terrific knockabouts with U-boats or Stukas, which did much to hone their martial arts but gave them scant opportunity to practise sexual skills. In dealing with women they were DBS. For dealing with women, one had to learn from Bogart.

'Yeah,' I had said again, lighting a cigarette and letting the smoke trickle through my teeth. *Play it again, Samantha...* 'I'm from England.'

The girl had stood before me, her bosom heaving nicely.

'You dirty, sodding, shitty, English mother-fucking bastard.'

It was a compliment I could not ignore. I flagged the taxi and escaped.

Yet, forty years on, with Stalin dead and Mikhail Gorbachov wowing the White House, I had scarcely dipped *Kylie*'s foot in Communist waters before there they were again, still getting at me.

'What ship?' they Morsed aggressively, the light flicking from a dark headland.

It was blowing twenty knots from the north-west at the time. I was on the foredeck, changing down from genoa to jib, too busy to reply. So before dawn they attacked me again, this time with a searchlight. It struck me rigid in the cockpit, one hand on the tiller. I froze for them obligingly, but after five minutes I wished the sun would come and thaw the situation.

'Shoot it in Technicolor,' I murmured at the searchlight.

When the sun rose it did not gild the land. Bulgaria and the sea were dressed in the same uniform of sepia and military grey, and the sky was sulphur-yellow and the cranes of Burgas docks were sticking up like spikes on prison walls.

The port sucked me towards it. With limp sails I dawdled at the harbour entrance until a launch bustled out, snatched my lines and yanked me to an oily crèche where it left me to sulk. It also took my shotgun and my passport and deposited a heavy policeman on the dockside to mind me.

After two hours I tried to step ashore. 'Bread,' I said; 'I want fresh bread.' But the policeman was unmoved. He took a bite from his sandwich and flicked a crumb from the holster on his thigh. I retreated to the cabin, re-read the instruction manual of my tape-recorder and thought about the chief reason for my visit. I wanted to interview George Georgiev, a Bulgarian yachtsman who had set a west-about circumnavigation record in 1977. I margarined a wedge of stale bread and daubed runny Turkish jam on it. Blobs of jam dropped onto the tape-recorder. I tried again to break the social ice between me and the policeman by doing a Charlie Chaplin dumb-show, alternately dabbing jam from the recorder and licking it off my finger, but he just went on glaring at me over his sandwich. I decided that the guard hadn't heard of Charlie Chaplin, or of Gorbachov's *glasnost* message, come to that.

'Where are you going?' they said when at last they returned my passport.

'Nowhere far today,' I said. It was too late to go searching for George Georgiev, and besides I was hungry.

'You cannot stay here,' they said. 'Round the corner there is a yacht club.' So I took *Kylie* to the yacht club of Burgas, and it was there that I met Ruslana.

'George Georgiev,' she said, 'sailed from Varna, forty miles north. Come with us to Varna regatta next week and we will show you the place.'

For several days I lay at the yacht club, which is in the lee of the ore-tips. I was unhappy about the dirty air and the scummy water but the kindness of Ruslana and her friends was a cleansing tonic. In between working on their own boats they helped on mine, attending to the engine, which had developed a sort of bronchitic wheeze. In the evenings we went into town to buy food, past a big notice which said in English,

BULGARIA IS AN ACTIVE FIGHTER FOR PEACE AND FREEDOM
AMONG THE NATIONS OF THE WORLD.

Give or take a noun or two, it was the same message that I had seen in Constanza, strung on a banner between two tannoys that were telling you what Josef Stalin had said to his caviar at breakfast.

The fine words did not seem to butter anyone's parsnips. I saw no parsnips, I could find no potatoes, and I had to queue for fruit. It was doled out by unsmiling stallholders in black plastic aprons.

'Things get worse,' grumbled an old woman. 'Now we have to queue even for cherries. Where have all the cherries gone?'

'To Russia...' whispered Ruslana into my better ear.

'...With Love?' I whispered back, but she did not smile.

We retired to a café where all the waitresses had square shoulders. They were just black oblongs from shoulder to knee whichever way you looked at them. They did not smile often, and when they did it was only to each other. Customers were given dour expressions and off-hand treatment, beer came late, and food came even later. Around me Bulgarians talked seriously about life. Alongside them, life-like babies in prams stared just as seriously at the grey skies. The only smile came when a dysfunctional young man swung a punch at a shadow and fell into his own beer.

But my hoard of spare boat-gear raised a lot of delight at the yacht club. It seemed I possessed bits and pieces of equipment they'd never even heard of. Ruslana fingered a twisted shackle as though it was a hand-out from Fort Knox.

'Would you...?' she whispered. And when I gave her two of them she looked into my eyes and kissed me warmly.

'Tomorrow,' she cried, 'you will be our guest for the passage to Varna!'

A bit exhilarated, I climbed to the masthead with a bucking hose to wash down every inch of *Kylie* before leaving.

The following morning Ruslana left without me, but I didn't blame her. Her boat had no engine, the winds were light, and I was still waiting to be dealt with by the passport controllers. I had stumbled to the immigration office at three a.m., high on Ruslana's vodka and a bowl of pilfered cherries. Uniformed men with oiled hair snored full-length on grimy settees, and someone was swishing a mop down the corridor.

'I am Turk,' he said, smiling proudly.

'*Merhaba*,' I replied. 'And when do they open?'

'At seven of the clock,' he said. I stilled my impatience and waited. A single fluorescent tube flickered and hummed. I ate cherries until five, and thought, 'Oh, well, what with the British MI6 and the American CIA sticking limpet mines here and there, it's no wonder they are edgy when Western boats start cruising their coastlines.' Things had not changed much in forty years. *Mariners are cautioned...* had said the British Admiralty *Pilot*, and the Black Sea charts made the paranoia plainer, for minefields the size of Suffolk were still lying off the shores of the Russian ports.

At five o'clock the settees were still snoring, and so I pretended to choke on a cherry. The officials awoke, smoothed their hair, and in ten minutes had cleared me for Varna.

By motoring hard across a windless sea, I caught up with Ruslana at noon, still more than thirty miles from our destination. Without putting the engine out of gear I passed her a line and took her boat and two others in tow. We got to Varna before dusk and berthed under the stern of a sleek Italian-built power-boat.

'It's the President's yacht,' murmured Ruslana, opening a tin of sardines. 'Will you eat?'

From the stern of the presidential yacht someone was looking down at us. The person was wearing a white boiler-suit and toting a sub-machine gun over the nearside shoulder. What put me off more was that the facial expression was even less welcoming than the one worn by my minder at Burgas. In fact, at second glance I decided it was only marginally more hostile than a full-frontal glare from an oblongular waitress.

'I'll eat later,' I said, putting down the sardines, 'when and if I return from Passport Control...'

Even before I'd got back to ingest the sardines they'd detailed another policeman to watch me. He was smaller than his Burgas equivalent and he was sporting a Stalinesque moustache, plus a twist to the ends of his lips which I thought might be a smile. It was. Also in his favour, he accepted cigarettes,

He was not the only one. A stream of Russians, Poles and Bulgarians trickled down the quayside, ignoring the two hundred gleaming feet of the Presidential yacht to inspect the twenty-six feet of scrubbed *Kylie*. Under the nose of the boiler-suited machine-gunner they took my Marlboro cigarettes and discussed among themselves the differences of gear and rigging between their boats and mine. One of them spoke English fluently.

He told me that his boat was the same size as *Kylie* and was based on the same Folkboat design. He invited me to inspect her. I was deeply impressed. Before seeing his boat I had thought *Kylie* to be a bit Spartan, but his boat was the most basic long-distance cruiser that I've ever seen. Self-built out of what might once have been discarded pallets, with a galley that comprised a single butane bottle lashed to a stanchion, it had nevertheless sailed to England and competed in a trans-Atlantic race.

'Please come aboard *Kylie*,' I said, 'and tell me all about it.' I motioned him to join me in the cabin, and I was already framing the questions and unbuttoning the tape-recorder.

The questions were never put. Just as the Bulgarian yachtsman was about to step aboard, the friendly neighbourhood policeman on the quayside palmed his Marlboro and made a small but unambiguous gesture. It was only a small, slow gesture but it was enough to stop my new friend in his tracks. He looked at me, shushed my incredulous protests and walked silently away. 'This is not happening,' I thought. 'We must be in a time warp.'

'It's like something from John Le Carré,' I told Ruslana, 'but I still hope they'll let me talk to George Georgiev.'

Ruslana put a finger to my lips. 'That will not be possible,' she said. 'Did you not realise that George Georgiev is dead?' And, still with her finger on my lips, she added, 'How or where he died, I do not know...'

Perhaps the policeman tried to make amends when I left Varna by throwing me the bights of my shorelines without wetting them, but his actions were too little and late, for by that time the paranoidal glumph was getting me down.

'Where are you going now?' prinked Passport Control. 'Nesebur or Pomorie?' These were the only other ports open to foreigners, I'd been told, so really they weren't giving me much choice.

'Both,' I said, and at the time I meant it. But I found that both those places were rather dull, and so, just to see what would happen, on the way back to Turkey I put into a harbour called Sozopol, which was near where they had cudgelled me with the searchlight.

I got into Sozopol alright. No mines blew me up, and, because it was broad daylight they couldn't make a to-do with a searchlight. I sailed in at the end of a rare and beautiful afternoon of blue skies and fair winds, mooring opposite three gunboats. On a huge parade ground a phalanx of sailors was doing Slavonic aerobics. When I reached the quayside a cloud came over the sun and it started to rain. I closed the forehatch, and the sailors started to chant slogans in time with their movements.

143

Before I had cleated the bow-lines the inevitable policeman was needling me. This one had no moustache and he refused cigarettes.

'Come with me,' he said, and so I went. Clutching a damp but well-upholstered passport containing formidable phrases like *Her Britannic Majesty's Principal Secretary of State... requests and requires... all those whom it may concern to allow the bearer to pass freely without let or hindrance...*, I slouched past coughing lorries and stalls offering unbreakable plastic combs until the policeman led me to face his superior officer. He was seated in a small room with a small window and straightaway I felt he was just the very chap to know a lot about let and even more about hindrance. He had tabs on his shoulders and his hair was oiled, but only very lightly.

He scrutinised my damp passport. Outside, it was now raining heavily but the sailors were still persevering with their aerobics. They seemed to be throwing telegraph poles at each other, while at the same time requesting and requiring their immediate return without let or hindrance at the tops of their voices.

'English?' asked the officer.

'British,' I corrected him.

The officer smiled primly, like a vicar remembering an indelicate joke. He foraged a while among the resonant phrases of the passport. I began to think that they might be impressing him, but I was wrong.

'If you are still in this harbour thirty minutes from now,' he said. 'I will make your life very difficult... *very* difficult indeed.'

The chants reached an aggressive crescendo. Telegraph poles rose above roofs. The officer eased his holster and handed back my passport.

After that little lot, I put to sea and stayed there, ghosting out through the rain. Before midnight the rain stopped, and I winged out an extra sail so as to get to Turkey more quickly. In a misty dawn I said an apologetic prayer for Mrs Thatcher and blew *The Red Flag* on my harmonica. As though in response, one of the Bulgarian gunboats slunk up out of the mist, growling softly. I stowed away the harmonica. The thing circled me slowly, keeping one red eye fixed on mine.

Through the mist a tannoyed voice crackled 'Vhere are you from?'

I shouted a reply. The red eye crept closer, eighty feet away and level with my masthead.

'At what hour did you leave?' it asked. Somebody was taking the cover off the gun on the foredeck.

'Four o'clock,' I shouted back, a shade more shrilly. The gunboat picked over the bones of my information. The person on the foredeck

'The officer smiled primly, like a vicar remembering an indelicate joke.'

elevated and depressed gun with impressive speed, and so I added quickly, '...with permission, of course.' I thought about reminding them of the *...without let or hindrance...* bit, but decided against it on the very linguistic grounds that if someone mistranslated 'let' as 'rent', he might think that I'd left behind some unpaid bills in Burgas.

Growling suspiciously, the gunboat digested my words. Between the throaty grumbles I tweaked the sheets and sidled southwards. When I was sure the gunboat was not following, I swallowed twice and tried to shout an impolite farewell but somehow I could produce only a squeak. I felt in my pocket for a handkerchief but my fingers found only Bulgarian coins. I tried to decipher the Cyrillic script on them but I failed. I could not comprehend even the smallest word of it.

I closed my hand and hurled the coins as far as I possibly could into the dark waters. Then I looked at the chart and thought warmly about Turkey, and especially about its markets.

One thing, at least, I could be sure of: in Turkey the stalls would be piled high with cherries.

10
Airs on a Harmonica

Unless we use mirrors we see only about half of what we look at. We infer that an entire cat is on the mat though we see only part of each. Given this wonky relationship between perception and reality, stereotypes are quite useful because they help us to get through the day without going mad. The trouble is, stereotyping can induce life-long tunnel vision; and chauvinistic spectacles do not improve it. In my school-room drawings of the world, all Germans had square heads, all Americans wore stetsons and the faces of several hundred million Chinese wore the same inscrutable expression. Thirty years later, when Cyprus had become a no-go area, I was still smiling at the favourite Turkish joke, which is the one about the crashing airliner. The story goes that after the American, the Englishman and the German have eulogised the honourable traditions of their respective nations and made the supreme sacrifice by throwing themselves out of the aeroplane in vain efforts to keep it at a life-preserving height, the Turk announces that he, too, will enact a similar sacrifice, whereupon he throws out the Greek.

My later discovery that not many Turks strolled around in Ottoman robes and carried scimitars to chop off the hands of Unbelievers who pinched parts of the Topkapi Palace as they wandered through it came, therefore, as a pleasant revelation, and so I decided to visit their country.

However, I didn't sail to Turkey directly but zigzagged there via Corfu, the Corinth Canal, the Saronic Islands, Crete, the Cyclades and the Dodecanese. Both the zigs and the zags involved far too much motoring to make them memorable sailing, but I met many memorable people who broadened my tunnel vision of the world. Among them was Philippe Fau, who was just starting his second circumnavigation in an engineless sloop the same size as *Kylie*.

'Before I fitted out my boat,' he said, 'I asked myself "Why do I need an engine?"' I could think of only six reasons for having an engine, but I thought of fifty-four reasons against, and so I did not install one. Apart from needing a tow through the Panama Canal, I have managed very well without. I can sail to all the places in the world I want to go.'

'What about the calms?' I said. 'Don't the Doldrums bother you?'

'The only time I was bothered by calms was here in the Mediterranean, when it took me three weeks to sail sixty miles during a passage from Sicily to Sardinia. A high-pressure area lay over Italy, and there was no wind at all. After two weeks I had read all the books aboard.'

'What did you do then?'

Philippe crinkled his merry elfin face. 'I started to write my own stories,' he smiled,' and I practised my guitar.'

Though I fell into several windless holes during the months that followed, I could not endure them with Philippe's equanimity. It wasn't only the meteorological calms that unbalanced me; sometimes it seemed that the people and domestic animals of the Eastern Mediterranean were living in a time bubble that had not been popped for thousands of years. In the Cyclades I saw farmers wobbling into town on donkeys that looked ancient enough to have once carried Jesus Christ, and everywhere east of Menorca the behaviour of cats and dogs would have thrown modern cartoon-animators into despair. Never did I see a dog chase a cat, let alone bark at one. Although the mongrels lying in the shade of the Turkish olive-trees were less classy than the Jack Russells of Southwold who went hysterical at anything that moved, they were much more civil towards cats. In Bodrum the two species lay down as closely to each other as they must have done in the 'tweendecks of the Ark before Noah turned them out on Ararat and Walt Disney goaded them to enmity.

One morning I motor-sailed *Kylie* to Rhodes, where I moored in the old harbour of Mandraki, beneath windmills whose idle sails confirmed that the wind had departed for ever. Having passed the afternoon lazing

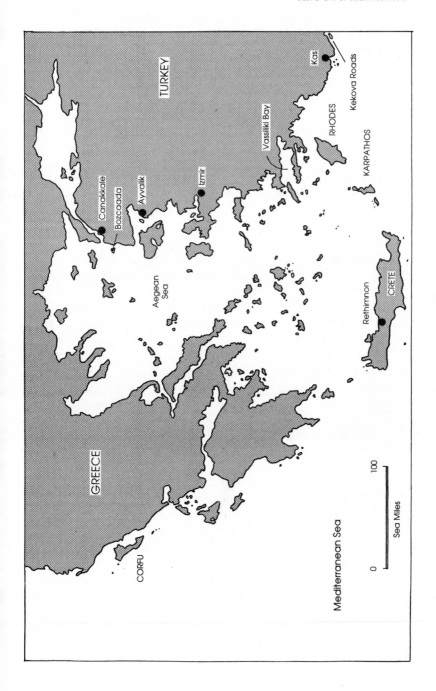

beneath the cockpit awning, in the cool of the evening I fashioned a Turk's head knot on the tiller, and for a while I added to the noise of the bustling city by practising *Nellie Dean* on my harmonica. The sounds of revelry in and around the old harbour went on until well after midnight, and so to escape the noise the following morning I bussed down the coast to the hamlet of Monolithos, where I embarked in a fourteen-foot boat with a fisherman and his eleven-year-old son. For four hours we hauled fleets of nets in the broiling sun but at the end our bucket was barely half-filled. I thought the catch a poor one, but the fisherman just sucked his lower lip and smiled. Having ordered a meal at the *taverna*, I selected a handful of small pebbles and beneath a wall that nodded with scarlet hibiscus I began to play jackstones, an occupation which, like juggling milk bottles and tearing-up treasury notes, is guaranteed to attract an audience. After a very few minutes the fisherman's son was asking me what I was doing, and we were soon engaged in friendly competition, which was brought to an end only when my *taramasalata* appeared on a nearby table and I went off to eat it.

The eleven-year-old immediately gathered up the jackstones, sought out an eighteen-year-old and taught him the skills of the game. The instruction was done unselfconsciously; there was no sense that the older youth was condescending or that the younger was being uppish. Watching them, it struck me that the only time in recent England I had seen a young boy start a conversation with someone outside his peer group had been in a school-dinner queue, when a first-former had distracted the attention of a fifth-former by babbling about the fortunes of Norwich City Football Club so that his pre-pubertal companion could sneak off with the last piece of what he later called dead man's leg but which was really jam roly-poly.

By the time I had drunk a glass of *retsina* the heat of the midday sun had driven the jackstone-players to the shade of the courtyard trees, but before they had completed another round of play a very old man had appeared on the road outside the *taverna*, moving with the luxurious slowness of one who has finished work for the day and is looking forward to putting his feet up. Without saying a word to each other, the two young contestants adjourned their game, fetched a chair and set it down in the shade. The old man wiped his forehead with his cap and sank onto the chair. Anywhere in northern Europe, the action of the younger people would already have been enough to persuade the middle-aged that not all boys were boors: age and infirmity had been recognised and the social dues had been paid in full by the setting-out of the chair. The hibiscus nodded agreement from the wall; now, I thought, the youngsters will take up the jackstones and get on with their game, but they did not. A murmured conversation ensued among them. I learned from the waitress that they talked about the yield of the old man's olive-trees, the price of cheese, the kidding of his goats and the moulting of his chickens. Only when these weighty subjects had been discussed and analysed did the young people resume their game.

When I boarded the bus back to Mandraki they were still beneath the shade of the trees, the eleven-year-old playing jackstones with the eighteen-year-old, and the aged man leaning forward, elbows on knees, commenting on the play. We sped along the tarmac highway, buffeting the scarlet hibiscus with our manufactured breeze that would settle another layer of dust on the already dusty dogs who scarcely raised their heads as we roared past. No doubt, I thought, there are poor people and distressed people on the island of Rhodes, but on Rhodes there are no cardboard cities, and granny-dumping is not a likely gambit. Although their health-care services are probably less elaborate than England's, they will not need psychiatrists so long as their people behave towards each other like the villagers of Monolithos.

After two windless days in Mandraki, during which time I practised *Nellie Dean* so assiduously that a tourist from Wyoming asked me whether some queen or other had died at Buckingham Palace and was I playing the *National Anthem?*, the *meltemi* came down from the north and *Kylie* set off for Réthimnon in Crete. The seventy-five-mile passage from the port of Rhodos to the island of Karpathos was the swiftest I made in months. Under the small genoa, *Kylie* slid over the glistening seas in the Karpathos Channel at five knots and swept through the narrow entrance to the Tristoma inlet with such panache that an over-excited farmer fell off a promontory and had to be hauled aboard and revived with neat whisky. He sat in the cockpit beneath one of *Kylie*'s blankets, sipping the whisky and waiting for his shirt and trousers to dry in the rigging. Between each sip of whisky his tongue cursored his teeth, as though searching for a starting-place in his life-script.

He never found the place. After half a glassful of whisky he was asleep and I was practising *Waltzing Matilda*. I rowed him ashore at sunset, and sometime after midnight *Kylie* motored past the winking light at Tristoma entrance and headed for Réthimnon, where the people were less often excited when boats entered their harbour under sail but, even without the inducement of single-malt whisky, were usually more voluble. After a pleasant enough 140-mile passage across the Southern Aegean in winds of between five and fifteen knots, I ghosted past the old Venetian lighthouse, anchored in thick black mud, threw a line to a waiter at the nearest restaurant and resumed my conversations.

They started with pleasantries. Over a *tzatsiki* I commented to the waiter, who said he had once lived in Middlesex, on the large numbers of very old Cretans who were parading the quayside. They looked, I told him, fit enough to take on Australia in a Test Match. My finger was hovering over the inventory of a *filet mignon* on the second page of the menu at the time. The waiter clicked his tongue, referred me to page three and pointed to a dish called *Sfiritha*.

'If you want to live as long as *they* do, you will order *that*.'

'What is it?'

'Grouper,' he said. And, seeing me look dubious, went on: 'You see that man over there? He is ninety-five and his friend is one hundred and three. You want to know why they live so long? They never eat red meat. They have never eaten a beefsteak in their lifes. They eat only fish and chicken. If you eat red meat, you shorten your life.'

'Garn!'

'Is true. All his life my grandfather never ate anything that walked, not even chicken. He ate only fish, and he was ninety-eight years old when he died.'

'Heavens! That was a good innings.'

The waiter shrugged and re-folded a napkin.

'You want to know how he died?'

'Yes, please.'

'He fell off his donkey.'

*

To avoid the summer *meltemi* of the South Aegean, which, according to a couple of gale-shocked British yachtsmen I met, sometimes blew at sixty knots, I sailed northwards again towards Asiatic Turkey, where I discovered that not only were old people as much respected as those of Rhodes but that the phenomenon of ageing was itself of such momentous interest as occasionally to get in the way of more practical matters such as, for example, dropping stern-lines onto bollards.

After beating for sixteen hours against a moderate north-easterly wind, late one afternoon I eased sheets, reached through the Dalyan Bogazi and entered the harbour of Ayvalik. Seeing a vacant berth on the quayside, I backed the genoa, hitched a couple of lines onto the stern cleats, dropped anchor, handed sails and fell back on the anchor warp towards the quay. It was not a particularly difficult series of manoeuvres, but by the time I had got *Kylie* almost in line with what I hoped would be a safe berth I had taken up a notch in my Marks-and-Spencer belt and was perspiring freely. Balancing myself between the backstays, I lifted the wind-vane from its mounting, stowed the vane out of harm's way below decks and requested a likely-looking bystander to take my lines. He cupped his hands to his mouth and shouted something I failed to hear. I stood between the backstays, the harbour slop jostling *Kylie* towards the other boats, six loops of rope in my left hand and three in my right, all of them ready to be hurled twenty feet to the quayside so that he could drop an end over a bollard and make my boat fast for the night.

'What's that you say?' I yelled at him.

'Hargle bargle yellow poo?' he said.

'Catch this!' I cried, heaving the line towards his windward shoulder.

'Hargle polder woo? Wowgle higher hargle poo?' he reiterated, winding the line around the nearest twig of what an encyclopaedia later suggested might be valonia oak.

When, in the fullness of Asiatic time, the line was transferred from the oak-twig to the bollard and *Kylie* was secured six feet from his nose, I found out that the all-important question he had been putting so insistently was: 'In Allah's name, how marvellously old are you?'

As I explained to Kemal two days later, it was not the first question that even someone like a pig-farmer from as far inland as Bungay might put to the skipper of a short-handed sailboat who was trying to make fast outside the *Harbour Inn* at Southwold, but it emphasised, in a nicely practical way, the relevance of age in Asia Minor. Or, as I put it afterwards to one of my children who was into marketing: one sells fewer bottles of *Grecian 2000*™ east of Istanbul.

It is fifty miles from Ayvalik to Bozcaada Island and another thirty from Bozcaada to Çanakkale on the Dardanelles. If the wind allowed, I intended to give Bozcaada a miss. Like Isla Cabrera off Majorca, it is a garrisoned island which, according to what I could understand of Turkish regulations, visitors need special permission to land on. Bearing in mind the short shrift that the Spanish military had meted out when I attempted the same on Cabrera, I did not want to give their Turkish counterparts a chance to do likewise, and so I left Ayvalik before seven o'clock in the morning, hoping to make Çannakle before midnight on the same day. Under a large genoa and assisted at times by the engine, *Kylie* motor-sailed the six miles to Günes Adasi in what, if my Japanese watch was right, was two minutes and ten seconds less than an hour, before altering to a more northerly heading towards Baba Burnu, a headland which, despite its pudgy name, is altogether spiky. I poled out the genoa and reclined in the cockpit, breakfasting on bread and honey in the early sunlight. For those who do not yet know it, no bread in the world tastes quite as good as newly-baked Turkish bread. Its firm texture and semi-sweet taste is contained within a non-splinter crust that is itself delicious, and it is one of the few breads in the world that I, for one, can swallow without garnish.

For an hour or two after breakfast the south-east wind strengthened to ten knots, and so I switched off the engine and reached through the Müslim Kanali, with the green hills of Lesvos to port and the less luxuriant Turkish mainland to starboard. This pleasant progress continued until an hour before noon, when the wind, after veering first south and then west, fell so light that I was compelled to start the engine again. It ran for five hours, pushing *Kylie* some fifteen miles towards Çannakale against an increasingly strong current until tea-time, when it began to mumble and spit, and in the space of a quarter of an hour had choked itself to an oily silence. For two hours I struggled to put the timing mechanism to rights, but at sunset I wiped the oil from my hands, chomped an uncut Turkish loaf between my teeth, set the large ghoster and made for the nearest mechanic, who happened to be living on the dour-looking hump called Bozcaada, which by then was only eight miles distant.

It took me more than six hours to cover those eight miles. At two-thirty the following morning, *Kylie* ghosted into the harbour and anchored in two and a half fathoms on sand. I scrubbed the oil from my finger nails and wondered how the army would treat me.

I was awoken at seven-thirty in a very un-military fashion. Instead of the usual thump of a soldier's Doc Martens onto the side deck there came a polite but insistent series of raps on the hull. I poked my head out of the companionway and beheld a freckle-faced, red-haired young man smiling at me from a bright red motor-boat.

'Good morning, sir,' said the young man, holding up a creature that looked like a mullet. 'You want a fish?'

I thanked him for his offer but declined it, adding that I was in greater need of a mechanic than of something to eat.

'Come with me, sir, and we find my friend Ali Kaya very quick.'

We did not find Ali Kaya at all quickly. The young fisherman scoured the tea-houses, peered into alleyways and quizzed bystanders. Some said

Ali Kaya had gone to galvanise an anchor in Izmir, others that he was sleeping at his father's, while a third group insisted that he had gone — and not, in Allah's name, before time — on a pilgrimage to someplace like Mecca. We found him eventually in a hut on the beach, where he was snoring over an empty wine bottle. After rinsing out his mouth with a liquid that I thought was water but my red-haired companion thought was something stronger, he hitched up his trousers and said that, if Allah willed it, he would put my engine to rights. I said I would row him aboard and, if Allah still willed it, he could make a start right away.

'And after, sir, you come back to drink *çay* with me,' said the young fisherman. I rowed Ali Kaya and his tools out to *Kylie*, and on my return found a sergeant the same size and demeanour as the Spanish NCO who had ordered me out of Cabrera waiting for me on the quayside. Sensing that there might be some difficulties brewing, the red-haired young man bore me into the port captain's office to record *Kylie*'s entry before the NCO had a chance to unbutton his pistol and send me packing.

Over glasses of hot, sweet tea the young fisherman told me that his name was Kemal and that, although he had lived with his father, mother and sister on Bozcaada for as long as he could remember, he had not been born on that island but near the town of Kas, on the southern coast of Turkey. Fifteen years ago, when he, Kemal, was four years old, his parents had migrated on donkeys from the Lycian coast of Turkey to Izmir in search of work but, not finding city life to their liking, after a few months had donkeyed further to the Aegean coast, embarked on the ferry to Bozcaada and settled there.

'...but all the time they talk about Kas, about the beautiful people of Kas. I, Kemal, want to see the beautiful people of Kas.'

'Why don't you go? The buses are good and it's not too far.'

'Peter *abi*, I have not yet the money,' said Kemal, picking up his morning catch and inviting me to watch him dispose of it.

Kemal spotted his first potential customer, a man in a brown boiler-suit who was pushing a bicycle from one side of the street to the other. When Kemal called to him, the man leaned the saddle of the bicycle against his hip and, as Kemal approached, explained in about a hundred words that he was pushing the bicycle because the chain had broken. Kemal shook hands and showed him his catch, which comprised two small lobsters and about six fish, each between one and three pounds in weight. The man selected one of the lobsters and, after telling Kemal in a further hundred words that, if Allah willed it, he was going to repair the bicycle at his brother-in-law's house, he shook hands and walked off, carrying the lobster in his left hand and pushing the bicycle with his right. At no time did any money change hands. Oh well, I thought, he must be one of Kemal's closest friends.

The next encounter looked more promising. An old man with fierce white moustaches summoned him across the street by holding a walking-stick aloft and waggling it. The old man was wearing a newly-pressed beige suit and gold-rimmed spectacles. This time there will be a sale, I thought, for it is not likely that such a high-class person could be a close friend of a humble fisherman. Kemal darted across the street, took one of the old man's arthritic hands to his lips and kissed the fingers.

'Mustafa *abi*,' said Kemal, 'what is your wish?'

The old man inspected the catch and selected a three-pounder worth, I supposed, at least a pound sterling. Kemal placed it on a nearby ledge, bowed his head slightly and said, 'Mustafa *abi*, may prosperity and peace attend you!' The old man nodded gravely and murmured a reply, but again, no money changed hands.

Everywhere we went the same happened: fish changed hands, but Kemal received no money for them. The other lobster was given to a ferrety-looking man outside a baker's shop, and two more fish went to a wizened creature with a black scarf over her head who scuttled from a shadowed doorway behind a mosque. But it was the giving-away of the last fish that I remember best. We had come to a street that was somehow different from the others. Perhaps the doors had been painted a harder shade of blue, perhaps fewer women wore scarves over their heads, perhaps the washing hung at a different angle to the sun: whatever the other reasons may have been, I am sure that the people stood differently in doorways and, instead of calling out to Kemal as they had done in other streets, they remained silent as he passed.

We made a left turn and came upon a crippled man sitting beneath a flaking wall that girdled a large building. He had propped his crutches against the wall and his damaged foot, brown-stockinged and twisted, lay in the shadow, amid dust and cigarette butts. The other foot, encased in a black patent-leather dancing-shoe, had been awarded a higher station. Cushioned on a straw-filled plastic bag, it gleamed in the sunlight, reflecting diamonds into the face of its wearer. At our approach the cripple laid aside a rag and looked up from the burnished toe-cap. His jaw was black with stubble, but the collar of his open-necked shirt was clean, and something gilt and pendant could be glimpsed at his throat. To Kemal he raised a hand, but although his lips parted, he spoke nothing. Kemal made a similar gesture, one that conveyed respectfulness rather than easy friendship, before placing his last remaining fish on the cushion. The mullet lay alongside the bright shoe, its eye dull and the sheen quite gone from its scales, but still almost as good to eat as when he had offered it to me earlier.

'Peter *abi*,' said Kemal, turning his face so that I could see his lips, 'we can return to Ali Kaya and the motor now.'

When we reached the T-junction I looked back and saw that the large building was a Christian church and realised that the gilt ornament at the cripple's throat must have been a crucifix and he a Greek.

*

The day's events so impressed me that before shaking hands with Kemal that night I suggested that later in the year, after I had visited the Black Sea and mainland shores of Greece, it might be convenient for him to join me in *Kylie* so that we could sail together to his birthplace at Kas.

An hour before I weighed anchor the following morning Kemal was back, tapping slightly more rapidly and loudly than before on *Kylie*'s hull.

'Peter *abi*, my father say I am to go with you to Kas.'

'Good. When shall that be?'

'My father say we go after the Black Wind of July. *Allahah ismalardik!*'

'I shall write you in July then, to tell you where *Kylie* will be lying. *Güle, Güle*, Kemal!'

When it reached Bodrum the Black Wind of July was a two-day north-easter that ripped the awnings of the charter boats, abraded the bright varnish work of the *gulets* and disrupted the island ferries. *Kylie* lay in a western corner of the harbour, not far from a mosque, and waited for Kemal. He arrived very early one morning, tapping on the hull before the *muezzin*'s first call issued from the minaret. I looked out of the companionway and he was standing on the dockside, puffy-eyed but cheerful, carrying his shoes and waiting to be invited aboard.

We sailed in the early afternoon, reaching across the Gulf of Gököva to Körmen in a wind that rose to twenty knots, wetting our shirts with spray and caking our hair with salt. Afterwards, we sat in the cockpit and ate a carrot cake that had been made by his mother.

'In two-three days I think I am very, very happy,' said Kemal, brushing crumbs from the chart. 'Tomorrow we cross Hisarönü Körfezi and after Marmaris we are near the beautiful people of Kas...'

His prediction about our passage-time was correct. Aided by a good west wind, *Kylie* sped across the Gulf of Hisarönü in less than six hours and after anchoring for the night at Çiftlik pressed on past Marmaris towards Kemal's birthplace, which turned out to be not Kas itself but a small village some miles east of the town and best reached, according to his father, from an anchorage in Kekova Roads.

We entered Kekova Roads very late in the day, wriggling through the narrow western channel before the sectored leading-light had started to blink but just in time to behold the magnificent ramparts of Kale Köy castle illuminated a fiery orange in the last of the sun's rays. Kemal stood in the bows, willing us to continue eastward towards the castle, but so late was the hour that I thought we should not be able to navigate between the rocks and reefs that were strewn at its feet.

'Anchor, Kemal!' I called, swinging *Kylie*'s head towards a western inlet where, by the time the castle walls had changed from orange to mauve, we had anchored in three fathoms and I was marshalling tomatoes for dinner. Kemal tidied the deck and clambered to the masthead to study the land of his birth. The far mountains of Lycia were invisible, but in the fading light the nearer steeps of land were the colour of burnt sienna. I ladled half a pint of sea water into a pint of fresh and thought that burnt sienna was a fittingly emblematic colour for the Lycian people, who had burned their cities and immolated themselves before the eyes of Brutus so effectively that Rome had given up its attempts at conquest and declared the region an independent state. As though to acknowledge the ancient valour of the Lycians, before the water came to a boil I played the *Londonderry Air*, which, in the opinion of some, is the most sadly beautiful melody in the world. Then I called Kemal down from the masthead and wondered if by any chance the ancient Lycians had been red-haired and freckled. He sat at the cockpit table and asked me what the tune was. I told him that it was a lament of a father for his son Danny Boy, who had died in a war.

'Oh,' said Kemal, 'it is a sad story. After we eat, Peter *abi*, please play for me a happy story, for tomorrow I am to see the beautiful people of my village and so I need to be happy.'

I recollect that it was the last time I heard him say 'happy'.

In a dead-flat calm the following morning, with Kemal perched on the pulpit, *Kylie* threaded into Uçagiz Liman and anchored half a mile west of the castle. I landed him at a jetty that was some three miles from his birthplace and, after returning aboard to re-sew the seams of batten pockets and patch the chafed foot of the larger genoa, I rowed ashore, ordered a glass of *çay* and settled down to wait for the return of the happy pilgrim.

He came at two, with his trousers thick with red dust and his brow furrowed.

'No person lives there,' he said. 'When I find the house, there is no glass in the windows and the *maquis* is growing in the doorway. The *köyu*, the village, it is...it is...' He fumbled at a dictionary. '...it is not alive... The peoples has gone away.'

While he was speaking, three others made their way into the shade of a tree outside. The lower part of the leader's face was covered by the loose end of a dark turban, and in his left hand he carried a shotgun. Two paces behind, a woman lifted a large bundle from her head and set it on the ground. The third, a dark-eyed slip of a girl, unbound a smaller bundle from her waist and laid it on top of the larger one. Out of the fierce sun, the man unwound the end of his turban from his throat and sank down on his haunches in the shade. The women stood close to each other and looked at him. The man coughed, spat in the dust and wiped his lips with the end of the turban.

'Kemal,' I said, 'please ask them to drink *çay* with us.'

When civilities had been exchanged we learned that they were on their way to Kas where, after the father had bought cartridges for his shotgun and rice for himself, his wife and daughter would engage themselves to labour in the cotton-fields of Adana, whence an agent would transport them by sea in exchange for a lien on their wages. It was, they said, only way they could get enough money to live on. Their own village was dying just as surely as Kemal's birthplace had died, the man was ill, his only son had fallen in Cappadocia fighting an insurrection and, *Inishallah!*, the man had discharged his last cartridge at a pheasant two hours ago and missed it.

Kemal did not comment on the encounter until we had turned in. Before I snuffed out the cabin lamp, he looked at me and said: 'After three months picking the cotton in Adana the woman will be dead and the girl will look as old as the mother.' Then he pulled the sheet up to his chin and turned his face away. Although he had not said so, I knew that we ought to leave Kekova Roads as soon as possible.

I did what I could to keep his mind on other things. Before sunrise I had him sluicing the decks and I gave him the helm as we motored down Kekova Roads, turned our backs on the castle and headed for the open sea. When the wind came I bade him set about tacking westwards towards Kastellórizon, but just before the peak of the island came abeam he fell to

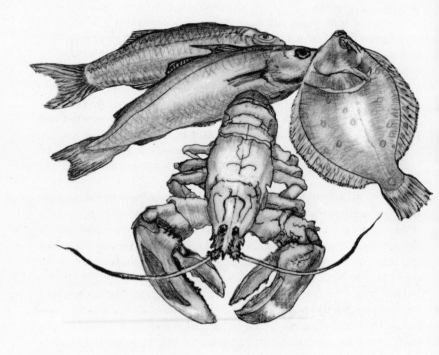

brooding. 'Watch the wind, Kemal!' I chivvied him, but I knew that it would not be long before he would come to some decision or other.

The wind strengthened as we moved out of the lee of Kastellórizon, and so I told him to bend on the smaller genoa, but he took a long time doing it, and by the time he returned to the cockpit he had made up his mind.

'Peter *abi*,' he said, 'please take me into Kas and leave me there.'

'You won't find them, Kemal. The boat for Adana will have left.'

'Go to Kas, please. It is written that I find them.'

We moored up near the port captain's office, and I made a last attempt to dissuade him.

'Don't sign off the transit log yet, Kemal; wait until the office opens tomorrow.'

'But the autobus for Mugla and Izmir will leave before the office opens tomorrow.'

'For Heaven's sake, Kemal, what will your father say?'

He creased his brow more deeply and looked at me in astonishment. 'What will my father say? My father will say *Merhaba* and give them fish. And my mother will also say *Merhaba*, but I think she will give them carrot cake.'

I warmed the remains of the spaghetti bolognaise at about nine that night, but after eating only a few forkfuls I scraped the remainder over the side and turned in. I did not awake until five-thirty, when, before the call of the *muezzin* had faded, there came a familiar tapping on the hull. Their tickets were bought, he said, and they would leave with him for Mugla at seven.

There was enough light for my camera to take a picture before he joined them on the bus. In the photograph, Kemal is standing on the quayside and *Kylie*'s blue sail-cover is in the background. There is enough clarity in the print to see Kemal's red hair sticking out from underneath his hat and, if you look closely, you can see that in his right hand he is holding the Beatles tape I gave him as a farewell present. He thanked me effusively for the Beatles tape, as though I had given him a million lira. I suppose that in the circumstances a million Turkish lira might have helped to change things for the better; but, on the other hand, it might not. A million lira might have altered Bozcaada for a day or two, but I don't think that all the money in the world would have made much difference to Kemal.

*

After the bus had rumbled off to Mugla I slid the harmonica back into its case and set off alone to the west under a full main and small genoa to re-cross the Gulf of Hisarönü, round Cape Krio and visit Kaptan Ibrahim, who runs a restaurant on the shores of the Gulf of Gököva. I went there in a quite unphilosophical mood but, having discovered a very rotten potato beneath the battery box on the way, I constructed the theory that the wry old Roman who first coined the maxim 'Nothing to excess' must have been the skipper of a short-handed sailboat with only a twenty-foot waterline. Nor, I thought, could his arms have been very long, because I reckon they couldn't reach the rotting potatoes in the outboard corners of his vegetable lockers. In the course of his travels, so my theory went, he acquired crowds of green-fingered friends who grew lots of fruit and vegetables in their backyards. At leave-takings the weeping multitudes gathered up their togas and filled them with hand-reared veggies which they dumped onto his decks before murmuring '*Ché sera, sera*' as the overladen craft lurched off into the sunset.

The tip of this hypothesis first emerged in the North Sea after ten kilos of time-expired Lincoln Whites had been dumped into *Kylie*'s cockpit by an oil-rig tender in exchange for eight cans of lager. Five months later I was still holding my nose and scooping goo from beneath the battery box. The experience of subsequent farewells had enabled me to refine the theory. My friend Alfonso filled *Kylie*'s cockpit with so many bags of oranges that she left Majorca with a seven-degree list and barely nineteen inches of freeboard. In Cagliari it was a bushel of parsley, in Corfu it was onions, and I left Kos with a liturgy of lettuce. After visiting Ibrahim I am certain that the wry old Roman made his final cruise to Vassiliki Bay on the Gulf of Gököva, where his ship was sunk by a mêlée of melons.

Kylie carries the wind to the head of Vassiliki Bay, which thrusts into Turkey at the same angle of incidence that Ibrahim's belly bulges into the twenty-knot breeze, and heads towards the rough wooden jetty that Ibrahim and his sons have built out from the restaurant verandah. He waves and beckons, inviting me to a glass of *ràki*, but I harden sheets and reach along the lee shore into a creek where the wind is less. I anchor in three fathoms, run a stern-line to a pine-tree and settle down in the cockpit with a bowl of black olives, Doluca wine and my harmonica.

Other boats moored there already are three Mirage charters flying Red Ensigns, a German ketch and a schooner with the Stars and Stripes. The creek gives all of us good shelter from the *meltemi* roaring among the pine-trees on the peaks but it will not protect us from Ibrahim, although he is presently invisible behind a rocky spur. At six o'clock the hills begin to pare the sun and Ibrahim boards his boat to hunt for custom. We hear him before we see him, the old diesel thudding his approach. The thudding becomes louder than a carnival drum, the launch rounds the point, and Captain Ibrahim's cabaret bursts upon us. Straddling the forehatch, a violinist jiggles a jocund tune, another musician puffs his cheeks and blows raspberries from a bulbous clarinet, while son number two beats on a wasp-waisted drum at his hip. Son number three lifts his hands from the tiller, claps them in time with the drum-beats and steers with his left great toe. Ibrahim himself, attired in wrap-around headgear, gold-spangled shirt and baggy black trousers, flaunts a finger-clicking fandango on the foredeck, partnered by son number one, whose every limb seems double-jointed as he go-goes in the bows.

'Allo, my friend! *Merhaba, Kaptan*! What time you come eat?' calls Ibrahim as he jigs among the tethered boats. Son number one breaks from his dance to take our orders: 'Five *calamar*, six sheeps, three fishes...? Okay! What time we come for you? *Yedi*? We come at seven, okay?' He grins his delight and does a handstand on the bitts. 'And after eats we have music, plenty music! And dancing, yes? After *yemek, dansetmek*! Okay? *Okay!*'

'That's fine!' I call back to him. 'I'll bring my harmonica.'

At seven-fifteen the launch carries its cargo of captives to the wooden jetty. It is already dark, but an Islamic moon hangs above the hill as we scrunch the gravel and climb the steps. Between a large and jolly German lady and a small, grim American lady I eat my *chops of sheeps*, drink my *sarap*, and am told alternately of the joyous strength of the Deutschmark and the doleful decline of the dollar. By eight-thirty we have ditched both the dollar and the Deutschmark and are chasing Turkish lira, on which we conspire to get forty per cent interest for a six-month deposit.

The men set up their instruments and *dansetmek* begins, led by a seven-year-old girl and the double-jointed son. Their partnership is unusual, for Turkish dancing is traditionally an all-male affair. The little girl dances with great seriousness, tossing her chin and stamping her feet imperiously at her six-foot partner. He takes her onslaughts gently, as a father would his daughter's, muting his movements so that her charm is not eclipsed, and when she finishes he leads the applause.

By this time the orchestra has plied itself with *raki* and *sarap*, and all the diners have switched their attention to the music. I flourish my mouth-organ at the American lady and begin to render *Battle Hymn of the Republic*, but am drowned out by the resident musicians, who seem to be playing *Pennsylvania Polka* in reverse. I stand up to protest at their tyrannous behaviour but my upstanding is mistaken by son number one as an application to fill the vacancy left by the infant Carmen.

'*Kaptan dansetmek?*' he cries, tugging me away from my chair. From then onwards neither I nor my mouth-organ stand a chance.

Under his tuition I am made to stamp my feet, slap my thighs, click my fingers, waggle my shoulders and wiggle my head twenty times over until I am dissolving in my own perspiration. Just as I am falling gratefully into the lap of the small American lady she puts on her Daughters-of-the-Revolution face and becomes suddenly coy about furthering the special relationship her late Presidents had forged between our democracies. Instead, she pours half a glass of *sarap* onto my shoulder, thrusts bread down my shirt and shoves me off the verandah into the sea. Bereft of his pupil, my dancing-master lets out a howl of dismay, plunges in after me and forces me to do a series of sub-aquatic staggers before he permits me to come up for air. If I do not then fall flat on my face it is only because he is using a fireman's lift to get me back to the verandah. Once there, I somehow regain the vertical and am rewarded by a crescendo of applause from the massed choir of diners, drinkers, resident musicians and itinerant carpet-peddlers. I finally collapse at the feet of hiccoughing Germania, who treads on my neck and bestrews me with overcooked vine-leaves.

After that I forsake my occidental connections, sit among a benchload of local farmers and think about embracing Islam. From my sodden pockets I extract a mouth-organ, a spectacle case and a venerable briar pipe. Though the objects are all gritty and wet, they become instantly coveted. While I am trying to blow most of Vassiliki Bay out of the mouth-organ, a thin-headed melon-farmer mops out my briar, admires the grain and requests that I make him a present of it. I explain that the recent hiatus between the English-speaking democracies has not yet created a void into which a Turkish melon-farmer can readily squeeze, however narrow his head or however small his melons. He is so downcast by my churlish refusal that he and his companions seem set on an instant secession from NATO. Amity is restored only when I take the pipe from his hand and replace it with my spectacle-case, over which he sheds so many tears of gratitude that I feel like an affluent heel. He dries his eyes and we pour liberal measures of *raki* into each other's glasses. Soon we are roaring out pledges of Anglo-Turkish friendship, employing the only truly international vocabulary we know.

'*Futbol*!' he cries.

'Liverpool!' I croon.

He waves his glass aloft, throws an arm round my shoulder, and, after a bit of thought, declaims triumphantly '*Shuffled Wens Die!*'

I am unable to record how and when Ibrahim got me back to my boat. All I know is that when I awoke I was lying on the cabin sole with an object the size of a medicine ball at my feet. Also, the afterdeck was encumbered with six others of similar weight and girth.

When I sailed *Kylie* out of the bay six hours later I still hadn't solved her latest loadline problem. Although I had managed to recoup some lost freeboard by giving away two of the heaviest, my boat was still overladen. How, I wondered, could a one-man crew hope to eat a poopful of melons at twenty-nine Celsius before they went bad?

11
With Orville off Mikonos

Orville's hands were the size and colour of day-old piglets, and they were out of control again. Blind, perverse and delinquent, they barged through the dishes, clattering the brown mug onto the cockpit sole. Although greatly attached to his hands, when they behaved badly he tried to disown them.

'Who did that?' he said before they plunged back into the cabin to ram-raid the galley lockers.

I rescued the brown mug, swilled the suds off it and stood it on the bridge deck to drain. Reminding Orville to up-end the crockery was a waste of time, for he would forget again by tomorrow. I won't multiply his problems, I thought; he has too many already.

While the mug was draining I contemplated the island of Siros. *Kylie* was lying in Ermoupolis, where there are some very fine buildings above the harbour, including, so Orville had told me soon after we left Levkas, an opera house that had been inspired by La Scala of Milan. He had joined *Kylie* by invitation in Levkas because, returning aboard one moonless night, I had fallen into an unfenced slipway and knocked myself out. Orville had wandered past by chance soon afterwards with his flashlight, and his hands, which had been obeying their owner for once,

166

had lifted me off the greasy rails and helped me aboard, where I had stayed for a whole day, nursing my head. In appreciation of his timely action I had asked him if he would like to sail eastwards for a week or two.

'I'd like to go to Mikonos,' he had said, and I had said that going to Mikonos would be fine. Although it had taken us ten days to get to Siros, *Kylie* was now only twenty miles from Mikonos, and soon he and his hands would be leaving me to photograph, so he said, its colony of windmills, but I now think they were likelier to have been photographing rather more gorgeously personable subjects.

Lying alongside was a sloop wearing an unusual ensign. As Orville's hands rampaged among the cutlery I remarked that it was the first time I had seen a Finnish ensign in the Mediterranean and, since the cabin curtains were still drawn, I wondered whether anyone was aboard.

'Someone was aboard at two this morning,' he said. 'I saw him stagger about in the cockpit.'

He slung his Olympus over his shoulder and said that he was going to photograph some Venetian façades and would I like to accompany him? No, I said, I would rather not. I had had enough of sightseeing and wanted to do jobs aboard *Kylie*, but would look forward to preparing him another stupendous dinner of spaghetti bolognaise for eight o'clock. After he had smiled lopsidedly and clambered over the pulpit I lit a pipe and tried to remember what the jobs were. I knew that I wanted to make a Turk's head for the tiller but at the back of my mind was a more important thing I needed to do while Orville was absent. I watched the pipe-smoke drift between the backstays and wondered what the job could be.

My train of thought was interrupted by the nosing of another boat into the slot alongside. I took its bow-line ashore and returned to adjust *Kylie*'s fenders while its crew were tidying the decks. After coiling the mainsheet, the skipper picked up a winch handle from the sidedeck, wagged a finger at one of the crew and replaced the handle in its pouch. His action reminded me that the job I needed to do was to find *Kylie*'s winch handle, which had disappeared from the stowage bucket alongside the engine cover in the cabin. *Kylie* carries only three winches: the two in the cockpit for the foresail sheets are bottom-action jobs with integral handles, but the handle for the mast winch which serves the foresail halyards was detachable. If we lost it and the spare handle fractured, the foresails would have to be swigged tight with a tack tackle.

I rummaged in the bucket but could not find the missing handle. The weighted monkey's fist for the heaving-line, the large spring-hook for

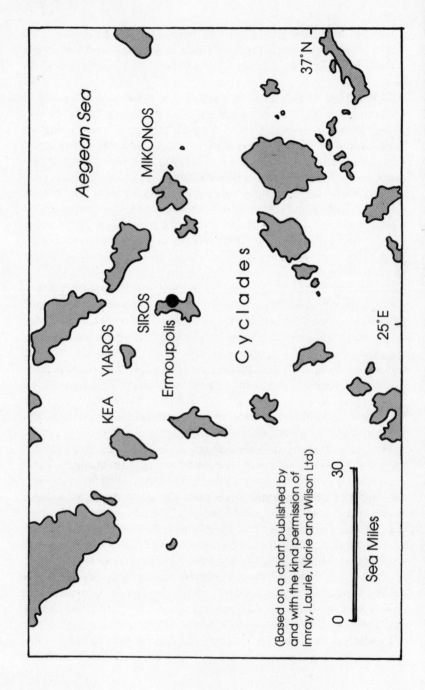

Aegean Sea

MIKONOS

37° N

KEA YIAROS

SIROS

Ermoupolis

Cyclades

25° E

0   30

Sea Miles

(Based on a chart published by
and with the kind permission of
Imray, Laurie, Norie and Wilson Ltd)

168

securing to mooring-buoys, and the spare, Mickey Mouse winch-handle were there, but the sturdy handle that had been aboard for fifteen years was not. On the off-chance, I moved Orville's dolphin-carving aside and emptied the locker under his berth in case one of his hands had cast it among the blocks and rigging-screws that lodged there, but still I could not find it. I closed the locker door and lit another pipe. I would have to mention it to him, I thought; forgetting about how to drain crockery or where to stow one's belongings is trivial, but the loss of a winch handle is a serious matter. His amnesia, I thought, is like nothing I have ever met. He can remember arcane details about dolphins, but he has a poor muscular memory. His fingers do not remember how to make sheet bends from one hour to the next, and now it seemed that his thumbs do not remember from one sail-change to the next how to flick-on the safety lock of winch handles so that they stay in the barrel. It must have gone overboard during my yesterday nap, I decided, somewhere between Kea and Yiaros, when I had been awakened by a clatter and found that Orville had changed up from the number two genoa to the number one. It had been a sensible thing to do, for the southerly wind had fallen from fifteen knots to ten. I had stayed in the cockpit long enough to check that the sail was drawing and the wind had not shifted and, after complimenting him on the sensible sail-change, had returned below to get on with my nap. Orville had not replied to the compliment, I recollected. He had just clamped his hands between his knees and looked away.

I stowed the dolphin-carving in his locker, where he should have kept it all along. It was incredible that he had left his precious dolphin lying about. He had made such a song about it when he had first carried it aboard, when even his hands had been respectful, stroking the bulge above the creature's bill as delicately as if it had been the forehead of a human child. It was a marvel, he had said excitedly, how *turisops truncatus*, the bottle-nosed dolphin, with its three-hundred pound bodyweight, was so very similar to man in its neck movements and in its brain-to-body ratio. Even more remarkable to Orville was that although their fins are torn off as they struggle to free themselves from fishermen's nets, dolphins had never been known to attack human beings. On the contrary, the dolphin's friendliness to man was legendary: Pelorus Jack had piloted ships through New Zealand waters for years, said Orville, despite the fact that people had taken pot-shots at him. Such loyalty, which in the opinion of himself and others might better be called devotion, was rarely found among the human species these days, although, he added carefully, it had been the lynch-pin of the ancient Greeks.

To displace my irritation over the loss of the winch handle, I took out a hank of codline and the sailmaker's bag from another locker and started to make a Turk's head on the tiller. Halfway through the second round of tucks I still hadn't reconciled myself to the loss of the winch handle. I wondered whether Orville might have slipped it into one of the cockpit lockers. To satisfy myself on the question I left my Turk's head and lugged out all the cockpit-locker bits and pieces: warps, chafing-gear, buckets, and even the fisherman anchor. Surrounded by a mess of lines and buckets, I stood upright in the cockpit, eased my aching back, scratched my head and became aware that my activities were being watched by someone in the Finnish boat.

'Ho humph,' said the watcher, his eyes twinkling, 'you are having a clean-up?'

No, I told him; I was looking for a ten-inch-long winch handle, and did he know of a yacht chandler's ashore that might stock one?

'Er...humph a moment,' he said. He ducked into his cabin and after a few seconds emerged with just the very item I was looking for. 'There is no yacht-chandler in Siros; only shackles for fishing boats and hardware for the home. Take this...er...humph...one, please,' he said, and seeing my hesitation, thrust the handle into my hand and added: 'I have...er...humph...others.'

'What,' I asked him, 'do I owe you?'

Well, he told me, he wouldn't think of accepting any drachmas but, if I had the time, he wouldn't mind ...er... humph...some decorative ropework on his own tiller...

I bore a hank of codline to his cockpit and began straight away. He opened two beers and told me that his name was Ünto, that he was an clarinettist in the Finnish State Orchestra, and that he was sailing single-handed from Piraeus to Mikonos, where tomorrow he would be joined by his wife, who was flying in from Amsterdam. What a stroke of luck, I thought; perhaps he will be able to give me some tips on improving the *Skye Boat-song*.

'She will be very... er... humph...good for me,' he said earnestly, 'because when I am by myself I have certain ...er...humph... problems: not...er humph... problems at sea, but problems in port. At sea I don't have ...humph...problems but,' he sighed over his beer and glared at it, 'in port I drink too much of *this*. Last night, having...er...humphed several litres of it, I damaged...er...humph...my

Ünto and his clarinet

clarinet while trying to...er...humph...Brahms on the foredeck. It was
too adventurhumph.'

'What happened?'

'I...er...bumped against a stanchion and broke a valve.'

By sunset I had finished the Turk's head and, using an elastic band or
two, Ünto had repaired the broken valve while I cooked a meal and laid
places for three on the cockpit table. By nine, when Orville had not
returned aboard, I was cling-wrapping his plated dinner and Ünto was
giving the reed of his clarinet a preliminary lick.

He played for two hours, ranging among the world's melodies with the
skill of the veteran professional, transmuting, transposing and
transporting. I sat in the cockpit entranced. The dulcet wood-notes rose
above the roofs of Ermoupolis and wound among the assembled stars
before swooping down between the astonished columns of the opera
house to stipple the waters of the harbour. The last notes died away and
the air was filled with applause: in cockpits of the gently nodding boats,
on the quaysides and on the afterdecks of silent ferries people clapped
their hands. What a wonderful talent, I mused, scraping Orville's dinner
over the side and wondering where he had got to.

He did not return until eight the following morning. Having exhausted
the Venetian façades, he explained, he had wandered to the far side of the
island with such engaging people that he had forgotten about the last bus
to Ermoupolis and been obliged to spend the night on the beach, where
two of them had been so bedazzled by his account of *Kylie*'s wanderings
that they had boarded the early-morning bus with him so as to meet her
skipper and buy him a drink.

Orville's new friends turned out to be Ellen from London and Piet from
Amsterdam, who were celebrating their recent engagement by back-
packing through the Cyclades. Ellen's face and legs were raw with sun
and midge-bites. While she dabbed lotion on her legs, Piet, whose skin
was younger, darker and smoother, surveyed me from a blander face and
drank only coffee, which, I noticed, Orville paid for. Seeing a darkening
of the water outside the harbour, I rose from my chair and walked twenty
yards to higher ground to get a better view of the sea. Orville joined me
and asked what I was looking at.

'The wind on the water. It's so light I can't see which way its coming
from. We ought to leave about noon if it fills.'

'What do you think of them?' said Orville, and then, without waiting for
my answer: 'They would like to get to Mikonos. Could they come with us
in *Kylie*?'

I hesitated. Four people would be a bit crowded, but Mikonos was only twenty miles away. Orville's hands were clamped out of sight, one in each armpit, and his eyes were bright with expectation.

'All right,' I said. 'After they get their gear aboard, you come ashore again to buy extra food and I'll go to the port captain, clear for Mikonos and make ready to leave as soon as the wind comes.'

Stowing their gear took longer than expected because after Orville's hands had pulled Piet and the two rucksacks below they got out the dolphin carving and started stroking it. While Ellen smoked a cigarette in the cockpit and I wrote out a shopping list, Orville's hands fondled the dolphin while Orville described to Piet the creature's handsome form and noble character.

I called into the cabin that the shopping list was ready. Piet, who was sitting nearer the companionway, took the list from my hand and held it out to Orville.

'You'll come with me?' said Orville, looking at Piet.

'He came with you already,' said Ellen, stubbing out the cigarette. 'He came with you last night, didn't you, darling?'

I picked up the transit log and the ship's papers from the chart table and said I would be back aboard by twelve or when the wind came, whichever was the sooner, and hoped that Orville would do likewise. Then I slid the documents into a plastic bag and left them to settle their scores in private.

In a *taverna* across from the port-captain's office I saw Ünto. Humph-humphing benignly over a beer, he asked me if I would be leaving for Mikonos that day, and when I told him I would be leaving as soon as the wind came he dipped a finger into the beer, held it up and said that I might have to wait...er...humph...a very...er...humph...long time.

When at eleven-thirty there was still no wind I finished my beer and went back to *Kylie*. Orville and Piet had not returned, but Ellen was lying in my berth asleep. Moving as quietly as I could, I unzipped the starboard sailbag, hanked the number one genoa onto the starboard forestay, stretched the foot along the sidedeck and lashed the bunt loosely to the guardrail, all ready to bend on the sheet.

Some stirrings of wind came a few minutes before noon, when Orville was handing the shopping from the dockside to Piet on the foredeck. Piet was wearing reflective sunglasses that looked like mirrors framed in blue spaghetti and a pair of new white shorts that had been turned up at the bottom. Judging from the white shave-line between his brown skin and the hair at the nape of his neck, Orville had also stood him a haircut. The deck-noise brought Ellen out. Before she could say anything I picked up

173

the tail of the genoa sheet and showed them how to make a sheet bend on the clew. Orville's hands leapt out straight away, leaving him to say: 'I can do it!' But, of course, they couldn't. They blundered about, and when I pulled it tight their effort fell apart. Piet's effort, on the other hand, worked straight away. His brown fingers formed a loop, tucked the end through and pulled it tight.

'That's okay,' I said.

'But you said you hadn't been on a boat before now,' said Orville.

'That's right,' said Piet; 'this is the first time.'

Orville's hands flapped about. 'It's incredible,' he said, 'how quickly you pick things up.'

'Oh, Piet picks things up very quickly,' said Ellen; 'he picks them up almost as fast as he throws them away.'

We left soon afterwards. As soon as they heard how I proposed to move astern out of the berth, Piet singled up the bow lines and stood ready to let go while Ellen stood at the mast, ready to set the genoa. I took in the warp on the stern anchor, Piet let go the bow line and coiled it on the foredeck. When we had made enough sternway Ellen hoisted the genoa and Piet backed it to port. Thus far, Orville hadn't done anything; not that he didn't want to — it was just that Piet and Ellen beat him to it. Before Piet could move aft and take over from me at weighing the stern anchor, I called to Orville to take my place. He did it with his usual eagerness, but deposited so much mud on himself and the sterndeck that it was not until we had cleared the harbour and the genoa and main were drawing to a very light northerly wind that he had bucketed the mud from the sterndeck and his person was clean enough for Piet to allow him to sit next to him in the cockpit, and then only on the coaming and not on the more comfortable slats.

The wind held for two hours then fell away to light variable airs. We set the ghoster and made one mile an hour towards Mikonos. Ellen sat in the bows, elbows on the pulpit and legs dangling outboard, gazing into the water. Piet went to the bows and put a hand on her shoulder, but when she pushed it away he shrugged and returned to the cockpit. Orville, who had remained perched on the coaming to keep an eye on what was happening forward, whispered to Piet 'What did she say?'

Piet made a face but did not reply. He removed the sun glasses and said to me: 'May I have a try, please?'

I explained how I was playing the ghoster sheet and moving the tiller. Piet slid onto the seat beside me and took over, laying the sheet in his right hand, resting his left hand lightly on the tiller and keeping his eyes on the ghoster. I smelled the hair oil, moved forward on the slats and set about filling my pipe. Piet watched the luff intently; just as intently, but for a different reason, Orville watched Piet.

'How am I doing?' said Piet when my pipe was alight.

'Not badly,' I said.

'How long is it to Mikonos?'

'All night,' I said, 'at this rate.'

'Good,' said Piet; 'that means there will be time for you to teach me a lot more things.'

Orville slumped down from his perch on the coaming and thumped so hard onto the cockpit seat that *Kylie* trembled and the luff fluttered.

'Elephant!' hissed Piet.

Orville's jaw fell open, and his hands flopped into his lap, looking like a couple of pork cutlets. Then he blinked, clamped his jaw tight shut and went below. Piet smiled and carried on steering. Ahead, a steamship with white upperworks and her masts in line was coming up fast from the east, but Mikonos was not yet in sight.

'I would like being a sailor,' said Piet. 'What do you think? Do I show an aptitude?'

'You're doing alright so far.'

'Only "alright"?' That sounds worse than my report on Algebra. Not even "Shows promise"?'

'Head north,' I said, 'out of the track of that ship that's coming towards us. Harden the sheet a little...that's right...that's good.'

When *Kylie*'s bows had swung and the ship's masts were no longer in line, he took his eyes from the luff, looked directly at me and got to the point: 'I'm between films at the moment, so if there's any chance of going on to Turkey...'

Films...? I thought.

After sunset the wind died. When Piet had disentangled the ghoster from the spreaders and bagged it, he curled up on the tiny foredeck with his sleeping-bag for a pillow. Below decks, Orville slept, his face covered by a T-shirt and his great hands clenched loosely on his chest. So slight were the waves that *Kylie*'s mast was almost motionless between the loom of the lights of Mikonos to the east and Siros to the west. I cleated the tiller lanyards and lit another pipe. Ellen leaned her face towards the flame, a cigarette between her lips. When it was drawing she rested her elbow against the winch and said: 'I can't go on with this charade. I should have known what he was like from the sort of car he's got. What have I got? A rented room in Kilburn, an Equity card and two nice legs.

175

What's he got? Apart from what you see, a white Porsche. How many nineteen-year-old men do you know who have white Porsches?'

'Would you like some orange juice?' I asked her.

'The engagement wasn't my idea, you know; it was his mother's. And after last night, I just can't go on with it.'

'There's no ice but it's quite fresh...'

'His family will be mad, but I don't care, because...well...you've got to draw a line somewhere, haven't you?'

I poured an orange juice from the Thermos and put it into her hands. Then I slid past Orville's hands and unstrapped a blanket from her rucksack.

'It gets chilly at sea after midnight,' I said, tucking it over her legs.

'What hurt most,' said Ellen, blinking in the glow of the cigarette, 'was that before the two of them got into Piet's sleeping bag, Orville let on that he thought I was Piet's mother...'

The cooling breeze came from the east-northeast at one in the morning. All three were so tired that the noise of the genoa hanks rasping the forestay did not awaken them. Piet pulled the sleeping-bag over his head and snuggled nearer the anchor, but Ellen, who had curled herself at the foot of the mast, did not move at all, even when the halyard thumped about her ears.

An hour before dawn, when the harbour lights of Mikonos were twinkling yellow above where the horizon would soon be, Orville's hands fumbled into the cockpit and sought to take the helm.

'Feel the way the wind is coming on your left cheek,' I told him, 'and keep it like that. There's no need to play the genoa sheet because I've cleated it. It doesn't matter if those harbour lights wander about a bit, just go by the wind; keep it the same angle on your cheek.'

I gave him the time it takes to rub a palmful of tobacco and said: 'Good, Orville. You've got the hang of it now; you're doing fine.'

'That's not true; I'm doing badly and you know it.'

I struck a match. 'Don't look at me,' I said, 'or you'll lose the wind. You're doing fine. The genoa's drawing and we're making two knots.'

'I've brought nothing but trouble aboard the boat. I do things all wrong. I can't tie proper knots. And I lost the winch handle overboard.'

'Ah, yes. But don't worry about that; I got another one as easy as pie. The thing is, you're sailing her fine at the moment. We'll be in port in a couple of hours if you keep on like this.'

'Whenever I try to light the stove,' he insisted, 'it goes up in yellow flames.'

'Shut up,' I said, 'and attend to the wind on your cheek...'

When my pipe was drawing nicely and we were still moving at two knots, I added: '...so that we can all have fresh yoghourt for breakfast.'

Orville was still at the helm when the dawn scooped grey hollows in the black sea and silvered the sky behind the dark hump of Mikonos. To the west the loom of Siros had faded but coming from the same direction were the lights of a vessel overtaking. At a quarter of a mile distant I saw through binoculars that it was Ünto's sloop, and by the time she drew thirty yards abeam I could make him out, standing in the cockpit, holding a coil of line above his head.

'What's he doing?' said Orville.

'Offering a tow,' I said. Then, cupping my hands to my mouth, I called out 'No, thanks!'

Ünto waved a hand in acknowledgement and increased the revs. Focussed as they were on the other boat, my eyes did not at first take in what had happened on the deck of my own. Although Ellen's blanket still lay at the foot of the mast, she was no longer under it. But — energized perhaps by my shout to Ünto — the sleeping-bag in the bows moved and briefly writhed. I was not the only one to notice it. Orville's hands absconded from the tiller.

'Orville!' I said sharply. 'Watch the luff!'

But hardly had I spoken when there came the sound of laughter; and though it should have been muffled by the sleeping-bag it came so clearly that even I could hear the elements in it. Ellen's was a deep chuckle of pleasure; Piet's was a higher note, almost a giggle. Taken together, however, the laughter was that of conspirators: intimate, knowing, and spiced with mockery.

I saw Orville's great fist clench and the knuckles whiten.

'Look over there, Orville!' I cried, directing his eyes to where the wave-tops were tipped with early gold. 'Here come your dolphins!'

12
The Missing of Malta

Many blue-veined sailors have sought respite in the Mediterranean from chillier seas and some have stayed to bask in its waters for ever. Now and then I thought to do the same. The people, the scenery, and the sense that in exploring the Mediterranean littoral I was re-discovering the roots of our civilisation were inducements I could not sniff at. And some authorities, it seemed, had awarded the Mediterranean nautical kudos too. According to the Admiralty *Pilot* it is '*...a favoured region, with protracted periods of fine, quiet weather and comparatively brief periods of storm and discomfort*'. But at the end of a sizzling summer during which *Kylie* wandered listlessly down the Argolic Gulf and headed for Ithaca, I sweated over facts which suggested that the favoured region was not as kindly to small-boat sailors as the Admiralty said it was.

By day I thumbed through logbooks, charts and pilots, and at night I re-read Homer's *Odyssey*. From the squiggles in the old logbooks I worked out that during *Kylie*'s 2,000-mile round-Britain cruise I had used her engine for eighteen per cent of the time, which had seemed an awful lot. Compared with the hours of engine-use in the Mediterranean however, the figures were small, for to cover the same mileage in the Mediterranean I had resorted to the engine for thirty per cent of the time — getting on for twice as much. The comparison was disturbing, but the figures were not too far out of line with the meteorological data for the two areas. According to the *Pilot*, the North Sea is windless for three per cent of July, which is bad enough, but when I read that the seas between Greece and Sicily have no wind at all for eight per cent of that month, I thought the Mediterranean even worse. Such weather may be well-liked by visitors who wish to peer at coral through the hulls of glass-bottomed motor-boats but it is not the stuff that sailing dreams are made on. I'm sure I can't be the first to think so. Odysseus, for one, must have thought Mediterranean meteorology was the pits. Even allowing for stop-overs with Lotus-eaters, Cyclops, Laestrygones, Circe and Calypso, his taking ten years to make good the 500 sea-miles between Troy and Ithaca doesn't say much for the Admiralty's claim that it is a favoured region. Whether Homer's figures are cosmetic implants to fill out his story-line, or the Admiralty's statistics are placebos for hypertense Chief Engineers, neither are good news for sailboats. I shut the *Mediterranean Pilot* and slid a spent match into the *Odyssey*. Then I re-filled the fuel tank and went to forage history on the island of Ithaca.

If the completion rate of modern Greek buildings is anything to go by, a lot of their more ancient structures could never have been completed. According to Homer, Ithaca is the island where Odysseus had his palace; but I could find no sign of it. I wiped a splodge of ice-cream from my guide book and wondered whether the palace had been just a creation of Homer's imagination. I had always taken for granted that the fissured columns on the hillsides elsewhere in Greece had once supported roofs, and that every catalogued pile of rubble had at some time been a chamber that had rung to the music of Homer. Sitting outside a *taverna* on Ithaca, I began to think that historians might have got some details wrong.

Elsewhere on the island I had come across the skeleton of an hotel. Someone had started its construction years ago but the steelwork was still unclad. Such deficiencies were not uncommon, for opposite my *taverna* most of the houses petered out after the first floor. At ground level they were replete with glaze-tiled porticos and pelargonium, but the terrazoed stairways led to boarded-up doorways, beyond which was only cement dust and tattered plastic baggery. If I stopped licking my ice-cream and lifted my eyes above the first storey I beheld only a stubble of rusting rods. When the wind blew, the longer rods swayed about like the feelers of cockroaches that had been crushed by rubble. Sitting in front of one of the houses was a woman with an El Greco face. She was eating olives and wearing a jazzy frock. I picked up my phrase book and crossed the road to

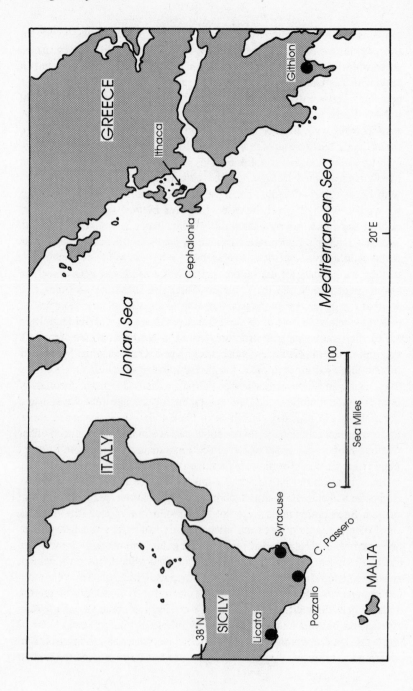

ask about Odysseus. She told me in English that although she had been born in Ithaca, for fifteen years she had lived in New York, and once in a while returned to her birthplace to eat olives and slip dollars to her builder. It had taken her ten years to pay for the first storey, but if the people of Brooklyn went on buying her kebabs in quantity, next year a start would be made on the second storey. She hoped the house would be completed before the time came to sell up the eating-place. I thought about the unfinished hotel and told her that, whatever happened, at least the olives were worth coming home for.

As for Odysseus, she said, if I followed that path upwards as far as I could go I would certainly find myself on the site of his palace. I could not miss it, she said, for it was now occupied by her builder, who stored his materials there. She was sure it is the site of the palace, for it was the only habitable place on Ithaca from which I could view three seas, just as Odysseus had done.

I ascend the path, which is not greatly different from scores of other paths that climb the flanks of other hills. It is steep, dusty and stony, and is skirted by spiky vegetation that appears to be kept down by goats. At the top I come to a wire-mesh fence surrounding a cuboid jungle of building-blocks, chipped bricks and steel rods. A concrete-mixer gawps at an empty sky, its mouth and undershot chin encrusted with dribbles of cement. I walk through a gap in the fence and look about for a view of the three seas, but can glimpse water in only two directions. To the west bulks Cephalonia; dimly to the east sprawls mainland Greece; somewhere in the northern haze is where Levkas ought to be. I scramble to the top of a pile of concrete blocks and Cephalonia lowers its head. My eyes are twelve feet above the ground now, the same height that the eyes of Odysseus would have been at if his palace floor had lain there. To the north and east the land is draped in haze, but I can see new areas of water: to the west shines the Ionian Sea, and at my back and to my right flickers the unnamed stretch between the Ithaca Channel and the Gulf of Patras. In all, it amounts to only two seas. Where is the third? The Ithaca Channel is only ten miles long and three wide. Unless Homer counted the narrow channel as a sea, I reckon that Odysseus must have dwelt somewhere else. I shake my head so vigorously at the confusing evidence that I lose my footing and dislodge a bit of my makeshift gazebo. An elderly goat lifts its head at the clatter, and when I climb down from my perch it waggles its ears and snickers.

By this time the woman with the El Greco face has gone indoors, and so I head southwards again to Githion, a small harbour on the Gulf of

Lakonia, where I lay-up for several days and cannot sleep because of the heat. At six o'clock every morning I rinse the sweat-soaked undersheet and ask myself: 'If I am so damn keen on sailing, why am I searching for phantom palaces on hot islands in windless seas?'

In my experience, small-boat sailors don't tell each other why sailboat voyaging is attractive, and I have never asked them. One attraction may be that it offers the prospect of working through a series of tasks using limited resources in a slightly unfamiliar environment. The more limited are the resources and the more distant are the goals, the greater is the satisfaction when they are achieved. There is, too, the fact that one is using the natural energy of the winds rather than mechanical power. For the intolerant and hard-of-hearing, there is the added recommendation that progress is less dependent on listening: you don't, I think, have to listen so attentively to the sounds made by winds and waves as you do to those made by engines. But without a modicum of moderate, reliable winds, life aboard a sailing-boat is something to be endured rather than enjoyed. As I wrung out the undersheet after yet another sleepless night it occurred to me that I had put up with the lack of wind for long enough.

I looked again at the wind roses of the Mediterranean and compared them with those of the Atlantic. The *Pilot*'s wind roses are not at all like the petalled flowers they are named after: they look more like a series of bubbles that are being injected by eight hypodermic syringes. The longer the syringe, the likelier is the frequency of wind from that direction; the longer the needle to each syringe, the greater the incidence of frustratingly light winds; and the longer the cylinder of the syringe, the likelier are the chances of stronger winds. I saw that the Mediterranean light-wind needles are commonly much longer than their North Atlantic counterparts, their cylinders of moderate winds are also shorter and, whereas the frequency of calms off Southern Greece is as high as nine per cent, many areas of the North Atlantic are never without wind.

On the third day at Githion I folded up the sleeping-sheet and wrote to my daughters that I was sailing westward again and expected to anchor off Katy's bar in Majorca and meet Sarah there in eighteen days' time. As things turned out, I was being too optimistic.

The Atlantic lay more than thirteen hundred miles away, and between Greece and Gibraltar both the winds and current are generally adverse to the westbound sailor. As much as sixty per cent of early autumnal winds will come from points well forward of his beam, from between north-west and west-southwest, and for much of the time will blow at less than ten knots. To hinder him further, for thirteen hundred miles an adverse current will be setting him backwards — according to the *Pilot* — up to fifteen miles a day.

During the fourth day in Githion the heat wave lessened and a breeze came from the north-east. Before the sun was a hand's-span above the mountains of the Elos Peninsula, *Kylie* set off southwards down the Gulf of Lakonia, under full sail for the first time in weeks. With the wake unravelling slowly behind, I set about preparing for the open-water passage across the Ionian Sea, partially inflating the dinghy on top of the coachroof and lashing within its folds a two-gallon water container, a small pack of flares and a worn but serviceable storm jib. Below decks I sorted charts into sequence and entered up the ship's log: 'Githion towards Majorca. Crew: nil.' Then, though I was still within territorial waters, I took down the Greek ensign from the starboard spreader and bundled it into the onion sack that serves as *Kylie*'s flag locker. Such a sack ought to be large enough to hold all the flags I need to cross three oceans, but somehow it never is. One or other of the flags always manages to wriggle free of its meshes between the time I leave one lot of territorial waters and arrive in the next. This time the escapee was a flag I hadn't looked at for years: a quartered ensign with a cross in the upper part of the hoist. I fingered it with faint stirrings of nostalgia. 'Alright,' I told it, 'let's call in at Malta on the way.'

The George Cross on the Maltese flag had been stitched there during my boyhood, awarded to the island by King George VI during the Second World War '...*to bear witness to a heroism and devotion that will long be famous in history*'. For me, these qualities were symbolised by the tanker *Ohio*. Holed by attacks from dive-bombers and submarines, she had limped into Valetta harbour with her decks almost awash. I remember running my eye over the photo of the crippled vessel. The seas around the *Ohio*, I had noticed, were entirely windless, and I had thought her lucky not to have met with a gale in the Malta Channel. Had the Admiralty *Pilot* been on my childhood bookshelves I could have discovered even then that gales are almost unknown in the Malta Channel at that time of year: Valetta had not seen a summer gale in thirty years, said the meteorological tables when I looked into them aboard *Kylie*. It was a sweet fact to suck on. A thousand miles of light head-winds and adverse currents would be quite enough to cope with, but unless the wind fell away for weeks like it once did for Philippe Fau, I thought I could expect to make good more than sixty miles a day. At least, I mused, I shan't be knocked about by gales: it must be several thousands to one against meeting any gales.

183

And so, without any thoughts about how deceptive statistics could be, I wiped the *Ohio* from my thoughts and blithely amended *Kylie*'s itinerary to include the island of Malta.

Six hours after leaving Githion I rounded Cape Matapan and the wind veered to east-south-east for a while before swinging round to the north-west quarter and increasing to fifteen knots. *Kylie* sliced westward through blue seas that sported small white forage caps at jaunty angles. I latched in the wind-vane gear, set the Walker log and took my last look at Greece, which seemed to be lying on the waters like a naked starveling who had collapsed on some Third World pavement. The spurs of its brown hills were famined ribs, and between them the wrinkled land sagged like old flesh between ancient bones. Nowhere was green and fresh; nowhere told of water. The way I saw it, the Peloponnesus of Greece could have merited ten seconds of prime time as a Freepost appeal.

Homer had pictured it rather differently three thousand years ago. *It is a pastureland for goats and more attractive than the land where horses thrive...* was how his Telemachus had described Ithaca. I re-read the words several times, trying to appreciate the ancient values, but they seemed very odd. Who would prefer thistles to grass? It was incredible that scrubby, dusty, rock-strewn hillsides could be more attractive than meadows. I prepared a crisp green salad, turned my back on Greece and settled down to the business of making westing.

For a day and a half the task went well. The wind veered and backed between north-northwest and north-by-east and though hardly ever stronger than ten knots it enabled *Kylie* to make good 112 miles from noon to noon. With the sheets freed and cleated, and with a cooling breeze riffling through the shady cabin, I felt more deeply content than at any time during the preceding months. In the forepeak a hammock of fruit and vegetables swung in the sunlight reflected through the open forehatch from the genoa. Sprawled in the lee berth, I sucked an orange and adjusted the telescopic mirror beneath the deckhead chart-rack so that without even turning my head on the pillow I could keep an eye on what was happening in the cockpit. The horseshoe-shaped companionway framed a picture I shall not quickly forget. Central to it was the white parallelogram of the steering vane, its counterweight sniffing the wind as alertly as the nose of any gun-dog. At the slightest change in the direction of the wind — whether caused by wave-action against the hull or by a shift in the apparent wind — the trim-tab of the steering vane wiggled acknowledgement below the waves and *Kylie*'s rudder responded. The tiller moved obediently to windward and back again amidships, a slave to forces it could not control, its lanyards swinging like the plaited locks of a hippie crooning a mantra. The nicest thing about it all was that except when I sucked the orange I myself did not need to move a muscle, and yet I was being transported in luxury across the seas at the rate of — if my sights were right — one hundred and twelve miles a day. I sucked the orange and closed my eyes. I did not need to invite any dreams.

After sunset the wind fell light and backed three points to the west, but by hardening sheets I was able to lay the course for Malta. Throughout much of the night *Kylie* edged westward at between two and three knots, but at two in the morning I was awakened from a doze by a change in the motion of the boat. I looked out. The sea was glassy calm and the wind-vane was idle. After handing the sails I went glumly back to my berth and stayed there until four-thirty, when I took the sextant from its box and busied myself with a series of star sights, but the dawn horizon was so fuzzy that the subsequent figurings produced a cocked hat that was half the size of Crete. Before breakfast a wind darkened the waters to the west, filling to a welcome ten-knot breeze that lasted throughout the day and polished the horizon so cleanly that a noon altitude crossed with a lattice of morning sun-sights told me *Kylie* had made good ninety miles from noon till noon and was only ninety-six miles from Cape Passero, the south-easternmost point of Sicily, and no more than 115 from Malta. If the wind held its strength and did not head me, it seemed possible that I might be sailing into Valetta harbour before sunset on the following day. I peeled another orange and wondered what Malta might look like.

My pleasant speculations went on until half-past nine that night, when the wind died again. *Kylie* flopped through the swell like a sated seal, gurgling westward at less than a knot, with the vane flapping like a nervous gull and the tiller snoozing. Rather than hand the sails, I hove-to on what the drifts of my irritated pipe-smoke suggested was the starboard tack and, without bothering to set the alarm clock and wedge it beneath my chin, I went below to sleep. For three hours I was haunted by the misfortunes of Odysseus. Compared with his, my delays were piffling. Though Malta was still about a hundred miles away, the next morning's ten-knot wind would surely get me there on the evening of the sixth day out from Greece. In five-and-something days I would have covered 380 miles against the wind and current, which meant that I would have made good about seventy miles a day. The passage would be nothing to shout about, but nor would it be anything to rail at. Odysseus, I thought, would have been pleased to make as many miles in such a space of time on his journey from Troy...

I don't know what awoke me. It could not have been a sudden burst of wind, for *Kylie* had not lurched, the sails had not cracked, and when I looked out I saw in the moonlight that the waves were still the same height they had been when I had gone below, the genoa was still backed to starboard and the tiller was still drowsing. I peered astern, looking out from the companionway. All seemed to be well, but I felt that something was amiss. I stepped up into the cockpit and saw what it was: about a mile away, the white masthead lights of a power-driven vessel were bearing down upon me. I ducked into the cabin, switched on electrical power to the engine and depressed the starter button. After a few hacks and gargles the motor fired. I cast off the tiller lanyards, engaged gear and made a ninety-degree degree turn to starboard. Minutes later the huge bulk of a container-ship thrummed past *Kylie*'s stern. Had I not motored out of its way it would have run me down. I eased back the engine-revs, handed the genoa and resumed my charted course.

For three hours *Kylie* puttered on towards Malta, her bows rising and falling in the low swell and the tiller vibrating lightly beneath my palm. Not long after the sternlight of the first vessel had disappeared, a passenger ship bedecked with fairy lights overtook me, and an hour later another vessel came up on a parallel course, going in the opposite direction. It dawned on me that I was in a shipping-lane. I stopped the engine, made a pot of tea and waited for the wind to come. It arrived at eight o'clock, but instead of blowing from the prescribed north-westerly quarter it came from just south of west, almost directly from Malta. I glanced at the chart. If I laid a course on the starboard tack I was likely to meet more shipping and stronger currents, but such a course would take me nearer Malta. A port-tack course, however, would not only be safer — for I would be diverging from the shipping-lane — but might also better tactically. Sooner or later the wind would surely heed the Admiralty's statistics and veer north-west, when I would be in a good position to make Valetta on a close reach. I backed the genoa to port and when the head came round sailed close-hauled, making a course of about 300° towards the Sicilian coast.

The tactic failed. For fifteen hours the wind stayed westerly, and at noon I discovered that although Sicily had moved twenty-six miles nearer, Malta was still as far away as ever. I held the north-westerly course until midnight when, still in light winds, I came about and headed 230° in the direction of Malta. The night was long and wearying, for the near-miss of

the container ship had made me so jittery that even with the alarm-clock near my ear and my eyes closed, I was unable to trust myself to sleep. In the dawn of the sixth day the wind at last strengthened, building to twenty-five knots by breakfast time. Wearied by nervous vigil, I made for the Sicilian coast. At two in the afternoon the wind abated, cloud covered the sun, and heavy rain filled the cockpit. I stripped off, and for a while soap-suds danced on the compass. Before sunset *Kylie* motored into the ancient harbour of Syracuse and anchored in three fathoms. Without bothering to write up the log, I switched off the alarm clock, covered my eyes with the Maltese ensign and slept, troubled by the knowledge that I had taken five days and six hours to make good only 380 miles and yet had not reached my intended port-of-call.

Though Syracuse merited a visit, I was too set on making Malta to land there. With little more than eleven clear days left if I were to reach Majorca on time, I paused only long enough to drink a cup of early morning coffee and inspect two impressively large spiders' webs strung between the backstays before weighing anchor and motoring south towards Cape Passero. The air was humid and still, and *Kylie* had to detour several miles from her direct course to avoid the tunny nets that a flotilla of acrylic boats had laid offshore.

I was so struck by the spiders' industriousness that I invested them with weather-lore. Although the webs had bent and vibrated for six hours while *Kylie*'s engine drove her along at four knots, not a strand had parted. At what wind-speed would they disintegrate? A fifteen-knot breeze, I thought, might be enough see them in tatters. This being so, it followed that the creatures wouldn't have spun such large webs if stronger winds were in the offing. Plainly, light winds were again to be the order of the day. In view of all this subtle nature-lore, what should *Kylie* do? Off Cape Passero I cut the engine and laid the parallel ruler on the chart. Valetta lay only fifty miles away, but the zephyrs coming from the south were against any ventures in that direction. If the spiders were to be believed, the morning's airs would not become any stronger, in which case it would take umpteen hours for *Kylie* to reach Malta. With Majorca still 900 miles distant, it seemed silly to indulge a whim to visit an outpost of the old Empire. I set the ghoster and laid off a course to run parallel with the lie of the Sicilian coast. Then I opened the logbook and deleted Malta from the itinerary.

The spiders were right about the wind. Its capricious antics kept me changing sails throughout that day and half the following night. Then, at about dawn, the webs disappeared and the wind built to twenty knots in the space of an hour. *Kylie* sped north-west through the Malta Channel under a full main and poled-out genoa, towards a bank of cloud that was scurrying in from the west. The wind dropped, and after a flurry of rain and lightning, swung through a full half-circle to blow from dead ahead. By noon I was down to the third reef, battling against a rising storm. At first the seas were as astonished and confused as I was. Summer gales, so they had been told by the Admiralty, had not happened here in thirty years, and the local waves were quite out of practice. Although some of them had the presence of mind to slip grey-green capes over their regulation blue uniforms when the rain came, the sudden reversal of wind bewildered them no end. They milled about like an army of fuddled pensioners who had been hauled out of their bivouacs and were searching for their dentures. The sound of cannon rolled in from unexpected quarters; orders which had required them to make a westerly advance in blue parade dress and white forage caps had been suddenly countermanded, and so the rankers were in a tizz. *What's it all about, then....? But we was supposed to be going for Gibraltar! Where's me teeth? Wot are those bleedin' generals up to? Have you seen my blessed teeth? Falling back on Alexandria is ridiculous! Fill-in the latrines? In this weather? Come off of it, Spud! Listen, you lot: what joker was it that went and pinched my teeth?*

As deaf as I was to the change of orders, a baggage train of heavy swells continued to lumber westward, barging the toothless, gabbling infantry. *Kylie* was ignored, waving a white rag among a confused and brawling militia. Then the easterly swells reared up and toppled backwards, like wrestlers who had been ankle-scythed. When the wind at last got its message through, the baggage train wheeled into line, the veteran infantry put its dentures in and tramped back eastwards, frothing at the stupidity of it all.

For a couple of hours I contended against the rising seas, hoping always that the wind would conform to the statistics. I wedged myself into the weather-going seat that fits on to the lower storm-board and peered through the streaming windows of the sprayhood. The sky darkened further and the leech of the storm jib began to judder. Whatever the *Pilot* said to the contrary, it looked as though I had found a gale. Because the nearest land was something of a lee shore, the gale was not without its dangers, but it had its beauty too. By a fluke of light reflected from the Sicilian landscape, Homer's 'wine-dark sea' was filigreed with amber jewels. Close-hauled, *Kylie* knifed through the crests, trying to reach the port of Licata. The town's factory chimneys appeared at intervals beneath the foot of the jib. Like lances seen above green hilltops, they streamed white banners and jogged against the louring sky. With my feet splayed the full width of the cockpit, I snatched a compass-bearing of the chimneys and recorded it in on the back of my hand. Half an hour later another bearing told me that we had made such beggarly progress that even if conditions did not worsen, *Kylie* would take ten hours to reach Licata; and so I wiped my spectacles and studied the chart.

The trend of the Sicilian coast is from north-west to south-east, which meant that in the westerly gale it was a dangerous lee-shore. Licata lies at the western end of a thirty-mile bight and is protected by a knuckle of land. Fifteen miles east of it is the port of Gela. Reportedly shallow, and unprotected by any headland, it looked a poor place to make for in such weather. The only other possible haven was Pozzallo. I opened the dividers and measured off the distance to that place. It lay more than forty miles away, but it lay downwind.

I unshipped the weather-going seat and slid all the storm boards into place. After disconnecting the wind-vane gear and uncleating the tiller lanyards, I looked ahead at the shape of the oncoming waves. On the crest of one of the few unbreaking seas I put the tiller to leeward, came about onto the opposite tack and bore away before the wind. *Kylie*'s head swung round and she surged eastward. By this time the veteran conscripts had got their battledress on. They had taken off their fancy forage caps and donned heavy bronze helmets topped with vast and floppy white plumes. Most of the breakers went about the business of conquest without any fuss, bearing down on the quivering acres in their path and subjugating them with textbook efficiency. But perhaps because *Kylie* herself did not appear to be paying the seas much attention, one or two of the more macho characters began to show off by rearing up and roaring paeans. The noise was awful. Starting with a growl thirty yards astern, it built up to a threatening belly-rumble and ended in a prolonged and open-throated shout that drowned the howl of the wind and set *Kylie* trembling with apprehension. A couple of panting sea-giants even tried to mount her, but in their eagerness they quite misjudged their distance and fell sprawling behind.

I headed for Cape Scalambri lighthouse at the eastern end of the thirty-mile bight, making shallow zigzags across the backs of the waves so as to pass at least two miles offshore. Spotting my approach, the lighthouse put out to meet me, but its bluff bows threw up such dense clouds of spray that *Kylie*'s mast was lost to view, and so it altered course and steamed rapidly westward in search of Gela, which seemed to have sunk without trace.

The white-legged pier of Pozzallo strode out in the sunset. Protected from the worst of the seas by a curve in the coast, *Kylie* skittered past its spindly shanks and beat towards a stone quay that was barely large enough to shelter the two yachts already moored in its lee. I backed the jib and hung fenders from the guard-rails. Though *Kylie* was only thirty yards from the quay and hove-to with little sail, the wind was strong enough to cant her mast ten degrees from the vertical. I creased my eyes against whirling gouts of sand while a figure climbed a leg of the pier and beckoned me onwards. Leaning against the wind, I bent the monkey's fist onto a heaving-line and hurled it towards the pier. The beckoning figure secured my second throw, and ten minutes later *Kylie* had nestled alongside, outboard of the other boats.

I hung my sodden gear in the rigging and between sips of neighbourly coffee reflected that in little more than six hours *Kylie* had covered forty-two miles. In other circumstances I might have counted it an achievement. The trouble was, I had been going in quite the opposite direction I had intended. Though I had finished up nearer Malta, the gale had driven me further away from Majorca.

I dropped an extra cube of sugar into my coffee. Then I listened to the wind in the rigging and hoped it would decrease.

13
Marsala and After

Sicily was the stomping ground of Homer's Laestrygones, a tribe of xenophobic cannibals who pelted Odysseus with boulders, sank eleven of his ships and afterwards dined on their crews. Perhaps because my boat is small and I am rather stringy and wrinkled, the cannibals hardly bothered me. After kicking dust and pebbles onto my deck, they howled inland to breakfast at the local radio station, where they throttled an announcer in the middle of the shipping forecast before plunging him, by the sound of it, into boiling oil. I switched off his dying gurgles and went out to gaze at the morning.

Even when the Laestrygones are not hurling boulders or scuffing dust, the air of Pozzallo is so thick with cement from a nearby factory that the land and its occupants are attired in compulsory grey overcoats whatever the weather. Whereas the Syracusan spiders' webs had been almost invisible, the strands that appeared between the backstays in Pozzallo were thick enough to rig a wind-jammer, and their eight-legged spinner looked like a dried pea in a mink muff. I spotted the creature as soon as I emerged from the cabin. Four well-upholstered limbs were gripping the backstay and two were clutching the web. The cement dust was so tenacious that none flew off the strands when I blew on them, although the spider itself stirred and blinked.

'Only flies with glaucoma would bump into that,' I told it; 'it's as obvious as the Forth Bridge.'

Kylie's tell-tales hung limply in the rigging, and the sky was like jeans that have been splashed randomly with bleach. Now the weatherman had been murdered, I should have to rely on the spider's forecast, but whatever was coming I had to get a move on. In fewer days than I cared to reckon, Sarah would be sailboarding across Pollensa Bay, looking for *Kylie*. If at sunset she stacked the board outside Katy's Bar and I had not arrived, I knew that behind her headband she'd be worrying.

While I was singling up the lines my neighbour came out to scowl at the dust on his decks, but when I pointed out the furry web in my rigging and enthused about the prescience of spiders he shook his head and laughed. He had passaged from Marsala and had meant to set off that morning for Malta, but was delaying things until his weatherfax had recovered from electronic amnesia. I didn't let on about the current appetites of the Laestrygones, or that only a couple of days previously I had been intending to go to Malta myself. It had been only a couple of days ago, but already it seemed like ages. He cast off my lines and I bade him goodbye.

Some spiders have lived fifteen years, but what with aggro from the cannibals and pollution from the cement factory, I thought that my Sicilian passenger would have a life-span of three years at most. If the creature's web-spinning augury of lightish weather turned out to be correct, I reckoned that the spider would have done proportionally better than any human meteorologist. To match the insect's achievement, the radio forecaster would have had to predict the weather ten days ahead.

The spider's divination was spot-on. By sunset it had travelled thirty miles westward, borne gently forward by the light wind it had predicted. For fifteen hours it reclined between the backstays, peering out of its furry cowl at the unravelling shoreline with the myopic boredom of a day-tripper on a mystery tour. From time to time — when a cloud obscured the sun, or when I changed the ghoster from one side of the boat to the other — it would twiddle at a filament of web, as though comparing its texture with the man-made stuff that its other limbs were attached to.

Cape Scalambri slid past, towing bargeloads of rocks large enough for the Laestrygones to practise with. Before the headland disappeared I attempted to take a bearing, but the figures of the compass were unreadable because a lens of the view-finder had gone missing. Since it

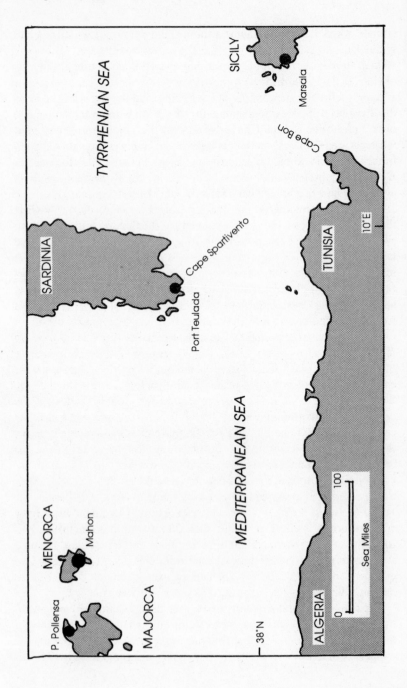

was less than the size of a contact lens for the human eye, I made no serious attempt to find it. To go searching, in late middle age, for objects intended to be looked *through* rather than looked *at* was rather asking for trouble. My father used to go mad regularly — about twice a week on average — just from the strains of searching for spectacles he was already wearing. If I started looking for the lost lens I knew I would end up in a strait-jacket. As a tranquillizer, I mixed myself a gin-and-tonic and tried to forget about the loss, but the navigator's craving for compass-bearings is as easy to suppress as the smoker's addiction to cigarettes. If someone else lights up, the addict's fingers twitch towards the pocket where he used to keep his cigarettes. So when a petroleum flare ignited on the Sicilian shore, mine reached for the hand bearing-compass. I stilled their indiscipline by wrapping them around the gin-and-tonic and fixing my eyes on the last shreds of sunset. For a minute or two the therapy worked: I contemplated an approaching continent of cloud and sipped my drink. Then, out of the corner of my eye I perceived the wink of Cape Scalambri. Ninety degrees from the petroleum flare, it would give a perfect fix; and if the cumulus did not disperse, such a fix might well be the last reliable one I would get for hours.

'Blast!' I muttered, raising the gin-and-tonic to my lips.

Something solid slid out of the plastic beaker and onto my tongue. I spat it onto my palm and fingered its edges in disbelief. Three minutes later the missing lens was cemented firmly back in its place and I was taking a dipping bearing of the light.

I altered course ten degrees away from the trend of the coast in case the wind increased and veered westerly to make Sicily a lee shore again. Affronted by my lack of faith, the spider pulled the cowl over its eyes and hugged itself to sleep.

My faithlessness was indeed wanton, for throughout the night the wind remained light from the east. Under a poled-out ghoster, *Kylie* sauntered up the Canale di Sicilia, trailing a languid thread of logline. At midnight things changed. In less time than it took to make a mugful of coffee, the breeze had fallen away and the logline had drooped further, and before I could swallow a mouthful the genoa was aback, pressed against the pole by a cool and adverse breeze. The pole juddered in alarm. I bundled the sail into its bag and waited...

The forerunners of the gale burst on me with shouts of frustration, stumbling out of the night like a rabble of thwarted gatecrashers. Angry and humiliated, they barged across the watery fields in the moonlight, uprooting white flowerpots and hurling them skyward, punching holes in the tent of cloud, flicking pellets into my eyes and spitting at *Kylie*'s lamp. There was much violence and noise, but there was no sense of purpose or direction. After a few chaotic minutes the rabble roared off southwards, dragging the tattered tent in its wake. And then the second gale strode in.

This gale had the demeanour of an elder statesman who was not going to be trifled with. In a very few minutes *Kylie* had made a diplomatic response by putting on a more business-like outfit of storm jib and deeply-reefed main, and was paying attention to the weighty proceedings, which looked as though they would drag on for hours. Hidden from the eye of the gale by the sprayhood, I made faces and swore. I couldn't afford the time to run away downwind from this one. I clipped on another safety-line, and when the wave-tops started to find their way between the sprayhood and the lee coaming I began to pump the bilge.

The gale blew from the west-northwest for fourteen hours at between twenty-eight and thirty-five knots. The seas were large, ponderous and orderly, and *Kylie* was able to ferret her way through their ranks without much help from me. The contest was a serious affair, but it was less stressful than most others I had been in. Sheltered by the sprayhood and wedged in by cushions on the weather-going seat, I felt almost comfortable, and so did *Kylie*. Guided by the windvane, her sleek hull clove the waves rather than breasted them, although the cliffier ones sometimes gave problems if her pitching rhythm was out of phase with the steeps above her bows. Faced with an unclimbable wall of water, she dug her nose in, tossed her head and drove through it. This action was accompanied by increased noise: the thuckity-clack of the anchor against its chocks, and the louder roar of water cascading onto the foredeck or rushing past the hull. As the hours went by such noises were not merely bearable: they were reassuring messages that she was coping with the Jekyll-and-Hyde forces around her. For the seas that sought to engulf her at one moment were the same that buoyed her up an instant later; the wind which tried to knock her down also invested her with the power to dodge its blows; and the waves were both bludgeons to crush the hull and cushions to soften its falls.

But even with cushions the falls were hard enough. Three or four times an hour a deviant gust would catch her awkwardly, or a juvenile wave would break ranks and scramble onto the shoulders of an elder to aim a punch at *Kylie* as she passed. When such lapses happened she tried to brush them aside, but sometimes the marauder could not be warded off. The blow would strike home, crashing against the hull so hard that the kettle would jump on its stove, the plates would rattle in their racks, and I would clench my teeth and share the pain. It didn't happen often, but when it did it hurt.

In such conditions horizons are as elusive as needles on glass, but at nine in the morning I hove-to, clipped myself to the shrouds and attempted a sun sight. From trough to crest the swells were about fifteen feet, and their interval ranged between six and eight seconds. For only three or four seconds was an horizon visible above the miles of moving hills, and for only the fleeting moment when I was teetering on a wave-top was it anything like stationary. After half an hour of squinting through the sextant telescope, shuffling colour-shades and dodging the worst of the spray, I managed to trap a fugitive sun in the mirror. From the formulae of Marcq St Hilaire and a resulting position line I estimated *Kylie* to be twenty miles from the Sicilian coast and to have made good sixty-five miles since leaving Pozzallo twenty-two hours before. Considering that she had been stemming a current and had been forced to sail at least forty degrees from her intended course since the coming of the gale, I did not think the progress bad.

During the late afternoon the wind strengthened and by six o'clock was blowing at more than thirty-five knots. Dazed by the hit-and-run attacks of marauding waves, *Kylie* panted forward gamely, but I was less stoical. After brewing a flask of tea I went about and settled her onto the port tack, hoping that in breasting the current at a different angle the hull would ride more comfortably. I re-positioned the seat on its washboard and, between draughts of tea, counted the frequency of the hull-slams. Before the mug had been drained I judged that the change of tack had reduced them by ten per cent.

Searching for even better news, I switched on the radio and tracked the air waves for a weather forecast. All I got were slurps. It sounded as though the Laestrygones, having consumed all the broadcasters in Sicily, were now devouring their mainland colleagues as well. Between prolonged belches and slobbers from his assailants, someone dying near Vesuvius eventually managed to gasp out an opinion about what could have been tomorrow's weather but might just as well have been a report of yesterday's activities in the Italian parliament. The words I heard did not encourage much meteorological hope. It seemed that a *depressione profond* had settled on Rome, and numerous *colpo di venti* had performed a *rotozione a sinstra*. I scratched my head. A profound depression resulting in a culpable and sinister rotation of wind? Was it a weather forecast, a debate on the Mafia or a description of dyspepsia? Any lingering fear that it might be about the weather was scotched soon afterwards when a radiant sunset was followed by a clearing sky and a lessening of wind. By midnight *Kylie* was wearing a small genoa and asking what all the fuss had been about. I set the windvane and went below to sleep.

The sun bustled through the companionway and slapped me awake at six. I squinted at the deckhead compass. We were heading north-northwest in what the gentle motion suggested was no more than eight knots of wind. While the kettle was coming to a boil I took a sponge to the foredeck and began to wipe the topsides, checking the sails and gear as I went along. We had come through the gale pretty well, I thought. The skipper, for once, had not suffered a single bruise and it seemed that *Kylie* had not been damaged either. The sailbags were still attached by their lashings to the guard-rails and — despite the side-swipes from undisciplined chancers — the stitching had not come adrift. The anchor, too, was still in its chocks. I squeezed out the sponge and went on wiping the coachroof and the side decks. It wasn't until I reached the shroud plates that I noticed something was wrong. One of the shrouds was slacker than it should have been. Thinking that perhaps a locknut had worked itself loose, I bent to inspect the bottlescrew gaiter and saw that the inverted 'U' of the stainless steel shroud-plate had broken clean across.

Replacing the broken shroud-plate should not have been a problem but it was. Two lockerfuls of spare bits and pieces ought to have contained U-bolt fittings of the right size, but they didn't. I wrung the sponge and swore, for in the gentle weather then prevailing it would have been only an hour's work to replace the broken shroud plate while *Kylie* continued on her way towards Majorca.

The oversight cost me two days. From the information in a pilot book I gleaned that the nearest blacksmith practised his trade in Licata, thirty miles distant to the north-east, and so I turned aside from my intended course and headed for Sicily again.

Although I arrived at Licata in mid-morning, by the time I had unbolted the shroud plate and presented my ship's papers at the port captain's office it was gone noon. The visit, I thought, would be either a disaster or a doddle, for Italian officials are either over-fussy about paper-work or neglect it altogether in favour of extended conversations about more important matters such as football and fornication. Despite my deafness and my ignorance of the language, I find Italians so very easy to understand that if the human species suddenly lost its voice box I believe that the Italians would be able to communicate with each other better than any other nation, for their body language is the world's best.

The port captain was indisposed, suffering, according to the lugubrious head-shakings and eye-rollings of his acolyte, from such tremendous toothache that his jaw was the shape and texture of a well-smoked Caciocavallo cheese.

I expressed my sympathy with his plight and enquired whether it might be possible for a deputy to write out a *Constituto* for a foreign yacht which had put into the port for emergency repairs. The acolyte raised his eyes to the ceiling and wandered upstairs, promising to return with an answer. Above the town a castle looked down on muttering tower blocks and a huddle of indolent trawlers. The dockside streets, which had been humming when I stepped ashore, sank into torpor, drugged by the heat. After waiting ten minutes I peered into the room next door. The acolyte was reclining on a window sill, leafing through a girlie magazine. I asked about the *Constituto*. It was quite impossible, his left eyebrow informed me, for such a document to be compiled at that time of day. Too many other things were going on. The port captain's head had apparently parted company with his trunk, the deputy port captain was engaged — if the wiggling of a forefinger was to be believed — in business of an intimate and private nature, and he himself, as I could very well see, was on a pornographic excursion to the Philippines Islands. I left him studying the posterior of a young lady who was brandishing, for no obvious nutritional reasons, a corn-cob, and hastened to the blacksmith's shop. I was too late. It was gone one o'clock and the place was deserted.

I retired to a nearby *trattoria*, where I slumped onto a table beneath a life-size colour-poster of a footballer from Palermo. Had a waiter not awoken me at five o'clock I should have stayed there all night, my head cushioned on my forearms, among the crumbs of a half-eaten meal, with the broken shroud-plate still clutched between my fingers.

The siesta and the abortive quest for a *Constituto* ate up so much time that the repaired shroud-plate was not bolted into place until twenty-four hours after I had borne it ashore. I left Licata as I had entered it, without the cognizance of the authorities, motoring between the supplicatory arms of the harbour at four knots to make up for lost time.   But even at two-thirds revs, progress was slow. During the ensuing thirty-six hours *Kylie* was contending against a current of between one and one-and-a-half knots as she pushed north-westwards through the narrows between Sicily and Cape Bon, a dislocated thumb of Tunisia. Had there been more time and

'I slumped.....beneath a poster of a footballer from Palermo...'

wind the passage would have been enjoyable, for it was enlivened with colour and incident: a sliver of moon rising above a wafered horizon like the illuminated sail of a felucca; comets streaking nakedly across an asphalt sky; and a leviathan standing on its head. The whale's enormous tail-flukes rose twice the height of *Kylie*'s masthead before coming down with a thwack that raised a wave which would have filled her cockpit if she had been any nearer. The expenditure of foot-pounds was so prodigious that I gave the creature a standing ovation. It was amazing, I thought, what lengths some creatures would go to just to rid themselves of itches.

And it was amazing, too, what distances some vessels would motor simply to investigate a radar blip. After the whale had done its headstand, a launch bearing the words *GUARDIA DI FINANZA* along its hull sneaked up from astern and stationed itself abeam. Behind its windows three watery-eyed officials were making peculiar chopping motions, as though telling me how to slice onions if I became as disconsolately immured in a small Italianate aquarium as they were. I was so entertained by their performance that it took me a while to understand that they were telling me to stop. I slid the engine out of gear and hung out my fenders. The launch burbled alongside and threw me its lines while two of its minders put on their caps and clambered into *Kylie*'s cockpit.

'Produce for our inspection,' they said, 'thy *Constituto*.'

'Oh dear,' I replied, 'I haven't got one. Your colleague in Licata was so far gone with toothache and neuralgia that he was quite unable to open his desk, you understand, and proffer one.'

'About toothache,' they said, 'we understand. But neuralgia? What is neuralgia?'

'It affects one something like this,' I said, standing on the bridge deck and reduplicating the performance of the port captain's acolyte. The officials opened wide their mouths and looked at each other in horror. During the ensuing silence I added: '...and the pain is so powerful that it blows his head clean off his shoulders.'

It took me a long time to convince them that I was neither someone pulling their legs nor a *contrabbandieri* running-in cigarettes under their noses. They returned to their rumbling aquarium, pulling faces at each other and tapping their temples. I unfastened the aquarium and took in the fenders. Safe behind the glass and using only their hands and facial muscles, my interrogators delivered a fluent, non-verbal account of their experience to their commander. From where I was standing it looked as though they were insisting that even if the port captain and I managed to regain our heads, neither of us was fit for a normal life. Indeed, they semaphored, the Englishman was of such limited intelligence that there was, in their opinion, only one occupation he might be at all good at. Curious about what this might be, I paused in my activity and stared through the window at a virtuoso display of finger-weaving and wrist-twirling. Then I engaged gear and puttered off, pondering on a new insight into my character. It had taken me long to discover it, but it seemed that I was blessed with the unique but useless skill of being able to disentangle hot spaghetti from the necks of low-flying geese.

*

Eventually my mind returned to other matters, such as wind, weather and fuel. Since leaving Licata the engine had been running continuously, for there had been hardly any wind at all, and now it had begun to rain. If the light weather continued, there would not be enough diesel in the tank to see us across the 150 miles of Tyrrhenian Sea between Sicily and Sardinia. I had hoped to be clear of Sicily four days previously, but now it seemed I would have to put into one of its ports again. I looked at the chart and headed for Marsala, thirty miles distant. Then I pulled tight the drawstrings of my hood and stared into the curtain of rain.

The engine commended the decision with Teutonic heartiness. *What a goodly ganter! Righty ho-ho! Top-up the old tank, Otto Diesel, Diesel, Diesel...Fillitup, fillitup till it tickles! 'Ave a gander at Marsala in the morning!* The mindless chatter got on my nerves. After two hours of it I stilled the engine and sank into the silent warmth of the cabin, peeling off my damp clothes and towelling myself dry in the mellow lamplight. *Kylie* settled herself among the pillows outside and nodded off.

We got to at Marsala on a saint's day — of which Italy has a profusion — mooring next to a shapely local boat that lay in water the colour of minestrone soup, though it was by no means as drinkable. Oil-spills and ordure had blotched the hull, and its uppers were infected with the malaise of peeling varnish and chalking paint. Despite the dirt and neglect, it seemed that people were living aboard, for the hatch was half-open, jeans were swinging in the rigging and an umbilical hoseline pulsed from the quay. In Britain such a boat would have been the chrysalis of a fifty-ish daydreamer like myself, someone who listened to *Sailing By* and the midnight-fifteen forecast before dreaming of voyages he would never make. The same boat in Italy, I supposed, would pupate the same kind of person. I squirted detergent onto the scummy meniscus and watched it rip open. Then the hatch was pulled back and three female crew-members emerged from below.

Such is the Italian genius for creating drama that the girls came up like Venuses out of sludge. They had lustrous cheeks, glistening lips and wonderful carriage that transformed the oil-stained deck into a designer cat-walk for a fashion parade. Two nymphs in white nylon lingered diaphanously at the end of the gangplank to await the third, a pale sylph clad in tights spun from what looked like threads of sunshine. The sight of such vulnerable beauty filled me with delight and terror. Would the virginal skirts be soiled by that oily stanchion? How could such dainty slippers circumvent the debris on the quayside? Somehow they did, and when they did I re-capped the detergent flask, wiped the dribbles from the deck and watched them go.

Toting empty cans, I followed them in search of fuel, which was dispensed, according to the harbour plan, from a pump outside the custom house. But when I got there the custom house was shuttered and barred, and the diesel pump locked. Why, in Heaven's name, I enquired of someone sitting on a plastic fish-box, was the place closed? Today was not Sunday but Wednesday, a day of labour. He spread his hands and raised his shoulders. Yes, he conceded, today was indeed Wednesday; however, it was also a saint's day, and so every office was closed. But a diesel pump, I pointed out, was not anything like an office. '*Quello non dice niente*,' he shrugged. 'It's near enough to the *Guardia di Finanza* to be taken as one.'

Defeated by this line of reasoning, I shaved off a three-day stubble and went into town to search for the nymphs. In this I was at first no more successful than in my quest for diesel fuel. The streets were so crowded with revellers that I could not reach anywhere I aimed for. Borne by warm currents of humanity, I was eddied into a smoky, cavernous eating-house, where sweating cooks shovelled a motley of pizzas into huge brick-lined ovens that looked like main-line railway tunnels. Had the cooks been hagiolatrous and their object of devotion Saint Catherine of Alexandria, they could have baked a pizza the same diameter as the wheel that the Emperor Maximus had tried to break her on. I sat down and ordered something. Out of the smoke appeared a *Margharita* as big as a satellite dish. Nowhere else, since then, have I eaten another pizza to match it. The flavours of each mouthful were unique, sealed in by flame and tangy with woodsmoke.

Although someone told me the name of the local saint whom the revelry was honouring, I became too tipsy on *Marsala Stravecchio* to remember it. Having downed several glasses of the honey-coloured liquid, I suggested to one of the boat-nymphs — who had materialised out of the smoke towing a bearded Dane — that John Holloway be canonized forthwith. After all, I argued, the Englishman had performed a saintly office by brandyfying the previously mediocre Sicilian wine and exporting it to London, where it had so elevated the minds of Victorians that they had built the Great Eastern Hotel and engendered Edward Lear, a contemporary, as both she and the Dane very well knew, of the illustrious Garibaldi. So let us, I insisted, drink a toast to all three.

'And,' said the Dane, 'this Edward Lear was also a revolutionary?'

'Sort of. He drew pictures and wrote limericks.'

'What are limericks?'

'They are absurdities, like hamsters on stilts.'

'We don't,' said the Dane, 'understand you. Please supply an example.'

'The only one that comes to mind,' I said, 'goes something like this:

> "There was a young man from Darjeeling
> Who got on a train bound for Ealing.
> It said on the door:
> 'Please don't spit on the floor',
> So he lay down and spat on the ceiling".'

The nymph evaporated, disappearing through the bottom of my glass as I drained it, tugging the Dane towards clearer air.

I bore another bottle of *Marsala Stravecchio* aboard and drank alone in the cockpit. The Italian boat lay in darkness and silence.

On awakening I was annoyed to find that someone had been throwing books and clothing around the cabin, had spilled wine over the chart table and had defaced a page of the logbook by scrawling, in a hamfisted mockery of my own handwriting,

> 'A Viking, consigned to Valhalla,
> Used to entertain nymphs in his parlour.
> After dining at nine,
> He immersed them in wine,
> Which he'd shipped by the tun from Marsala'.

The nymph did not re-decorate my life until mid-morning. Still in a diaphanous skirt, she flitted aboard the Italian boat while I was stowing away the diesel cans and wiping the fuel drips from the deck. The skirt, I was pleased to notice, had not been stained by wine.

'*Buon giorno*,' I called. Her fingers rose to shoulder height and flickered, a smile twinkled above the grimy hatchway and she was gone.

Kylie motored into a flaccid sea and headed for Sardinia. I hoped again that the wind-strength would heed the guide-lines of My Lords Commissioners, but the Tyrrhenian weather turned out to be no different from what had gone before: hours and hours of calms were followed by vicious puff-adders that coiled down at sunset and spat poisonous gales at midnight. *Kylie* draped herself in an awning and plodded on, with the windvane jittering to the whirr of the engine and my sweat dripping onto the glassfibre coamings. For two days I saw nothing: not a boat nor bird nor fish. Though the awning shielded me from the sun, the heat belaboured my head with rubbery truncheons until it seemed that I and my boat had parted company with the world, and that we were on a glazed tectonic platter from which everything else had slithered.

Below decks was darker. Going down to escape the glare, I saw a crumb of dirt glide across a white surface and disappear into a crack. I closed my eyes and shuddered. *Kylie* was more earth-bound than I had thought; despite my precautions, a cockroach had got aboard.

Cockroaches had crawled out of world's first rocks, and would be around at its last moments, scuttling filth among its fallen palaces and dislocated graves. I had seen them before by the squillion. Once, most unforgettably, I had switched on the lights in the kitchen of a platinum hotel and the floor had rippled. Back in the bedroom, we had huddled in a corner and tucked our knees to our chins, and when one had crawled out of the skirting we had crushed it with a shoe but it had never quite died. The waving feelers infiltrated my dreams long after the holiday had ended.

The only poison aboard was oxalic acid, used for cleaning the teakwork. A half-teaspoonful of the crystals mixed with sugar would be more effective than a shoe, I thought. I tipped the mixture onto a cardboard tray and placed it on the cabin sole. Then I shuttered the cabin and retreated to the cockpit, where I remained for eighteen hours, unwilling to face such odious creatures but also detained on deck by another gale.

This third one lasted only four hours, long enough to leave me weary but not long enough to drive away my fears of what might be lurking below. When the wind had subsided to twenty knots I unshuttered the cabin and scrutinised the poisonous white pyramid. No doubt about it, the stuff had been disturbed, but whether by the motion of the boat or the crawling of a cockroach was impossible to know. I slid into the cabin and, still with one eye on crevices, had just enough time to work out that I was some twenty miles from the southernmost point of Sardinia before a speck of dirt sliding across a locker lid drove me back to the cockpit.

My body did not attempt to enter the cabin again until I had anchored in Port Teulada, to the west of Cape Spartivento, by which time I was so weary that I could have slept with a tin of maggots writhing on my pillow.

'I should have been there yesterday,' I explained on the morrow, having dinghied across to an American power-boat, 'but Majorca is about two hundred and fifty miles away, so I'm running a little late. Where's the nearest fuel outlet?'

'Too far for you to row. Come aboard for waffles and honey while I decant you five gallons of mine.'

The tankful lasted for twenty-eight hours, carrying me at half-revs across another endless blue plain. Emboldened by gin-and-tonic, I blustered into the cabin and threw away the scuffled poison. Not until weeks later, when I discovered the corpse of a half-inch cockroach in — of all unlikely places — the kerosene locker, did I move about my home with the certainty that I was its sole occupant.

With the fuel cans empty again, I puttered into Mahon, secured at the Club Maritimo and re-filled the tank. It turned out I needn't have bothered, for at breakfast time a strong wind set in from the north, rattling the halyards and raising white-caps in the harbour. With two reefs in the main, *Kylie* scooted out to sea and headed for Pollensa Bay. In the flat-water lee of Menorca she averaged six knots and kept her decks dry, but when she entered the shallow channel between the islands, clouds raced in from the north-northeast, the mountains of Majorca disappeared in rain, the wind rose to thirty knots and I donned my oilskins. For the fourth and final time in 1,300 miles, *Kylie* was amid a gale. I thought about the Admiralty statistics and poured a liberal measure of rum.

In the lee of Cabo Formentor I unpeeled the oilskins, and at sunset anchored in six-and-a-half feet of water on a familiar patch of sand, only ten oar-strokes away from the mooring I had left a lifetime ago.

Ashore, things were arranged much as I had imagined they would be. Alfonso was strolling the promenade, the lights were on in Katy's Bar, and a sailboard was propped against a tree.

'I'm sorry,' I said towards some figures at a table, 'to be a little late.'

'Hello, Dad,' said Sarah. 'What would you like to drink?'

National flag of Antigua.

14
To the Lips of Antigua

At a different time on another day, the wind was gusting through the gap in the mountains, jostling the palms and riffling the pages I had spread out on the table. Having stood Joe Miller's beer on the met notes and Sarah's on the Admiralty's statistics, I looked around for a third paperweight. As John Leach was cradling his *Cienta y Treis* brandy quite possessively by then, I was obliged to position my own glass on the passage notes to hold them down.

'It's true,' I said. 'I went through the logbook twice to make sure.'

'Say the figures again,' said Joe, feeding what he called a cookie and I a biscuit to one of Katy's dogs.

'For fifty-seven point five per cent of the time the winds were at or below force three, which means less than ten knots, which is awfully poor stuff.'

'I got that.'

'And for ten per cent of the time it was blowing more than twenty-five knots, which is rather too much.'

Sarah picked up her beer, and pages of Mediterranean statistics turned themselves over. Joe picked up his, and the met notes blew away so fast that only the dog went after them.

'So I think I'll go back to the Atlantic again,' I said.

'You'd love to sail in the Gulf,' said Joe. 'Absolutely. Also, believe it, you'd love the Cajun cooking.'

'Tampico to Vera Cruz was alright,' conceded John Leach, 'but sailing the West Indies is better.'

'Therefore I'll go to New Orleans for the cooking and the Virgins for the sailing,' I said, lifting my glass from the table. As if to validate my decision, the wind blew my passage notes onto the sand.

*

A few days later Sarah and Joe flew back to their Anglo-American duties while John Leach and I set off for Gibraltar and the Canaries. I was glad of his company, for although we differed on minor matters such as the durability of socialism or whether murderers should be hanged or helped, we were in complete agreement on the tenets of a happy life, which are that tobacco is best enjoyed after the washing-up is done, and that log-lines should be coiled anti-clockwise.

That being said, it has to be allowed that we sometimes reacted differently to identical circumstances. After we had put into Tarifa, for example, we came across a rather grand restaurant. Whereas I demurred about going in, John did not hesitate.

'How's your Spanish?'

'About GCSE grade five,' I said. 'How's yours?'

'Much worse than my Malay. Can manage, though. I just keep on saying "*Quiero*..." and wave my arms about.'

He strode through the mahogany portals, requisitioned a table at fifteen paces simply by glaring at it, and even before a menu had been produced, had ordered beer and *tapas*. Two *quieros* and a hand-motion describing an asymmetrical carrot rolling off a gas-holder resulted in the appearance of two nicely garnished portions of chicken. After consuming them, we smoked our pipes and were quite miffed to find that the waiter spoke English.

Apart from its more comfortable wave-shapes, the bit of the Atlantic between Gibraltar and the Canaries seemed no better than the Mediterranean. In light airs that were punctuated by occasional midnight hoolies, we idled towards Lanzarote, grinned at by a lop-sided moon. Had John not been aboard I would have found the passage a trial. I particularly liked the moments when I could snuggle deeper into my sleeping-bag

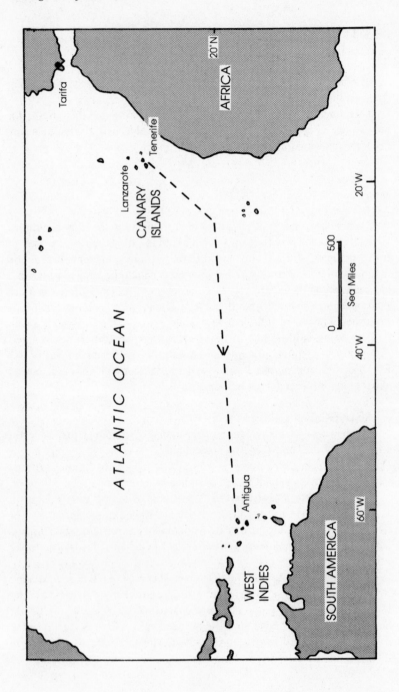

while he was busily repelling, by the sound of it, a legion of armour-plated octopods.

'...and you didn't hear *anything*?' he said to me afterwards.

'No,' I said, nursing my cocoa. 'When there's a crew aboard I... Gracious! You are looking rather wet again.'

'It bucketed down. The first inkling I had of its approach was the noise of an express train, a *steam* express train, somewhere behind me. Couldn't see a thing...'

'Can't say I'm surprised. You don't eat enough carrots.'

'...then we took off...genny poled out...thought seams would burst...sheets like iron bars...wavetops up to the spreaders...'

'Please lift your left foot a moment, I want to get at my tobacco.'

'...and by the time I got the pole in, it was all over.'

'That's all right, then. So I don't need to put on my plastic mac, do I? Do I, John? John...?'

But he was already snoring: accumulating credit, as he is wont to say, in his sleep-bank.

Opening an eye in the sunlight, he discovered me muttering at a silent engine. It had started making noises, I told him, similar to those emitted by his cat the time I dropped a samovar on its tail.

'...and then it started to vomit,' I said.

The other eye opened. 'Injector's mucky. Where d'you keep the spanners?'

We could have had way on again in a quarter of an hour if I hadn't misplaced an important washer. John had spent ten minutes doing some very deft things to the engine and had then asked me to hand him back the injector, which, to the best of my remembrance, had been lying quietly in my palm, wrapped in a piece of kitchen-roll. When I gave it back to him, however, it was minus a washer.

'Where's it gone? I swear it was there a moment ago,' I gabbled. 'It must have flung itself overboard.'

'It can't have done. You haven't been outboard of the cockpit. And though you are greatly agitated, you have not been waving your arms in the air.'

I scrabbled about, clattering the cockpit duckboard and poking between slats. John sucked a mint and snorted.

'Come to think of it,' he said, 'the immobility of your arms is another of your failings. Even in *Lear*, where rages are supposed to be epidemic, you were incapable of shaking a decent fist.'

'That's a disgusting slander. The press were quite complimentary. The *Yellow Advertiser* gave me two column-inches...'

'Do stick to the point. The washer must still be in the cockpit. Sit down, have one of these mints and feel around your bottom.'

In no time at all we had found it, sticking to the underside of my tobacco tin. While John clipped on the fuel lines, I crunched the mint and fumed at his insulting remarks. Above the whirr of the starter motor, I went on: '...and the *Maldon Chronicle*, I'll have you know, ran a photo of me and Cordelia. It was mostly of me, with just Cordelia's downstage cheek and shoulder.   I was asking the faithful Kent to undo my button, and sort of looking into the middle distance. I was at death's door, of course, by that time... Quite incapable, really, of moving a muscle...'

'What I like most about Shakespeare,' said John, edging me gently aside and revving the engine, 'is that even though his characters no longer wear old-fashioned clothes, one still sees them around today.'

*

John left the boat at Lanzarote, and at his departure my days became suddenly pitted with holes, some of which I slithered into. Between Lanzarote and Tenerife I brooded on the immensity of ocean that lay between me and the West Indies. The idea of crossing it excited hopes and fears as powerful as any I had felt in the hours before I married the woman I loved. Blue lagoons of prospective bliss were muddied by rivulets of doubt as I teetered on the brink of both adventures. How was I going to survive in bed or on board when I was so ignorant of their mysteries? Where on earth was this blessed 'E-zone' that the glossy magazines were alluding to? And, thirty years later, what the hell went on in the Bermuda Triangle? The lagoons were muddied, too, by leachings of distaste when I thought about the messy tasks I would need to do in servicing both of the adventures. The prospect of changing *Kylie's* engine-oil was as off-putting as that of changing a baby's nappies. All in all, when I contemplated both the altar and the Atlantic, I wasn't sure I wanted to push anything much further.

By the time I got to Tenerife I had floundered into classic small-boat nightmares. What would I do, I wondered frantically, if the mast failed, the shrouds parted or my appendix misbehaved? It was all very well for dockside couples to shout blue-water encouragement into my thick ears; when *they* set off they'd be able to drink mugs of mutual tea and sympathy if something mucked up their innards or their engine. Unlike them, once I had left Tenerife I couldn't look for any encouragement except, perhaps, from a passing dolphin, and even then I'd hear only one syllable in ten of the reply.

On the credit side, though, *Kylie* had come through the several Mediterranean gales and was now as staunch and tuneful as a miner's canary. Even my chronic worries about the engine had been resolved at last, I thought, by the obvious but costly expedient of replacing it with a new one. Two burly Spaniards had lowered it into the bilge, twirled their spanners for an hour and soon had it purring as smoothly as a coddled cat. It was only when it was asked to do some work that it failed. They put it into gear and Clunk!, it stopped. No, I told them, there weren't any ropes fouling the propeller; the problem was that their new installation was fractionally shorter than the old one and so the prop was now impinging on the outboard studs of the stern-gland assembly. They scratched their heads, noticed that the working day was ending, and solved the problem in ten minutes by drilling a new set of holes for the engine mounts and shifting the unit half an inch towards the stern. After that it purred easily again both in and out of gear. I wrote out a cheque and with it signed away my last excuse for not going west.

With all these oceanic matters to dwell on I didn't bother about the dangers that lay in wait ashore. If the shore-going mariner sprinkled fungicide in his socks every Tuesday and Friday, never patted strange dogs and never permitted any part of his anatomy to approach foreign lavatory pans closer than three Imperial inches whether they were provided with seats or — as was more often the case — not, he would, I was sure, come to no great harm. The question of what would happen to the mariner if he lost his identity was never thought about, let alone raised. It was something that could never happen. I mean, if Columbus had had to waste his time and strength in Santa Cruz de Tenerife insisting that he was Christopher Columbus and not, give or take a few years either way, the apostatical Martin Luther in disguise, he would not have had the energy to set off into the great unknown at all.

The city of Santa Cruz de Tenerife is a bewilderment of wide avenues, warrened streets, haughty shops and snarling traffic. Having come to terms with the last of my nightmares by working out, on squared paper, that I could construct a jury mast out of the genoa poles and the boathook, I rode by coach to the city to purchase stores, obtain clearance and fill my body-belt with traveller's cheques. Clutching my passport, I joined the queue of other visitors in a *bureau de change*. The queue was long, the day was ending and my varicosed legs had started to throb. To complete my discomfort, the noise-level was so high that I couldn't hear the clerk's

213

questions and had to have them shouted into my better ear by, firstly, an impatient man from Hamburg who had a taxi waiting, and secondly but no less pressingly, by a clutch of girls from Upsaala who wanted to climb Mount Teide before sunset. Not wishing to unbutton my shirt in such mixed company, instead of returning my passport to its usual place in my body-belt I dropped it into one of my four plastic bagfuls of miscellaneous stores and hurried out towards the nearest bus-stop, intent on getting back to *Kylie* and putting my feet up.

The bus was full of spitting images of myself, all encumbered with similar plastic bags and equal weariness. For the distance of three bus-stages we trundled along tree-lined avenues, pausing now and then to tumble perspiring lookalikes, their wives, their several children and their numerous plastic bags out of the throbbing vehicle.

My turn came outside the coach station. I struggled out of the bus and deposited my plastic bags on the pavement. The doors hissed shut and the bus sped away. I took out my pipe and reminded myself that the ordeal was nearly over, that all I now had to do was carry my four bagfuls of stores into the coach station, sink into a reclining seat and be taken to my boat. I picked up my bags and started across the avenue, walking with a springier step than I had expected. It seemed that my varicose veins were not as bad as I had thought them to be.

Not until my feet were about to board the coach did the notion strike me that there might be a non-physiological reason for the sudden access of strength to my legs. I looked down at my shopping and saw that I was carrying not four plastic bags but three.

There was absolutely no need, I told myself, to panic. During the flickering, breathless seconds it took me to rummage the bags, a taped celestial voice higher and louder than Semprini's violin was insisting that there were at least three chances to one against the passport going missing, and that it would be no trouble at all to replace six D-sized batteries, five bagged potatoes, four tinned pilchards, three canned tomatoes, two sliced loaves, or — even a month after Christmas — a partridge in a pear tree.

All of which sounded very well, but when I looked into them the three remaining bags did not contain my passport. Even then the blow did not strike home. A passport, when all was said and done on my dad's factory floor, was nothing but a bloody piece of bloody paper. There were at least six people in England — which, thanks to Margaret Thatcher's hand-baggings, was temporarily at or near the axis of the world — who would be prepared to vouch that I was whoever I said I damn well was. After a minute, though, the far-fetched barricade collapsed. I stood amid the flattened bags and their scattered contents, the taped voice fell silent and I had to admit that as far as the immigration, the customs and the port captain were concerned, without a passport I was probably not even a classifiable ghost. Without a passport I had no credible identity; for practical purposes, I might as well be dead.

'*Una problema grande,*' I said, trying to wave my arms like John would have done. The bus inspector backed away and blinked. 'Lost it. On one of your buses. Five minutes ago. GOT TO GET IT BLOODYWELL BACK.'

At last he was responding. His eyes glinted with unmistakable sympathy and concern.

'Please assist me,' I muttered hoarsely. '*Ayudarme!*'

He raised his arm and pointed to a nearby toilet.

It was a clean, well lighted place, and there were plenty of paper towels there. I wrote '*AYUDARME!*' on one of them and flashed it in front of a clerk who was standing in the window of the first tourist agency I could find. Her reaction was slow in coming, but when she had grasped the gist of my story she hurried me back to the inspector and delivered him such a galvanic account of my loss that he leapt into a breakdown truck, switched on its revolving lights and roared off in pursuit of my lost self.

The yellow flashes disappeared among other glittering constellations along the snarling boulevard and I tried to recollect when life had last seemed so desolate. Losing one's passport was, I thought, more debilitating than having mumps or measles, for though you had then felt that death was imminent, you had at least escaped a week of boiled cabbage, religious education and double woodwork. On the scale of character-assassinations, losing your passport ranked somewhere between failing your driving test and the ultimate death of being seen wearing trousers you could get out of without first having to take off your shoes.

I massaged my aching veins and groaned. Before I straightened up I envisaged Mrs Ezra telling Katy that it was a dolorous tragedy of gastronomic proportions, J M Barrie slamming down a window on Peter Pan's shadow, and among the scattered bags, Peter and the Lost Boys insisting so shrilly that I was now admissible to the Never Land that I did not hear the breakdown truck roar back into the station.

'*Señor,*' beamed the inspector, holding up the plastic bag by its ears, '*lo he fundado.*'

'*Muchas gracias,*' I replied. 'You are quite a magician.'

Whereupon he drew out a watch and blew on his whistle. I stepped quickly forward, and the assembly of coaches dispersed towards the sea.

*

I sailed from Tenerife one lunch-time when the tour-packaged visitors were making for the pizzerias. If they even so much as glanced at the small sailboat that was edging out between the breakwaters it was only because a swarm of buzzing water-scooters seemed to be attacking it like wasps going at a split plum.

The irritants dropped behind, two by two. In the wind-shadow of Tenerife the howling Kawasakis fell away, the concrete shoreline sank beneath the sea and by the time I pumped the Primus for my evening meal only the smooth green sides of Mount Teide were there to watch me go.

I expected to have the mountain's company for days. On my coming to Tenerife from the north I had sighted the 12,000-foot peak at a distance of sixty-five miles, so clear had been the visibility. But when I left Tenerife the mountain stayed in view for only eight hours, for dust carried by the easterly wind had blotted it from view by sunrise on the following day. Losing something the size of a 12,000-foot mountain was a little careless of me but it didn't hinder progress. In the first twenty-four hours of her east-west trans-Atlantic passage *Kylie* averaged four point eight knots over the ground. I reefed the mainsail and carried only a small headsail during the hours of darkness, for we were still in the Horse Latitudes and I did not want one of John's midnight squalls to catch me napping.

Of greater concern than the loss of Tenerife was that I also misplaced the horizon. The wind had backed a point north and puffed itself up to more than twenty knots: that was the good news, for *Kylie* could now make six knots. The bad news was that the same wind had also rouged the sky and powdered everything with all the acres of Sahara that lay west of Timbuktu. The dust gathered in little piles in the corners of the cockpit, it filmed my spectacles and scummed my afternoon tea, which was bad enough. What was worse, it gummed-up the horizon as well. For six days I beam-reached in a rising wind that peaked at thirty knots. The skies were grey, the sun invisible, and the waves that broke aboard chilled me to the bone. Where were all the sunlit seas and the fluffy trade-wind clouds that Hiscock had written about? I slotted-in the storm boards, warmed my hands above the galley stove and went by dead reckoning. It was no better than the North Sea in winter.

Six days out from Tenerife *Kylie* had covered about 650 miles in a south-westerly direction. Erratic sights and scribbled figures told me I was at 21°N, 26°W. The Admiralty's *Ocean Passages for the World* suggested that I should keep on going south-west for some days longer before heading due west for Barbados, the nearest West Indian island. To head west any earlier, said the pundits, would detain one's boat among winds which did not quite know where they were going. It seemed to me that the winds I was experiencing were altogether stronger and more certain of their direction than those the pundits had met with, but their passages had usually been made at the end of autumn whereas I was crossing some months later. I went by the wisdom of the ancients for another hour or two but the increasing wind eroded my faith in the printed word and before long I had turned decisively to the right, had brought the wind on my starboard quarter and was steering a composite great-circle course for Barbados, sailing by the seat of my pants in thirty-plus knots of gale.

Although the seas were high, under only a storm jib *Kylie*'s motion was not too uncomfortable and I was able to nap quite restfully, lying on the cabin sole with the alarm clock tucked beneath my chin. This mode of rest is eccentric only as regards the alarm clock. People with normal hearing would give it a more comfortable lodging in a hammock or on a shelf; my problem was that I couldn't hear the bell unless it was within eighteen inches of my better ear. With the clock lodged between chin and collar bone I slept confidently, for I knew that even if the acoustics didn't alert me, the vibrations of metal against bone would jar me awake at half-hourly intervals.

Calculations may suggest that half an hour is too long a period for a small boat travelling at six knots to be without its look-out. If you can see a steamship at five miles, and your combined speed of approach is, say, twenty knots, then the barest minimum between look-outs should be...what? twelve minutes?

Well, yes, of course it should. But much depends on where one is sailing. A vessel in the English Channel will need a pair of alert eyes on watch all the time, but the further she is from the shipping lanes and fishing grounds, the lower is the likelihood of encountering other vessels. Away from the shipping routes I will sometimes heave-to and sleep for half a day. On the other hand, near land or the likely tracks of other ships I'll perhaps not close my eyes at all for fifty hours. At this particular stage of the voyage, where I hadn't quite cleared the north-south axis of the routes from South Africa to Europe, I reckoned that half-hour naps were pitched at an acceptable level of risk. So saying, I glanced up at the masthead light and went complacently below.

A day later I had no masthead light. The failure wasn't the fault of either the bulb, the wiring or the battery; it was all to do with the brand-new engine. The engine had been designed and made by German engineers of international fame. When installed in cars, such engines seemed to carry all before them; in boats they didn't do much good at all. This opinion is not altogether my own; I later found out that it was also the view of the manufacturers who, unknown to me, had given them up as a bad job and withdrawn from the marine market altogether, which perhaps explains why their one-time agents in Tenerife were so anxious to sell me a replacement engine at such a huge discount. And it also explains why, like its predecessor, the new engine conked out almost as soon as it heard the awful news that Atlantic waves were slightly higher and bumpier than the sleeping policemen it ran over on land.

While playing the flip side of the voyage I need to mention that other unhelpful things happened too: I tore the luff of the genoa while changing sails, I fractured another shroud plate in heavy seas and I lost most of an upper-left back tooth while chewing a stick of gum. For a time my natural buoyancy of character deserted me: on the eighth day I vowed in the log that I would surely sell the engine and buy a pair of carpet slippers with the proceeds when I reached the West Indies.

Despite the set-back I didn't once doubt that I'd get there. Until the tenth day I was heading for Barbados but when I re-read my borrowed copy of Hart and Stone's *Caribbean Pilot* and learned that Barbados offered little more than an open-roadstead anchorage I opted for Antigua instead. I think I was right to do so. English Harbour at Antigua was totally protected; there, *Kylie* could lie alongside for engine-repairs without being at the mercy of waves and wind. Though it added 200 miles to the voyage, I altered course to north of west and headed for Antigua. Then I lit the cabin oil-lamp and played the better side of that day's disc. The music was tuneful and the lyrics sounded good: *Kylie* was averaging five point nine knots under a deep-reefed main and working jib, the bilge was dry, the bedding was warm and a lovely stew was simmering on the stove. What more could I want? I towelled my pink and wrinkled skin and yearned for the sun.

It burst through the grey-papered sky like a clown through a hoop, all spangles and smiles. I stripped off my shirt, hung the sextant round my neck, lashed myself between the mast and shrouds and prepared to take a sun-sight. With my feet spread wide and my body swaying to *Kylie's*

'I chivvied the sun down towards the horizon.'

plunges and rolls, I chivvied the sun down towards the horizon, but the horizon was bashful and elusive, which wasn't altogether a surprise considering that the two parties hadn't seen each other for weeks. Every time the sun got close, the horizon slid herself behind a fold of sea, and whenever she popped up again the sun covered his embarrassment by zooming off into a cloud. 'Stay still!' I admonished them. 'Keep your minds on the job.' At last, however, I got them to touch each other. Although the encounter was only brief, it was decisive. The sun stole out from a cloud. By twiddling the tangent-screw on the sextant arc I persuaded him to place a kiss on her naked flank. I stared at them critically through the telescope. When I saw the kiss was not a deeply wet one I started counting off the seconds. Then I lowered the sextant and left them to it.

Back in the cabin, the sextant was dabbed with fresh water, dried off and stowed away in its box before I wiped my hands and set-to with the figures. After twenty minutes I was pencilling a cross on the chart. The crosses were pencilled on the chart noonday after noonday, sometimes less than two inches apart. The dusty air cleared, and with each successive day the sun became brighter and the seas lower until on the eleventh day after leaving Tenerife I was able to spend a whole afternoon in the cockpit for the first time and think about distance run and distance still to go.

According to the accounts of others, the time taken to sail from the Canaries to the West Indies can vary greatly, depending on the strength and direction of the winds and, to a lesser extent, upon the waterline length of the boat. An admirable set of benchmarks are those chiselled out by the Hiscocks, a couple who have practised standards of seamanship that others can only strive to equal and never excel. Their first ocean-crossing from La Palma to Barbados took twenty-six days and eight hours. It was made in *Wanderer II*, a vessel 26ft 5ins on the waterline, during October and November of 1952. Thirty years later my friends Laurence Clegg and Vanessa Banks in their 39-ft Ohlson *Ganadero* took only a few hours longer to make the same passage at the same time of year. Both vessels were beset by calms, and *Ganadero* had to contend against headwinds during the latter part of the crossing. These and other experiences seem to show that passages made before Christmas are generally rather slow but pleasant affairs, while crossings during winter and spring are often much faster but less comfortable.

I was therefore not surprised to find that even on her short waterline of twenty-one feet, by noon on the eleventh day *Kylie* had sailed some 1,200 miles at an average speed of four point seven knots. I wasn't out to break any records but if the wind remained constant in strength and direction it seemed possible that we might make the crossing in less than twenty-four days.

I did not try to help her do it; for one thing I was tired, and for another I was timid. Even when the wind decreased to a steady fifteen knots I chose to idle along under the smaller genoa and often — to my shame — a double-reefed main. Why, I thought, should I try to go faster? My consumption of only three point three pints of water a day meant that my tea-kettle would not be dry until at least three more weeks had passed. I had time and enough to doze, to practise my harmonica, to admire the sunsets and to read about the dolphins I ought to be seeing but wasn't. Together we passed a lovely, unstressful time, punctuated by some unlooked-for delights, and a visit from someone whom I knew well. Under-canvassed though she was, on her fifteenth day at sea *Kylie* covered 142 miles at five point nine knots. I measured half a pint of water into the kettle, popped a tea-bag into the orange-coloured mug and lit the Primus stove. While waiting for the kettle to boil, I bore a small brandy into the cockpit to celebrate a new 'best day's run'. A bevy of girlish clouds flounced by, holding down their skirts. Gazing after their fluffy outlines, I wondered loudly whether I might make Antigua in less than 22 days.

'Mind the kettle, else it will boil dry,' said a voice.

'I hadn't forgotten,' I said to her. 'And will you have a cup?'

'Yes,' she said, looking no older than the day we wed.

But by the time I tipped back the brandy she had gone.

My timidity and torpor were evident in the galley as well. I like eating red meat, but only if I haven't had to bone it and clean it beforehand. I will eat fish if it is offered, but the idea of catching one and butchering it in the cockpit does nothing to set adrenalin racing round my limbs. On the other hand, I have no qualms about cracking eggs, de-gutting melons, skinning tomatoes or stripping-down a lettuce. Most of all, I go mad for corned beef, and have been known to empty a chain locker of forty fathoms of short-link cable just to get at an eight-ounce tin of it in time for supper.

For all these reasons *Kylie*'s menus might be thought stodgy, repetitious, unbalanced and dull. Mondays and Thursdays are spaghetti bolognaise, Tuesdays and Fridays are beef stew, Wednesdays and Sundays rissoles. By way of excitement, Saturdays are tinned sausages. Sometimes the meat is graced with salads, but only if in season and when less than four days out from port.

Not only do I never tire of such food but in sixteen years of cruising I have never suffered stomach upsets or any dietary disease that flesh is heir to. On this voyage I took particular care to buy several pounds of oranges and lemons before leaving the Canaries. These lasted well, and I ate the last of the citrus only two days before I arrived at Antigua.

At half-past eleven in the morning of our nineteenth day at sea we crossed tracks with another vessel, a laden tanker creaming eastwards, with high plumes rising from the widely flared bow. I longed to speak to her watchkeeper, for the encounter offered my first chance of talking with another human being after almost three weeks of silence. But although I looked briefly at my hand-held walkie-talkie I could not bring myself to take the instrument from its rack and switch it on. Old fears die hard; if I couldn't see the speaker's lips I knew I might not be able to understand what was being said. Instead, I settled for the safer thrill of taking a bearing of the tanker's masts in transit. By relating the bearing to *Kylie*'s charted position, I deduced that the vessel had passed between Martinique and Guadeloupe. I thought that perhaps she was laden with crude oil from Curaçao and bound for the English Channel.

Before the excitement of meeting another ship had died away my spirits were raised further at sunset when the wind backed a point to the north. I adjusted the poled-out genoa and over the ensuing three hours the Walker log recorded speeds of six point five knots. My elation lasted throughout the night, but by ten o'clock the following morning I had again reduced to a storm jib. With the wind gusting at thirty knots, *Kylie*'s cockpit was once more a wet and dismal place but I was not unhappy for the North Equatorial Current was running at full spate and my boat was making six knots over the ground.

At sunset on the twenty-first day I knew that I was not far from land, for that evening a lone gannet skimmed among the swells to the north. Made eager by its coming, I shook out a reef, hung a lantern in the backstays and tried to imagine what Antigua would look like.

At half-past seven on the morning of the twenty-second day I found out. The island came up fine on the starboard bow, just a grey-green smudge on a slate-grey sea, riven by rods of rain. It was not a picturesque landfall. In fact, even an up-market copy-writer might have called it rather drab, but after 2,700 miles of ocean my tired eyes could not have wished for anything better.

Before midday the rain lifted. In bright sunshine I reached into the lee of the Pillars of Hercules and wound my way among the anchored boats.

In Ordnance Bay I backed the jib and struggled to prise the swollen plug out of the navel pipe.

From the shore a black man smiled at my clumsy impatience.

'Take it easy, man. You got all the time in the world here.'

I smiled back and relaxed, for I had seen what he had said. Not only had I *seen* the words, I had also *understood* them. Antigua, I decided, was a good place for my ears to get to, for I had read those wide West Indian lips at twenty yards.

L' Envoi

Beneath the euphoria, an air of regret steals among the anchored boats at the end of their ocean crossings. When the sails have been covered, the sextant stowed and the beer drunk, the navigator's mind turns to the ruling-off of pages. Although another twenty thousand miles of sea may still lie between him and his final goal, he will work out his elapsed time and average speed for his first ocean crossing with elaborate care, stroking his chin over the figures with the mien of one who has just discovered the origins of the universe, or devised a neat way to open a bag of peanuts in a crowded bar. But however many times he may traverse the same wide waters in the years to come, and however easier or more arduous those crossings may prove to be, his memory will still cherish the sad sweetness he tasted when he completed his first voyage across an ocean, for that moment will never come again.

And when the ocean miles have been totted up and the columns ruled off, he will shut his logbook and, likely as not, he will put it on a shelf awhile, and address himself to the trickier business of covering miles on land, in the same way that I am now laying aside this narrative before risking my neck on the narrower but more dangerous highway that winds from Southwold down to London.

But *Kylie*'s odyssey is unfinished, and to end this account with her arrival at an island which, for all its sun and fun, is most commonly nothing more than a stopover on the way to someplace else, smacks of literary fraud. A story half told, you may very well say, is worse than no story at all. So I will tell you why it is right for me to lay aside *Kylie*'s tale for a year or two.

I will tie the matter up briefly, so the ligature will avoid embarrassing stains, and we can be on our ways ashore.

My marriage was not fashioned in heaven, but in England. During the years between the wedding and her death, Pip and I sometimes gored each other deeply, but our hearts were robust and, despite the blood-letting, our marriage did survive. We kept our charted course for our children's sakes, and because we wished to hold fast to our promise, and because we loved one another. Loved one another, that is, not as the snarling animals we often were — for neither of us was forgiving enough to love the other *despite* the faults, nor agile enough to love the other because of them. Rather, we loved one another because of the power, the logic and — I might as well say it — the music of such words as *Let me not to the marriage of true minds admit impediments.*

'The coupling of minds,' we agreed, 'is what it's all about; not just willies and pussies, but minds...'

Well, our marriage managed to survive, but as Pip fought against death it did more than merely that. On the drear hills of her sickness, love flowered again, vividly and surprisingly, like yellow gorse in the grey days of winter. As I lay tenderly beside her in the curtained room, only hours from when the warm flesh I was embracing would be clay, she wrenched her mind from the cancers which were pressing on her brain, tore down the veil of darkness hanging above us and, with her hand clasping mine, lifted us both into a world where all was pleasing to the senses and agreeable to the mind. For five short days and nights she described it to me, methodically and in detail, before her body became cold to my fingers forever. And in learning of this world from her lips, on her deathbed I loved her anew.

After her death, with my hopes kindled by a man with a scythe, a man who had prophesied 'Nothing dies; everything grows...' when fowls of the air were entombed in ice, I hungered for more news from my dead bride. I was sure it would not be an utterance I could read with my eyes: there would be no comets seen, no burning bushes, no tablets of stone, no fireworks from heaven. My eyes would be useless; any message would come in spoken words, for *In the beginning*, we had been taught by St John, *was the Word*.

Yet no words had come. In the gales of the North Sea I had heard only the roar of chaos. Beyond the Biscay's 100-fathom line, though I had listened long, I had heard nothing from her. During the crossing of that bay, other friends had tendered advice, but never a word had come from the friend I had loved most. I had drifted into the Valley of the Shadow in Majorca and had not heard her voice among those of lesser princesses from Acre, Aquitaine and Peru. And with the passing of years, resentment had overlain hope, settling like dust on crystal, until it seemed that I had been wilfully cut off from the most articulate mind I had ever known.

But suppose that she was, after all, speaking from beyond the veil, and was not getting through to me? I became prey to the notion that my deafness was not partial, but profound and entire; that it proceeded not from a deformity of my acoustic nerves but from the weakness of my spirit; that however faintly I might hear her voice, my flabby soul would not heed it.

Then after fourteen years, at a time when I was so preoccupied with seafaring pleasures that I had forgotten to rehearse my daily script of resentment and guilt, she had slipped into *Kylie's* cockpit and homed in, as she always did, on the practicalities of everyday life:

'Mind the kettle,' she had said, 'else it will boil dry.'

Closing the logbook, I laid it in a locker and pulled on a clean shirt. The words were not what I had expected to hear, but at least they had pierced the veil.

I shut *Kylie's* cabin and went to stretch my legs at Nelson's Dockyard. By sailing there, I had voyaged to the thresholds of lands which, in the days of William Pitt her ancestor, had been called The New World.

Well, the New World must await my coming for a while. For the moment, all that mattered was that I had sailed out of a very long silence.

15
Glossary of Nautical Terms as Used in this Book

Aback : A sail is aback when its clew is to windward. Inattentive helming or a sudden change of wind may cause the sail to be *taken aback*.

Abaft : Towards the stern of a vessel in relation to some other position; e.g. *abaft the beam*.

Abeam : Having a bearing or position at right angles to the fore-and-aft line of the ship.

About : A sailing vessel will *come about, go about*, or *put about* when she goes through the wind from one tack to the other.

Adrift : A rope or line is adrift when it becomes loose or unfastened from its intended place.

Aft : Towards the stern.

Aloft : Above; overhead.

America's Cup : Prestigious trophy, competed for internationally by large racing yachts since 1870.

Amidships : The centreline of the vessel. *To put the helm amidships* is to centre the tiller.

Anti-fouling : Paint that inhibits the growth of weed and other marine organisms, applied to the underwater parts of the hull.

Astern : In a rearward direction; behind.

Awning : Plastic or canvas cover spread above the decks as protection against sun and rain.

Back, to : (1) To sheet the clew of sail to windward. (2) In the northern hemisphere, the wind *backs* if it changes its direction anti-clockwise; i.e. by shifting from, for example, south to south-east.

Backstay : A wire rope supporting the mast from aft.

Ballast : Weight carried in or immediately above the keel to give the vessel stability.

Bar : Shallow area at the mouth of a river or a harbour.

Batten : Usually, a wooden or plastic strip inserted into a horizontal pocket in the roach (i.e. the curved leech of a sail) to prevent it from flapping. *Full battens* stiffen the entire width of a sail.

Beam : (1) The widest transverse dimension of a ship. (2) A transverse member of the ship's frame.

Bear away, to : To alter course away from the wind by moving the tiller to windward.

Bearing : Angle in degrees or compass points between the direction of the True or Magnetic North Pole and the direction of an object. In *Kylie*, as in other small boats, bearings are taken by using a hand-held magnetic compass. At night, the navigator may fix the vessel's position by taking a *rising* (or *dipping*) bearing of a light of a known elevation immediately it appears above the horizon (or just before it disappears below it).

Beat, to : To sail to windward in a series of zigzag courses, with the wind on alternate bows.

Beaufort force : Scale used for measuring wind-strength, devised by Rear Admiral Sir Francis Beaufort. On the scale, force 0 is calm and force 12 is a hurricane, i.e. more than 65 knots of wind.

Bend : A knot which fastens one rope to another, a sheet to an eye, a line to a spar, etc.

Berth : (1) A sleeping-place aboard. (2) A place where a ship may lie.

Bight : (1) A loop or curve in a rope. (2) A very wide bay.

Bilge : (1) The space beneath the cabin sole. (2) The curve of the hull between the sides and the keel.

Bitts : A pair of stumpy pillars attached to the deck, and on which mooring lines are secured in figures-of-eight.

Block : A pulley with one or more sheaves.

Boathook : A pole with a metal hook at one end, used for latching onto mooring buoys, etc.

Bollard : A stumpy pillar set into the ground, to which mooring lines are secured.

Boom : A horizontal spar for extending the foot of the mainsail.

Bo'sun : (Shortened form of Boatswain) Senior person in charge of all deck-working crew, taking orders from the ship's officers.

Bottlescrew : A screw used to adjust the tension of standing rigging.

Bow-roller : Sheave mounted in the bows, over which passes the anchor cable.

Bows : The forepart of a ship's hull.

Bowsprit : A spar on which a jib is set, projecting beyond the bows.

Break out, to : (1) When weighing anchor, the flukes of the anchor will *break out* (become free) of the seabed. The vessel will then be *under way*. (2) To unfurl, by a tug on the halyard, a flag which has been hoisted rolled-up.

Bridge deck : Aboard *Kylie*, the term is a grandiose euphemism for the horizontal surface of a watertight box at the forward end of the cockpit.

Bring up, to : To anchor.

Broadside : Sideways on.

Bruce (anchor) : An anchor of relatively modern design, looking like a three-fingered claw.

Bunt : The middle section of a sail.

Cable : (1) Unit of measurement: 600 feet (approx. one-tenth of a nautical mile). (2) Chain or rope attached to anchor.

Capping or *Toe-rail* : Strip of wood running along the top of the vessel's sides. In *Kylie*, two inches above the deck.

Cast off, to : To let go; unfasten.

Catamaran : A twin-hulled craft of shallow draught, having a deck between the hulls. Capable of higher speeds than a conventional monohull craft, but sometimes less well able to progress upwind.

Caulk, to : To drive cotton material into the seams of wooden decks or hull planks to make them watertight.

Centreboarder : A relatively shallow-draught vessel, having a pivoted board or plate on its centreline. When lowered, the board increases the lateral resistance of the hull, so enabling it to sail better into the wind. However, such a vessel is likely to have a higher centre of gravity than a deep-keel boat, and thereby has less inbuilt stability.

Chafe : The rubbing together of, for example, sails and ropes.

Chafing-gear : Material such as rubber or plastic tubing, or strips of canvas, used to prevent chafe.

Chain locker : Compartment below the deck for the stowage of the anchor cable.

Chocks : Wooden blocks used to prevent deck gear such as anchors from moving about in rough weather.

Cleat : Deck fitting on which halyards, sheets, etc., may be secured.

Clew : The lower rear corner of a fore-and-aft sail.

Clinker : Wooden boatbuilding method in which the edges of planks forming the hull overlap each other.

Clipper : Very fast 19th-century sailing vessel.

Close hauled : A vessel is *close-hauled* when sailing as nearly as possible into the wind, yet with her sails still full.

Coachroof : The cabin top.

Coaming : The sides of a hatch, cabin or cockpit that project above the deck.

Cocked hat : On a chart, the triangle formed by three bearings.

Cockpit : Well near the stern in which the helmsman stands or sits while steering.

Codline : Small-diameter line.

Colour-shades : Red or blue shades on the sextant to reduce the glare of the sun or its reflections on the sea.

Companionway : The opening from the cabin to the cockpit.

Course : The direction in which a vessel is sailing, measured in degrees (or compass-points) from 000° (or North).

CQR (anchor) : Trade name (a phoneticization of 'Secure') of a patented anchor resembling two ploughshares placed back-to-back and joined together along their upper edges.

Crown : The part of the anchor where the arms join the shank.

Cutter : A single-masted vessel with a mainsail and two foresails.

Danforth : An American anchor with large pivoting flukes.

Davit : A small crane for lifting a dinghy aboard.

Dead reckoning or *D.R.* : The arithmetical account of the ship's position, using only the course steered and the log-distance run through the water, and making no allowance for the effects of currents, tidal streams and the wind.

Deckhead : The underside of a deck; the 'ceiling' of a cabin beneath the deck.

Depthsounder : Electric instrument which transmits sound-waves to the seabed and, from the time taken for the sounds to bounce back, measures the depth of water.

Dhow : A sail-trading vessel of the Middle East and Indian Ocean, having one or more masts with a backward-raking, high-pointed triangular (*lateen*) sail on each.

Diaphone : The prolonged bellow terminating in a grunt that is emitted by light stations in foggy weather.

Dinghy : Small open boat, driven usually by outboard motor, oars or sail. *Kylie's* dinghy is like a rubbery doughnut inflated by a foot-pump. Used as a tender to ferry crew and stores to shore.

Distance run : Distance travelled through the water.

Dividers : Measuring-compasses.

Doldrums : The belt of equatorial calms between the northern and southern trade-winds.

Double Matthew Walker : A knot formed at the end of a rope to stop the rope from running through an eye.

Drag, to : An anchor drags if it fails to hold a vessel in position.

Draught : The depth of water in which the vessel becomes afloat; i.e. the distance from the waterline to the deepest point of the keel. *Shoal-draught* vessels such as catamarans *draw* (i.e. occupy) a lesser depth of water than do vessels such as *Kylie*.

Draw, to let : To slacken the weather sheet of the jib and take in the lee sheet so that the sail fills and drives the vessel forward.

Duckboard : Low platform resting on cockpit sole to keep one's feet dry.

Ease, to : To slacken.

Ebb : The flow of the tidal current as it recedes. *Quarter ebb* and *half ebb* are intermediate stages of the process.

Ensign : The vessel's national flag.

Estimated Position or E.P. : The Dead Reckoning Position after adjustment for the effects of wind, currents and tidal streams. A navigator will use an Estimated Position as a basis for his *sun-sights* and *star-sights*

Fair : (Of winds, tides and currents) : Favourable.

Fall : The hauling part of a rope.

Fathom : Former unit of measurement (six feet, or 1.8256 metres) for depths of water or lengths of rope. Still used aboard *Kylie* for practical as well as philosophical reasons, but little used elsewhere.

Felucca : Mediterranean vessels with lateen sails. Now almost extinct.

Fender : Plastic, air-filled cushion hung overside to prevent damage when lying alongside a quay or another vessel.

Fin-and-skeg : A deep and narrow keel, (the "fin"), plus a shorter, protective piece immediately forward of the rudder.

Fine : (Of a relative bearing or direction) : At a small angle (e.g. *fine on the bow*).

Fisherman (anchor) : The basic, traditional anchor with curved, fixed flukes.

Fisherman's bend : A knot sometimes used to secure a rope to a ring.

Fix, to : To determine a vessel's position by taking bearings (by eye or radio-waves) of charted features or celestial objects, or by satellite-navigation systems.

Flood stream : Flow of the tidal stream when the tide is rising. *First of the flood* is the beginning of such a flow.

Flog, to : (Used of a sail) : To beat about uselessly in the wind.

Flukes : The triangular, digging parts of an anchor.

Foot : The lower edge of a sail.

Fore-and-aft : In a direction from the bows to the stern, and parallel with the keel.

Forehatch : Covered opening in the deck in the forward part of the vessel.

Forenoon : The period between 8 a.m. and noon.

Forepeak : Under-deck compartment in bows of the vessel.

Foresail : Aboard *Kylie*, any sail set forward of the mast.

Forestay : Wire rope running from the upper section of the mast to a deck fitting in the bows. Acts with backstays to brace the mast in a fore-and-aft direction, and provides track for hanks of foresails.

Freeboard : Height of the ship's side above the water.

Gaff : On a fore-and-aft rigged ship, the spar at the top of the four-sided mainsail.

Gaiter : Cover for a bottlescrew.

Gale : On the Beaufort scale, a wind of between 34 and 47 knots.

Galley : A ship's kitchen.

Gelcoat : Outer coat of glassfibre constructions.

Genoa : Large foresail, the clew of which overlaps the mainsail. *Kylie* carries two genoas, number 1 being the larger.

Ghoster : Large, light-weather foresail.

Gimbals : A mounting and suspension system which permits galley stoves, compasses, oil-lamps, etc., to remain more-or-less horizontal when the ship is canted from the vertical.

Great circle : Any circle (e.g. the equator) that girdles the earth's surface and has its centre in the middle of the earth. In theory, the shortest distance between two ports will be the arc of the great circle on which the ports lie. In practice, motor-driven vessels on long-distance voyages will plan to steer a series of rhumb-line courses that approximate to the curve of the great circle. Sailing vessels, however, have to make the best they can of the wind and weather, and great-circle sailing is much less relevant to their navigational decisions.

Ground tackle : Inclusive term for a vessel's anchors and the chain and/or line attached to them.

Groyne : Wall built at an angle to the shore to stop the scouring of beaches by currents and waves.

Guardrope : Rope passing through stanchions at the ship's sides to prevent people falling overboard.

Gulet : Type of Turkish boat, these days almost always driven by a powerful engine although possessing masts and sails.

Gunwales : Edges of the boat's side above the level of the maindeck.

Gybe, to : To cause the mainsail to swing across the ship's stern by allowing the wind to catch the sail on the opposite side. The stronger is the wind, the more necessary is it that the gybe shall be carefully controlled, otherwise much damage may occur.

Halyard : Rope for raising and lowering a sail.

Hand, to : To take in a sail.

Handy Billy : Mechanism of pulleys and ropes which triples or quadruples the effort applied.

Hang in stays, to : To remain overlong head to wind while tacking.

Hank : (1) A clip used to hold the luff of a foresail to a stay. (2) A coil.

Harness : Safety harness is of strong webbing, and is clipped on to a deckline or other strong fitment to prevent the wearer being lost overboard.

Hawser : Rope with circumference of five inches or more.

Head : (1) The ship's bow. (2) Upper corner of a triangular sail.

Headsail : Aboard *Kylie*, any sail (such as a jib or genoa) hoisted forward of the foremost mast.

Heave-to, to : To set the sails and rudder so that the vessel is lying almost stationary.

Heaving-line : Light line, often with weighted end, cast to the shore when coming alongside so that a mooring-rope attached to the shipboard end can be hauled ashore.

Heel, to : To lean sideways.

Helm : Another name for the tiller, used for steering the vessel. To put the *helm down* is to move the tiller away from the wind, thereby bringing the vessel's head farther into the wind, while to put the *helm up* is to do the opposite.

High water : The top of the flood tide.

Hoist : The part of a flag nearest to the flagstaff or the line of the halyard.

Holding : A good holding is a sea-bed in which an anchor will remain firm.

Hull : The body of the vessel.

Inboard : Towards the centreline of the vessel.

Irons, to be in : To lie stationary with head to wind, unable to pay off onto a tack.

Jaws : The 'U'-shaped inner end of a gaff that enables it to pivot on the mast.

Jib : Triangular headsail set on the forestay. *Kylie* carries a working jib and a smaller, heavier storm jib.

Jill about, to : To sail round and about the same area, with the sails barely drawing.

Jury mast : A makeshift mast.

Junk : Far Eastern sailing vessel, having low bows, a high stern and quadrilateral sails stiffened with battens.

Keel : Lowermost section of the sailboat's hull. In *Kylie*, an integral part, incorporating the ballast.

Ketch : A two-masted, fore-and-aft rigged vessel, having the after (or miz(z)en) mast mounted forward of the sternpost.

Knockdown : The action of a sailing vessel being rolled over onto her side by the wind or waves until the mast lies in the water.

Knot : (1) A speed of one nautical mile (generally taken as 6,080 feet) per hour. (2) Used loosely to refer to a motley of bends and hitches in ropes.

Latitude : Angular distance north or south of the equator. A *latitude by observation* or *observed latitude* is one which has been calculated by taking a sun sight at noon or a star sight of Polaris at twilight.

Lanyard : A short line.

Lay, to : (1) A navigator will *lay off* a course on a chart. (2) A vessel can *lay* the course if she can keep to it without tacking.

Leading light : A light guiding the way through a navigational hazard.

Leech : Rear edge of a triangular sail.

Lee : The side of the object away from the wind.

'Lee-oh!' : Warning given by helmsman to crew as he pushes the tiller downwind (or puts the helm down) so as to bring the vessel on to the opposite tack.

Lee shore : Any coast downwind of the vessel; one which is, therefore, potentially dangerous because it is difficult to get away from.

Lee-cloth : Canvas side-pieces attached to berths and braced to the deckhead by lanyards to prevent occupants from being thrown out by the vessel's motion.

Leeward : In a down-wind direction.

Levanter : The strong easterly or north-easterly wind of the Mediterranean.

Lie-to, to : A vessel *lies-to* when, in a gale, she sails about 60° off the wind, making just enough headway to prevent the seas catching her broadside on.

List: A sideways inclination from the vertical.

Log : (1) Instrument (sometimes referred to as *Walker's log* or *patent log*) for measuring the distance a vessel has progressed through the water. Comprises in *Kylie* a 'clock', to which is attached a rotator towed on a logline. (2) Short for logbook.

Logbook : Daily record-book of navigational, weather and other relevant information.

Longitude : Angular distance East or West of the Greenwich meridian.

Longshore : Of a boat which works near the coast.

Loom : (1) The inboard part of an oar. (2) The vague first appearance of land or a light from a light-station.

Loose-footed : (Of a sail) : not having its lower edge attached to a boom.

Luff : The leading edge of a fore-and-aft sail.

Luff, to : To bring the vessel's head closer up into the wind.

Magnetic : In navigation, used to differentiate between bearings or courses which are True (i.e. related to the geographical poles) and those which relate to the magnetic, or compass, poles. To convert from the one to the other, the navigator applies *Variation* and *Deviation*.

Main beam : The principal transverse support beneath the deck. In *Kylie*, it is beneath the heel of the mast.

Mainsail or *main* : The principal sail; in a sloop such as *Kylie*, the sail on the after side of the mast. A *full main* is an unreefed mainsail.

Make fast, to : To secure firmly.

Make good, to : To cover distance over the seabed.

Marcq St Hilaire : French naval officer who introduced a method of fixing a vessel's position by constructing intercepting lines derived from astronomical observations.

Marina : A harbour specifically for pleasure boaters.

Mast hoops : Wooden rings circling the mast and attached to the mainsail luff, so enabling the sail to be raised and lowered.

Meltemi : The summer wind of the Aegean Sea.

Mercator chart : Type of sea-map devised by Gerardus Mercator, the 16th- century geographer, having the virtue of allowing rhumb lines to be drawn as straight lines. An even more necessary invention than sliced bread.

Monkey's fist : *Turk's head* knot made around a ball, used as a weight at the end of a heaving-line.

Mooring : A lying-place secured alongside a quay, or between buoys or piles, or attached to anchors fore and aft.

Navel pipe : Deck pipe through which anchor cable emerges from its stowage place below decks.

Neap tide : The smallest range of tide, occurring about half way between full moon and new moon.

North Equatorial Current : In the North Atlantic Ocean, a broad west-going current impinging on the West Indies and the northern coast of South America.

Null : A meaningfully silent part of the arc of an R.D.F bearing.

Oilies : Waterproof clothing, formerly of oiled canvas but now of plastic.

Offing : The distance a vessel keeps away from the land.

Open roadstead : An offshore anchorage lacking protection in onshore winds or swells.

Osmosis : The absorption of moisture (and hence the weakening) of a glass-fibre hull.

Outboard : Outside the vessel.

Over-canvassed : Having too much sail up.

Painter : Line used for securing a small boat, e.g. a dinghy or tender, to a larger boat or to the shore.

Parallel rule : A navigational tool for laying-off bearings and courses on the chart.

Parcel, to : To bind canvas or tape round a rope to make it watertight.

Pay off, to : (1) To allow the ship's head to fall away from the wind. (2) A seaman is paid off when he is given his wages and discharged from service at the end of a voyage.

Pay out, to : To ease out, to slacken.

Peak : Upper outmost corner of a four-sided mainsail.

Pendant : A hanging rope used, for example, to reef the mainsail.

Pilot : (1) One who navigates a ship in sight of land, especially where the water is shallow and the land is close. (2) Short for pilot book.

Pintle : Metal pin on leading edge of the rudder. Dropping into a metal ring or gudgeon on the vessel's stern, it fixes the rudder in position.

Pitch : The distance a vessel is moved forward by one revolution of the propeller.

Pitch, to : To see-saw in a fore-and-aft motion in the waves.

Pitchpole, to : To roll (or, more exactly, to be rolled) end-over-end by a wave.

Point : A compass has 32 points, each of 11¼°. Relative bearings or directions may be given as, e.g. two points on the starboard bow, three points abaft the beam, etc.

Point, to : Generally, to sail close to the wind.

Pole : (1) The mast. During a gale, a vessel will be under bare pole(s) if she has no sails up. (2) A spar used to extend the clew of a foresail outboard. Hence expressions such as to *pole out the genoa.*

Pontoon : A floating structure alongside which a vessel may moor.

Poop : Used loosely to refer to the afterdeck beyond the cockpit.

Port : The left-hand side of a vessel as viewed when facing forward.

Position-line : A line, usually a terrestrial bearing or resulting from an astronomical sight, at some point on which a vessel is lying.

Preventer : In *Kylie*, a temporary rope stay between the boom-end and the bows, to prevent a gybe in following winds.

Pulpit : A metal safety frame in the bows, acting as end-support to the guardropes.

Purchase : A rope, most often used with pulleys (or blocks) to achieve a mechanical advantage.

Put out, to : To sally forth.

'Q' flag : A yellow flag worn on entering harbour from abroad, telling the port authorities that the vessel is free of infectious disease and requesting permission to enter.

Quarter : The two after-parts of the vessel on each side of the centreline.

Quartermaster : Experienced seaman with special duty of steering the ship, especially when entering or leaving harbour. Also, the trade-name of *Kylie*'s wind-vane steering gear.

Race : Swift and confused currents, commonly occurring in tidal streams off headlands.

Radar : A radio system which detects the presence and movement of objects.

Radio Direction Finder (or RDF) : Navigational instrument which enables a bearing of a radio beacon to be taken at ranges of up to about 200 miles.

Rail or *toe-rail* : see Capping.

Raise, to : To sight a feature of a coast, a shore-light, a navigational mark or an island.

Reach : A point of sailing where the wind is on the beam, or just forward of the beam. Generally, a vessel sails fastest when *reaching*.

'Ready about!' : Command uttered by helmsman to crew, telling them to prepare to tack.

Reef, to : To reduce the area of a sail exposed to the wind by tying-down (or rolling-up) one or more of its sections. In *Kylie*, to *single-reef, double-reef* or *deep-reef* the mainsail.

Reef points : Short lengths of line on a sail to tie down the surplus material when the sail is reefed.

Rhumb line : A line which crosses all meridians of longitude at the same angle, and is drawn as a straight line on the usual shipboard (Mercator) chart.

Rig : General term used when referring to different numbers and arrangements of masts and sails, e.g. *square rig, fore-and-aft rig, sloop rig, ketch rig*, etc.

Rigging : The wire ropes supporting the mast comprise the *standing rigging*, while the ropes and lines used for raising, lowering and trimming the sails are the *running rigging*.

Rigging screw : See *bottle-screw*.

Roller-reefing : A system by which the area of a sail is reduced by revolving a drum connected to the luff of the sail.

Rudder stock : The part of the rudder between the blade and the rudder head.

Sailboard : A sporty sailcraft comprising a buoyant glass-fibre board on which is mounted a pivoted mast and sail controlled by a wishbone-shaped boom in the grip of its one-person crew.

Satnav : A navigation system which depends on radio transmissions from a number of space satellites.

Scandalize : In *Kylie*, to reduce the area of the mainsail by lowering the head and raising the boom-end.

Scantlings : The dimensions and weight of the parts used in the building of a vessel.

Schooner : Two-masted, fore-and-aft rigged vessel, having a mainmast taller than the foremast.

Scope : The length of cable to which a ship lies when anchored.

Scull, to : To drive a small boat forward by moving an oar from side to side over the stern.

Scuttle : Glazed circular opening in the side of the cabin or hull to admit light and air.

Scuppers : Holes in the ship's sides at deck level allowing water to drain into the sea.

Sea : Wave produced by the wind in the immediate vicinity of vessel.

Self-drainer : Pipe allowing water in the cockpit to flow outboard without the labour of pumping or baling.

Semaphore : System of visual signalling in which the positions of the person's extended arms conveys letters of the alphabet.

Set : (1) The direction a current is flowing. (2) The direction in which a vessel is moved by such a current.

Set, to : (1) To hoist and trim a sail. (2) To set the anchor is to anchor securely, often by motoring hard astern to dig-in the flukes.

Seven-eighths rig : Sloops with a foresail on a stay which runs from a position somewhat below the masthead are said to have a *seven-eighths rig* (as contrasted with a *masthead rig*).

Sextant : Hand-held navigational instrument for measuring angles, most commonly the angle between the sun or a star and the horizon, (a *sun-sight* or a *star-sight*).

Shackle : A 'U'-shaped or bow-shaped loop of steel or bronze, closed at its mouth by a pin, for securing halyards to sails, cables to anchors, etc. A twisted shackle has its pin at right angles to the body.

Shank : The part of the anchor joining the arms to the ring or cable shackle.

Sheet : A line to the clew of a foresail or the boom-end of the mainsail which enables the sail to be trimmed according to the wind, by *sheeting-in* or *hardening sheets*, or, conversely, by *easing sheets*.

Sheet bend : A sort of knot used to secure a rope's end through a small eye; most commonly used aboard *Kylie* for securing a sheet to the clew of the foresail.

Short-handed : Having too few members in the ship's crew.

Shroud : Wire rope supporting the mast laterally.

Single up, to : To reduce the number of mooring lines to one each at the bow and stern.

Skiff : A small, lightweight but firm-hulled rowing or sailing boat.

Sight : A sextant altitude of the sun, moon or star, together with the Greenwich Mean Time (now called Universal Standard Time) of the observation.

Slat : Aboard *Kylie*, wooden strip atop the cockpit seats.

Sloop : A single-masted sailing vessel which carries a single headsail forward of the mast.

Sole : The floor of the cabin or cockpit.

Soundings : The depths of water as shown on the chart. A vessel is in *soundings* when her equipment (e.g. an echo sounder) is able to measure the depth of water beneath her, or is within the 100-fathom contour.

Spinnaker : A three-cornered, full-bellied sail set forward of the mast but not attached to the forestay, used when the relative wind is blowing from abeam or abaft the beam.

Splice, to : To join together, finish the ends of, or form eyes in ropes by weaving together their strands.

Sprayhood : A protective cover at the forward end of the cockpit.

Spreader : A strut from the mast to widen the angle of a shroud to the upper mast.

Spring, to : (Of a mast) : to crack.

Stanchion : Vertical supports at the vessel's sidedecks to carry the guardropes, or a cabin pillar.

Starboard : The right-hand side of a vessel as viewed when facing forward.

Stem, to : A vessel holding her own or making slight progress against a current is *stemming* it.

Stern : The rear end of a vessel.

Sternsheets : The rearmost seats in a open boat.

Sternway : Backward movement through the water.

Stormboards : Boards slotted into or bolted over openings such as cabin entrances (companionways) as protection against heavy seas.

Stringer : Fore-and-aft members which give longitudinal strength to the hull.

Strop : A sling of rope whose ends have been spliced together.

Superstructure : Those parts of a ship above the upper deck, (e.g. funnels, deckhouses, etc.)

Swig, to : To tighten a rope (usually a halyard).

Swell : A longer wave, the result of wind blowing over long distances for hours, and one which may be running at a different angle from the seas on top of it.

Tack : (1) The lower forward corner of a fore-and-aft sail. (2) The closest course which a vessel is able to sail to the wind. Usually, this is somewhere between 40 and 50 degrees from the wind.

Tack, to : (1) To bring a vessel's bows through the wind until it is blowing effectively on the other side of the sail. (2) To work upwind in such a manner, going alternately from port tack to starboard tack and back again.

Tackle : System of blocks and ropes to increase the effective power of the effort applied. A tack tackle on *Kylie's* foredeck may be used to tension the luff of a foresail.

Tail : A rope's end.

Take in or *up, to* : To haul on a line.

Tangent screw : Mechanism on the arc of a sextant, allowing the navigator continuously to adjust the movement of the arm when taking a sight.

Tell-tales : Ribbons of light fabric used as wind-indicators.

Tide : The rise and fall in the sea-level caused by the gravitational forces exerted by the sun and moon.

Tiller : The horizontal bar, secured to the rudder-head, by which the vessel is steered.

Topsail : In gaff-rigged vessels, a sail set above the mainsail.

Topsides : The sides of the hull above her usual waterline.

Transit : Two charted features in transit provide an accurate bearing.

Transit log : Document issued by some foreign countries recording the itinerary of a visiting yacht while cruising territorial waters.

Trade wind : A belt of steady, regular winds on each side of the equator, blowing from the north-east in the northern hemisphere and from the south-east in the southern hemisphere.

Traveller : The movable iron ring on the mainsheet horse to which the mainsheet is attached.

Trimaran : A shallow-draught craft having a central hull and a float on each side. Capable of very high speeds.

Truck : Used loosely to refer to the mast-head. More correctly, the cap on some mastheads.

Turk's head : An ornamental knot.

'Tweendeck : Used loosely to mean the confined space between the principal decks.

Under-canvassed : Carrying too little sail.

Unship, to : To remove a shipboard fitting from its working position.

Veer : In the northern hemisphere, if the wind changes in a clockwise direction it is said to veer.

Wake : The path made by the ship's hull in the water astern.

Wardroom : Officers' lounge.

Warp : A strong rope for towing, anchoring or securing a vessel.

Washboards or *stormboards* : Planks which slot into grooves in the companionway to prevent water from entering the cabin.

Watch : Division of the ship's day, most commonly of 4 hours' duration. Thus, the *middle watch* (or *graveyard watch*) is from midnight to 4.a.m., the *morning watch* is from 4.a.m. to 8 a.m., and so on.

Waterline : The water level on the sides of the hull when the vessel is afloat. Also, the length of this line measured from the bow to the stern.

Way : Generally, the movement of a vessel through the water in such phrases as *making way*, *gathering way* or *having way on*. However, a vessel is said to be *under way* as soon as the anchor is broken out of the seabed or when the last shore-line has been cast off, even though she may not be *making way*.

Wear, to : (1) In sailing, to put the vessel on an opposite tack by putting the stern across and through the wind. (2) To display a flag, or to carry a sail.

Weatherfax : An electronic machine capable of receiving and reproducing weather maps.

Weather side : The side on which the wind is blowing.

Weather-going : Going against the wind.

Weigh, to : To raise the anchor from the bottom.

Whip, to : To bind twine round a rope to prevent the strands from unlaying.

Westing, to make : To progress westward.

Winch : A mechanism comprising a drum mounted on an axle. The drum is turned manually by a handle to produce increased power when taking in ropes, most usually sheets and halyards.

Wind rose : Chart symbol depicting the average prevalence and strength of the area's winds. Before the magnetic needle came into use, Mediterranean seamen relied on a 32-point wind rose as their compass.

Wind-jammer : Colloquially and loosely, any large, square-rigged sailing vessel.

Wind vane : Wooden aerofoil that communicates changes of apparent wind-direction to other parts of the steering gear.

Wing out, to : To extend the clew of a foresail outboard with a pole.

Yankee : Set on the forestay, a Yankee is usually a light-weather sail, narrower than a genoa, with a higher clew, and is often used in pairs for downwind sailing in the trade-wind belts.

Yaw, to : To wander from the desired course through the action of following winds and seas.

Yoke lines : In *Kylie*, lanyards and bungee attached to the tiller to cope with the stresses of steering.